The Lives, Lore, and Literature of Cranes

A Catechism for Crane Lovers

Paul A. Johnsgard

School of Biological Sciences
University of Nebraska–Lincoln

Photographs by

Thomas D. Mangelsen

Zea Books
Lincoln, Nebraska
2020

Abstract

This book provides basic information on cranes that should be of interest and importance to crane-loving birders ("craniacs") as well as to ornithologists and wildlife managers. Primary consideration is given to the sandhill and whooping cranes, but all 13 of the Old World cranes are also discussed. Special consideration is given to the relative abundance and conservation status of all of the world's species, of which nearly half are declining and a few are in real danger of long-term survival. More than 80 refuges and preserves in the United States and Canada, where the best chances of seeing cranes in the wild exist, are described, as are several zoos and bird parks with notable crane collections. Descriptions of 16 North American annual crane festivals and information on more than 50 bird-finding guides from regions, states, and provinces where cranes are most likely to be seen are included. Lastly, there is a sampling of American, European, and Oriental crane folklore, legends, and myths. The text contains more than 50,000 words and nearly 350 literature references. There are more than 40 drawings and 3 maps by the author and 19 color photographs by Thomas D. Mangelsen.

Text and drawings copyright © 2020 Paul A. Johnsgard
Photographs copyright © 2020 Thomas D. Mangelsen

ISBN: 978-1-60962-175-9
doi: 10.32873/unl.dc.zea.1103

Composed in Constantia types.

Zea Books are published by the University of Nebraska–Lincoln Libraries.

Electronic (pdf) edition available online at
https://digitalcommons.unl.edu/cgi/cview.cgi/zeabook

Print edition available from Lulu.com.

Page 1: Sandhill cranes with three-month-old young.
Below: Sandhill crane chick and egg.

UNIVERSITY OF **Nebraska**
Lincoln

Dedicated
to the memory of

Ronald Sauey (1948–1987)

&

James T. Harris (1950–2018),

who made the world a
safer place for cranes
and a more caring
place for humans

Contents

I. Major Aspects of Crane Life and Biology

II. Observing and Enjoying Cranes

III. The Old World Cranes: Their Populations and Conservation Status

IV. Cranes in Lore, Legend, and Myth

References

Maps

Drawings

Photographs

Following pages: Sandhill cranes, flock over Platte River, Nebraska

Preface

The fact that many crane-loving persons have given themselves the somewhat self-deprecating title of "craniac" provides a clue to the passion with which these people view their favorite birds. Certainly no other group of American birds has so many festivals (16 as of 2020) devoted to seeing, studying, and talking about them, and few people would be so willing to spend hours in usually cold, unheated blinds, patiently and quietly waiting for the rare magical moments when cranes begin to descend and land on their nocturnal roost as the evening clouds are stained with scarlet, or to suddenly depart at dawn amid a flurry of wings and excited calls as the rim of the sun first breaks the horizon. On such occasions I often think to myself, "If I were God, this is the kind of animal I would have invented to demonstrate to all others of Earth's creatures just how beautiful the biological world really is."

Who other than craniacs would travel halfway around the world to watch just one more group of cranes dancing with all the apparent joy of carefree teenagers, or to gaze at a circling flock as they soar effortlessly and lazily a thousand feet above, almost invisible among the cottony clouds of summer? These are experiences of a lifetime, to be stored away permanently in one's memory and retrieved during the most frigid days of winter, or when life seems too painful to endure.

It is for such people that I decided to write this book, which I hope will answer many of the questions that its readers might have about cranes. I cannot answer them all; cranes are so complex and inscrutable in their behavior that they exceed the boundaries of human understanding. Cranes have a continuous history of long-term survival that extends back to at least Oligocene and probably to Eocene times; they reap the benefits of prolonged parental care and remarkable adult longevity. They also have an ability to transmit important survival knowledge across generations as a result of maintaining long pair and family bonds. In many ways cranes are models of what humans should strive to attain but very rarely do.

No wonder so many people are entranced by cranes and so many persons' lives have been affected by them. Among these people are some of my dearest friends, such as George Archibald, Linda Brown, Jackie Canterbury, Karine Gil, George Happ and Christy Yuncker Happ, Josef Kren, and Tom Mangelsen, to all of whom I give my thanks for the time I have spent with them and learned from them, especially when we have also shared it in the rarified and regal company of cranes. I especially thank Tom Mangelsen, with whom during 50 years of friendship I have the longest history of shared crane watching and who kindly provided a group of his wonderful crane photos for inclusion in this book. As usual, I must offer my special and eternal thanks to Paul Royster, Coordinator of Scholarly Communications, University of Nebraska–Lincoln Libraries, and his intrepid and invaluable editor, Linnea Fredrickson, who together seem able to move the earth and who have kept me writing rather than sleeping for the past decade.

I also thank several of these same people for critically reading parts of the book's manuscript, especially Andrew Caven. While writing it I have relied heavily on my long out-of-print *Cranes of the World* (https://digitalcommons.unl.edu/biosci-cranes/), which has been described as the craniac's bible, and which in relative age now somewhat resembles the Old Testament. However, like the *Jefferson Bible*, my books exclude all miracles. Cranes don't need miracles to be fascinating; their simply being cranes is more than enough for mere earthbound humans to adore them. All the maps and drawings are my own and are in my copyright.

Paul A. Johnsgard
Lincoln, Nebraska

I Major Aspects of Crane Life and Biology

1. How are cranes unique and why are they so fascinating?

I believe humans experience certain moments—like seeing your first comet or hearing that you have been admitted to a highly respected academic or social group—that are then remembered for the rest of your life. It was thus for me at my first sighting of some special birds known as cranes.

When I arrived in Lincoln in the autumn of 1961 to teach at the University of Nebraska, I had never seen a wild crane and had viewed only a few in zoos. I was then preoccupied with waterfowl and hoped to one day make a significant contribution to waterfowl biology, such as by writing a book. I was assigned to teach an ornithology class during the 1962 spring semester, and I decided this would be an opportunity for me to encounter some unfamiliar bird species and begin to explore some of Nebraska's habitats. I soon accepted a graduate student and ornithology teaching assistant, Roger Sharpe. Roger was a longtime birder from Omaha who suggested some local places to visit with my ornithology class for Saturday field trips.

March in Nebraska is too early in spring for many migratory birds to be present, but near the end of March Roger suggested we head out to the central Platte River valley to look for waterfowl and perhaps sandhill cranes, which he had heard might be present. That was an exciting idea, so on a cold and blustery Saturday morning I loaded him and my class into a 12-passenger van, and we headed west 100 miles to Grand Island, where we first crossed the Platte River. No waterfowl were to be seen on the river, which was in spring flood, so we continued on another 40 miles to Kearney. The river at Kearney was also nearly bird free except for some common mergansers, and I was by then ready to give up on a fruitless wild crane chase.

But the day was still young, so we continued on west another 15 miles to the small town of Elm Creek, where I decided that, after 150 miles of searching, it was time to turn around and start back to Lincoln. Thinking that it would be worthwhile to stay close to the Platte River while driving back to Grand Island, I turned south onto a county gravel road that took us two miles to a long bridge that was barely remaining above the swollen Platte. While crossing the bridge, I glanced over to a nearby wet meadow and suddenly saw hundreds of foraging sandhill cranes! Others were flying in loose flocks in the distance, and after lowering the van's windows, we heard a chorus of crane voices overhead, seemingly coming from some distant angelic choir.

I was simply dumbstruck. It was as if I had been transported to some foreign land inhabited by strange new birds. In that instant, my perception of the earth seemed suddenly shifted, and my life was forever changed. I sensed how Howard Carter must have felt when he first peered into King Tut's treasure-laden tomb or John Colter when he first encountered the geysers, boiling mud pots, and other wonders of Yellowstone. We watched the birds for a long time, while I began to realize that my love for waterfowl must hereafter be shared with a passion for cranes, and that I must learn as much as possible about this wonderful group of American birds.

Among American cranes, there are two crane species only: the sandhill crane and the whooping crane, although the Eurasian "common" crane is an increasingly reported visitor to North America (Howell, Lewington, and Russell, 2014). No cranes exist in South America, although their probable nearest living relative, the marsh-dwelling limpkin (*Aramus guarauna*), occurs widely across the tropical parts of the Americas. Cranes are much larger than limpkins (which are about two feet

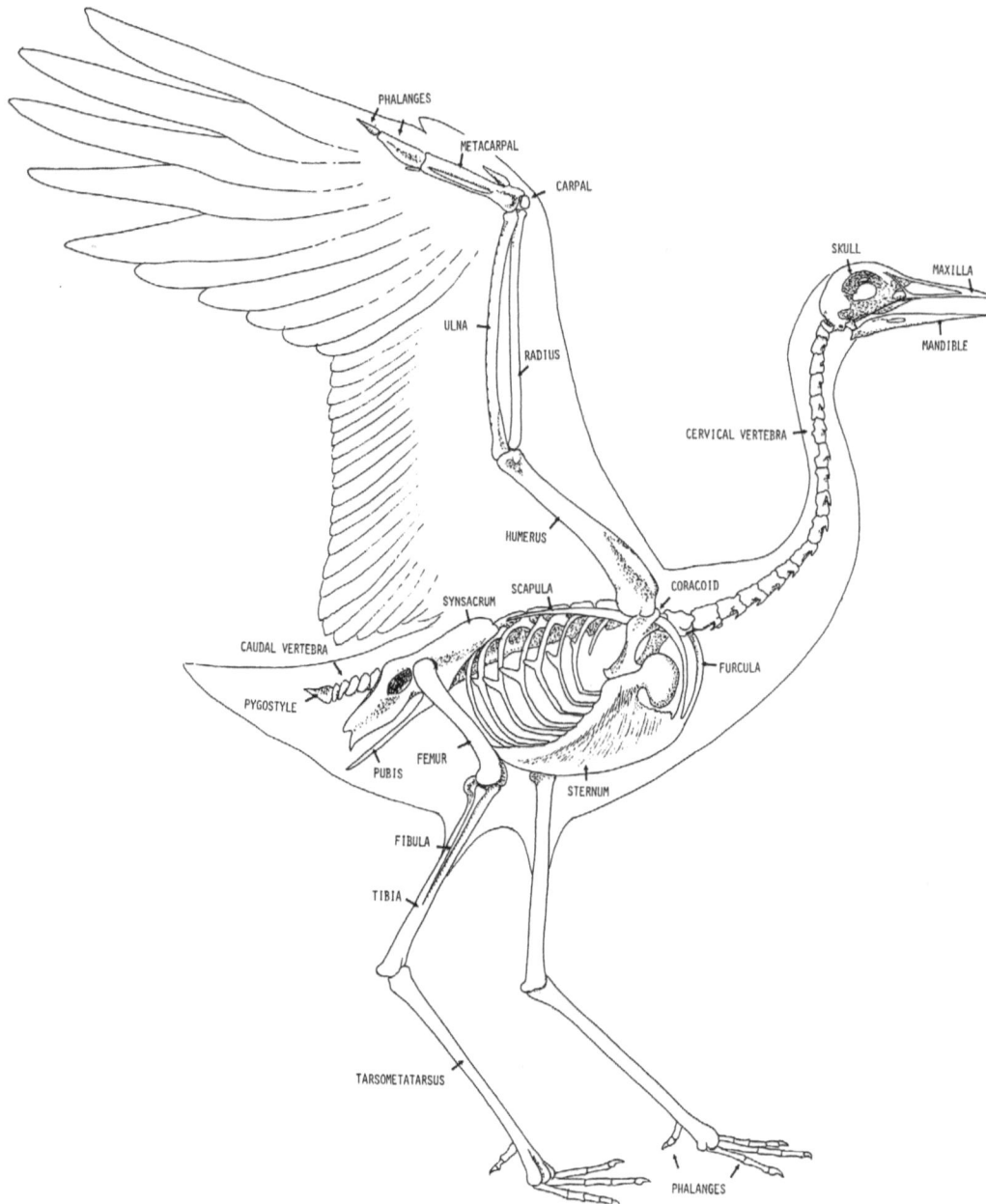

Fig. 1. Skeletal anatomy of a *Grus* crane.

tall); the smallest crane species, the demoiselle, stands about three feet tall. The tallest, the sarus crane of India and southeast Asia, is nearly six feet in height, and the heaviest, the red-crowned crane of Japan and China, may exceed 20 pounds as an adult, about equal to the heaviest of Canada geese.

Many structural features of cranes are of obvious adaptive value. Their skeletons have reduced numbers of wing and leg bones owing to fusion, which increases their rigidity, but have about three times as many neck vertebrae as most mammals (Fig. 1), which provides extreme neck flexibility. Like nearly all birds, cranes have mostly hollow bones, which reduces their overall weight. However, their bones are much denser in calcium than are those of mammals and thus are very resistant to breakage in spite of being hollow.

Among cranes, the skeletons of the African crowned cranes (*Balearica*) differ several ways from those of other more structurally advanced

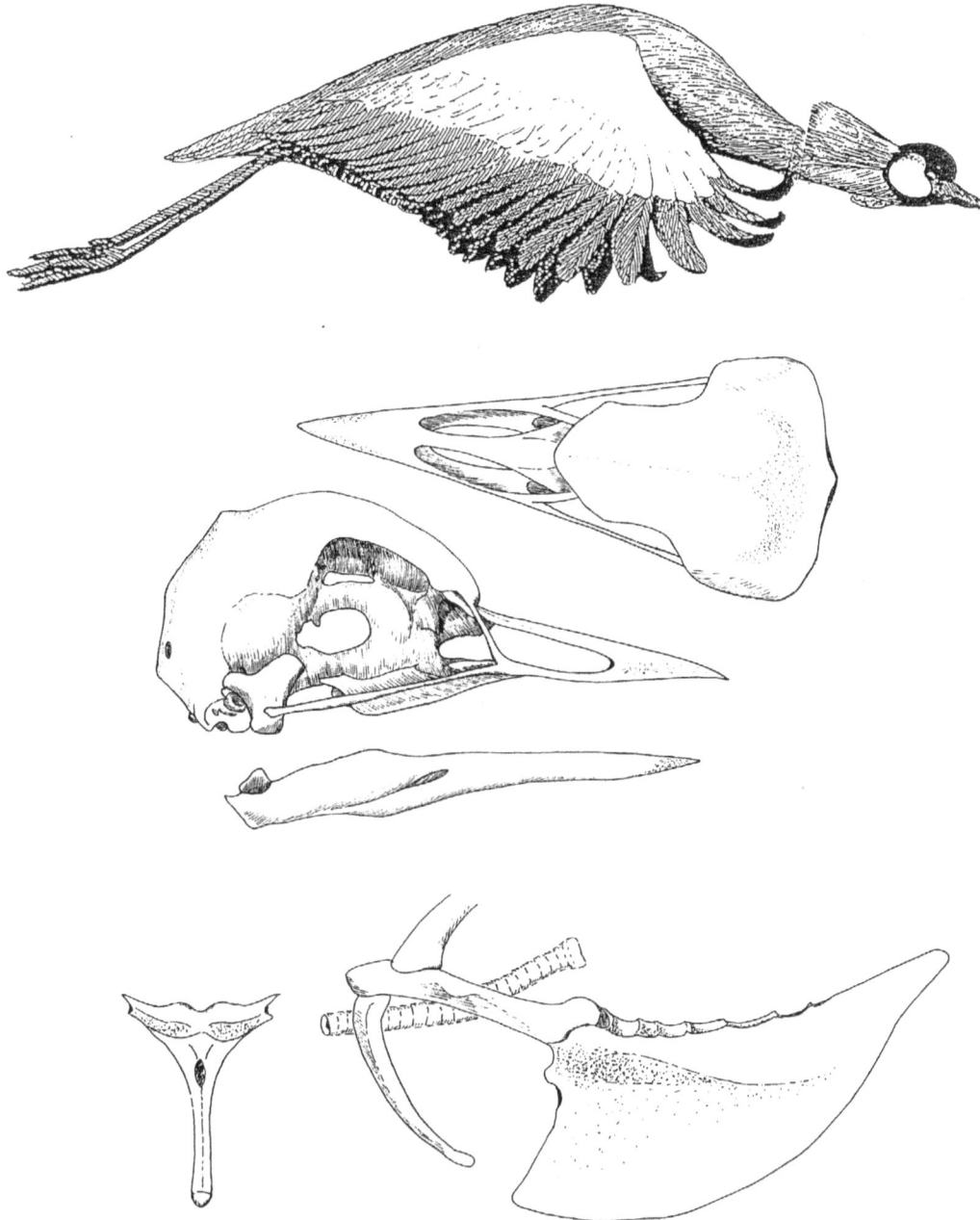

Fig. 2. External appearance (top), skull anatomy (middle), and sternal-tracheal anatomy of crowned cranes.

species that are classified in the large and typical crane genus *Grus*. Compared with *Grus* cranes, the beaks of crowned cranes are shorter and less pointed, their hind toes are longer, the furcula (the fused clavicles, or "wishbone") is not connected with the keel of the sternum (breastbone), and the trachea ("windpipe") does not penetrate the keel of the sternum but rather passes back directly from the glottis to the bronchi and lungs (Fig. 2).

Cranes have broad wings that are rather oval in shape, which results in maximum wing area and lift capabilities. This generalized wing shape and its airfoil characteristics limit the birds to rather slow flight speeds of about 40 to 45 miles per hour but also allow for highly effective gliding and soaring.

Following pages: Sandhill cranes, large flock, Nebraska

In spite of their large size and sometimes heavy weight (up to about 22 pounds in the red-crowned crane), cranes are among the finest of all birds in their soaring abilities, owing to their large wing surface area relative to their body weight. They can easily soar to 15,000 to 20,000 feet by using the updrafts caused by warm, rising columns of air (thermals) or by exploiting updrafts produced by air masses deflected upward as they pass over mountains. It is one of the joys of crane watching to see hundreds of cranes wheeling above in lazy spiraling circles, like a slow-motion cyclone, as they slowly gain altitude and disappear among the cumulus clouds of spring or fall.

The upper limits of crane soaring are still poorly documented. In the United States, sandhill cranes that winter at an elevation of about 7,000 feet in eastern Colorado must fly over a pass at about 12,000 feet in the Front Range of the Rocky Mountains to reach breeding areas in northwestern Colorado and western Wyoming. Species such as the demoiselle crane that breed in Asia and winter in large numbers in India regularly fly over the Himalayas, where the alpine passes are likely to be 20,000 feet or higher (Higuchi and Minton, 2017), and the Eurasian crane has been seen flying at an amazing height of 10,000 meters (33,000 feet) about the Himalayas (Carwardine, 2013). Matsuda (1999) described a photographic team stationed at 5,700 meters (18,700 feet) that videotaped (using ultra-long telephoto lenses) demoiselle cranes crossing the Himalayas high above.

One of the secrets of high flying and long-distance flights by birds is related to their highly efficient respiratory systems. Birds have several large abdominal and thoracic air sacs connected with their lungs that provide a huge air storage supply and an open-channel system of oxygen exchange that is unique among vertebrates. This efficient ventilating system is also connected with air spaces in some major limb bones, such as the humerus. Bird lungs are smaller than those of mammals, but mammals lack open lungs and air sacs and are unable to flush their lungs completely with each breath. Birds also have more densely concentrated red blood cells than mammals, and they are unusually rich in hemoglobin. The circulatory system is powered by a larger heart and operates at a higher pulse rate, and their body temperatures are higher than occur in comparably sized mammals.

The vocalizations of cranes emanate from paired and vibratory membranes—the tympaniform membranes—that are part of the syrinx (voice box). The syrinx is located where the trachea (windpipe) splits into two short tubes (bronchi) that in turn connect with the lungs (Fig. 3).

The high vocal diversity and complexity of crane vocalizations comes from two major sources. The most important is the paired tympaniform membranes, which are brought into vibration as air from the lungs is blown past them. Vocalizations are produced by passing air over the tympaniform membranes, which are held under varied degrees of tension and vibrate at correspondingly varied frequencies. The speed and amplitude of their vibrations control basic pitch (fundamental frequency) and volume (amplitude). Additionally, complex secondary vibrations of the membranes introduce a varied number of overtones (harmonics), which results in greater sound richness in the same way that a great violin differs from one that was poorly made.

Related to their highly efficient air-exchange capacity, most cranes (all those of the genus *Grus*) have unusually long windpipes (tracheae). Their long tracheae are in part the result of the long necks of cranes but also because in these species the trachea curves back and passes into the keel of the sternum, where it is coiled to varying degrees, depending on age and species, before exiting and passing back to connect with the lungs (Fig. 3). In the whooping crane this trachea length might exceed five feet.

This rare anatomical adaptation for lengthening the trachea (which otherwise occurs among North American birds only in the equally strong-voiced trumpeter and tundra swans) nearly doubles its length and has the acoustic benefits of producing an effective sound chamber for modulating and amplifying the birds' vocalizations.

In a manner similar to the way a French horn or a pipe organ operates, a long sound chamber is

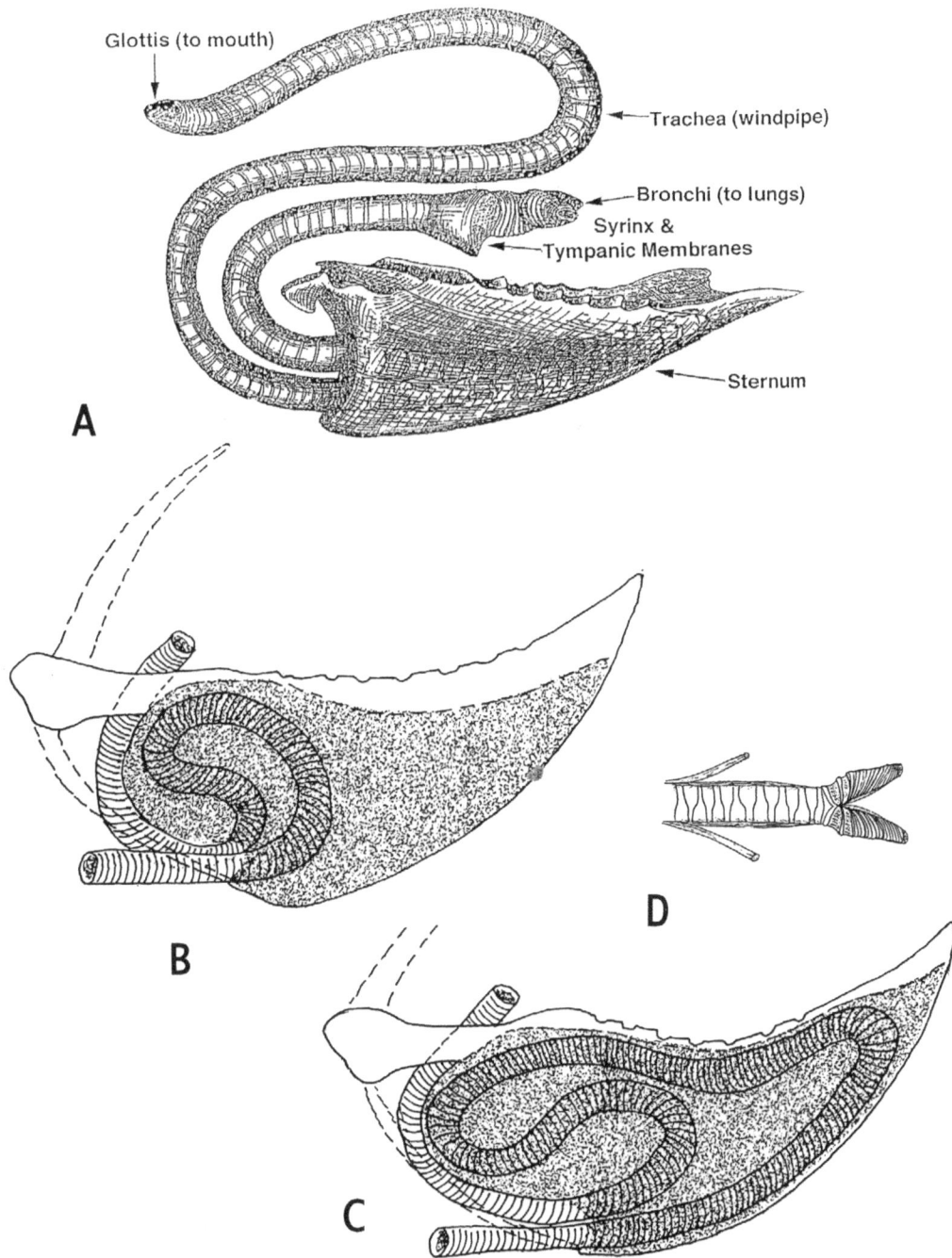

Fig. 3. Sternal and tracheal anatomy of a tundra swan (A) compared with intratarsal looping of a sandhill crane (B) and whooping crane (C) and tracheal-syringeal anatomy of a sandhill crane. Also shown are details of the syrinx and bronchi of a sandhill crane (D).

able to amplify and resonate low-frequency sounds that can be heard over distances of up to about two miles in some cranes. For highly territorial birds such as cranes and swans, the resulting advantages of efficient long-distance communication far outweigh the minor disadvantages of tolerating the dead air space that is always present in the tracheal cavity.

An important source of vocal complexity in *Grus* cranes comes from individual variations in the length and air capacity of the trachea, which influence the sounds produced by the syrinx by modulating their harmonic structure. The overall result of all these variables is a unique vocalization that can be more easily recognized by pair members or within a family group (Klenova, Volodin, and Volodina, 2008).

Different crane species vary substantially in their intrasternal tracheal lengths (Johnsgard, 1983a), but it is greatest in the largest species, such as the whooping crane (Roberts, 1880), in which it reaches nearly four feet (120 cm). The tracheal incursion into the sternum begins during the crane's first year, and as it grows the bird's voice changes from the high-pitched piping calls of a juvenile (fundamental frequency about 3 kHz) to the lower, louder, and richer-sounding voice typical of older birds (below 1 kHz), although the exact timing of this change is not directly correlated with the changes in tracheal length or body growth (Niemeier, 1979; Klenova, Volodin, and Volodina, 2007). In various cranes this voice-break might occur between 5 to 11 months of age (Klenova et al., 2010).

Cranes molt all their body, wing, and tail feathers once annually after the breeding season, which means that unlike many songbirds, for example, they don't seasonally change significantly in plumage color or pattern. With some exceptions, cranes also molt their major flight (primary and secondary) feathers gradually, so the birds never lose their flight capability. However, in most species, including the sandhill and whooping cranes, the annual fall wing molt sometimes occurs sufficiently rapidly, and with enough flight feathers simultaneously missing or not fully grown, that it makes the birds flightless for a period of up to several weeks. For example, whooping cranes have a six-week flightless molt that occurs every two to four years during summer.

It is possible that the incidence of flightless periods during the annual molt varies regionally in different populations of the same crane species, perhaps as an adaptation to the length of the breeding season. Additionally, not all the wing covert feathers are molted every year, so adult sandhill cranes that bred the previous year often exhibit some old brown-stained wing covert feathers visible as holdovers from the previous year's breeding plumage scattered among their newly grown gray wing coverts.

Like most flying birds, cranes have 10 long and outer flight feathers (primaries) that are attached to the largely fused "hand" bones (the carpo-metacarpus), and 17 to 18 feathers attached to their double "forearm" bones (the radius and ulna) (Fig. 4). These secondary flight feathers are mostly fairly uniform in length, merging inwardly into back feathers, as in most birds. However, in most cranes the innermost three or more secondaries (the so-called tertials) are variously elongated, curved, and pointed. In the whooping crane there are also 3 to 4 feathers arising from the humerus (humerals) that are airy, elongated, and recurved (Urbanek and Lewis, 2015).

This feather curvature and lengthening of the inner secondaries is scarcely evident in crowned cranes, but in the demoiselle, blue, and wattled cranes the tertials are extremely elongated, forming a trainlike effect. In several other cranes, such as the red-crowned, Eurasian, and black-necked, these feathers are more decurved, and their vanes are quite frayed and broken up into airy plumes. The visual result is a distinctive ornamental "bustle" that can be conspicuously raised during social display. By comparison, the tail feathers (rectrices) of cranes consistently total 12, are short and inconspicuous, and are usually hidden from view by the ornamental tertials, except when the birds are in flight.

Additionally, the adult plumages are of the same colors and patterns in both sexes, although juveniles initially differ considerably from adults in plumage color. Following the molt of their initial golden, tan, or brownish downy feathers, juveniles are usually more brownish to cinnamon in plumage color than adults, especially in species whose adults have largely white plumages, such as whooping cranes. However, even otherwise white-plumaged cranes have black primary feathers (Fig. 5); the melanin granules in the feather barbs provide added structural strength.

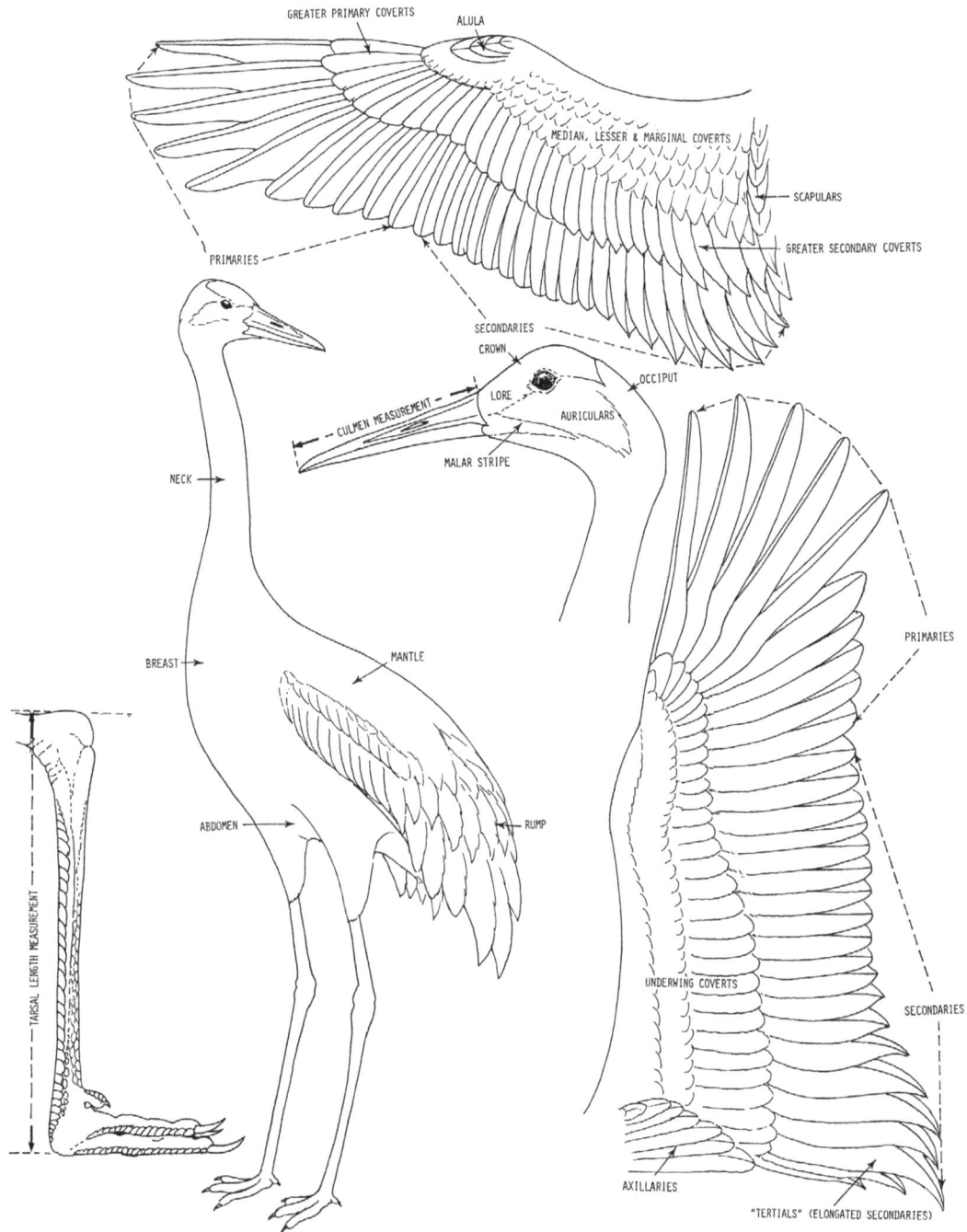

Fig. 4. External anatomy of a *Grus* crane.

The fledging period (the time elapsed between hatching and initial flight by juveniles) varies greatly, from about 65 to 150 days. It is generally shorter in Arctic-breeding species and longer in tropical cranes, such as the wattled crane (150 days) and sarus crane (120 days). Another two to four years or more might be required for the birds to mature fully and begin breeding.

In a very few species, especially the sandhill crane, breeding birds "paint" their body plumage with rotting organic matter prior to nesting by spreading it over their body feathers with their

Following pages: Sandhill cranes, dawn roost, Platte River

beaks. This activity stains the feathers with varied brownish hues, depending on the materials used. Painting behavior seems to have the purpose of developing a more camouflaged appearance while incubating or hiding in dead vegetation.

On a few occasions I have walked within about 25 feet of an incubating sandhill crane without seeing it until it stood up, or at least not recognizing it as an incubating crane. By remaining motionless with head and neck outstretched on the ground, incubating sandhill cranes sometimes closely resemble large, rounded, and brownish sandstone rocks.

Among other cranes, the Siberian and Eurasian cranes are also said to perform limited feather-painting behavior. The largest crane species don't engage in feather painting. This may be because they are strong enough to defend their nest from nearly all predators, and indeed it might be more important for the birds to advertise conspicuously their breeding colors and patterns to achieve their greatest effectiveness than it is to be well hidden while incubating.

In all juvenile cranes up to about a year of age, the body and head are entirely covered by feathers, but when the young of *Grus* species approach their first annual molt and lose their juvenile feathers they become variably bald. In sandhill cranes the crown then consists of bare pink to reddish skin that extends from the base of the beak back behind the eyes, whereas in the whooping crane and Eurasian crane the area of red is smaller and less conspicuous among the darker head feathers (Fig. 5).

As the juvenile grows older, this bare patch of skin in *Grus* cranes becomes an important external clue to the individual's physiological state. When angered or sexually aroused the crown becomes brighter red and more wartlike from blood engorgement, and at least in the sandhill crane it is also expanded and pulled back farther behind the eyes, making it more highly conspicuous.

Similar conspicuous crown patches are present in the whooping, Eurasian, and black crowned cranes, whereas the hooded crane has a small area of bare skin directly above the eyes. The eyes of the

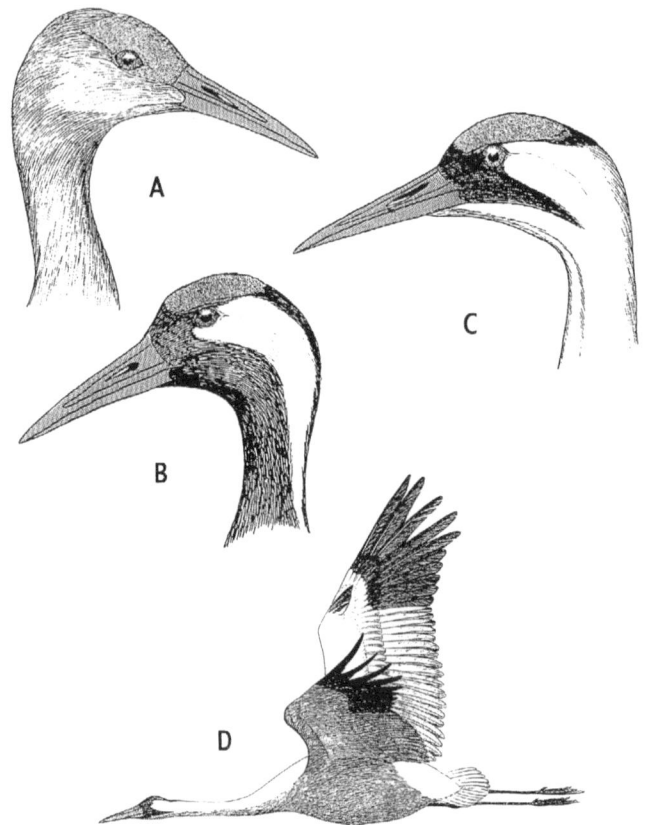

Fig. 5. Head profiles of sandhill crane (A), Eurasian crane (extralimital) (B), and whooping crane (C), and whooping crane flight profile (D).

white-naped crane and Siberian crane are also surrounded by a large patch of bare skin that in turn is surrounded by a ring of black feathers. In the sarus crane and brolga almost the entire head is bare and mostly red, which becomes brighter during the breeding season. The wattled crane has bare red skin in front of and below the eyes, and the bare skin extends down along the front of its pendant wattle. In the whooping crane there is also a strip of red to carmine skin that extends back from the lores and malar region to the sides of the throat, which varies individually in size and color intensity (Urbanek and Lewis, 2015).

In contrast, the crowned cranes have bare white to reddish cheek patches and bright red throat pouches that can be inflated while making honking sounds. The demoiselle and blue cranes have entirely feathered heads, but the demoiselle has conspicuous bright red eyes. Probably all of these variably colorful and distinctively patterned features provide important information about the bird's current physiological state and perhaps also its overall fitness.

Juvenile cranes typically have brown eyes, but in adults the iris color varies from pale bluish in crowned cranes to yellow in whooping cranes and bright red in demoiselle cranes. These eye-color changes might be important social signals among cranes for judging the age and overall physical or sexual condition of others.

All cranes have relatively large eyes and no doubt also have excellent color vision, judging from the social importance of the facial skin characteristics just mentioned. They also obviously have surprisingly good nocturnal vision, considering their basic diurnal activity pattern. During periods of a full or nearly full moon, I have often watched them approach and land at a roost without difficulty, even several hours after sunset and under conditions of nearly total darkness. I suspect they can use the light reflecting off the river surface to orient by and are also guided by the calls of already roosting birds.

However, nocturnal flying has its dangers. During a night of strong winds and freezing rain one spring in Nebraska more than 20 years ago, many birds panicked and left their nocturnal roost, flying blindly into trees and even crashing into the sides of buildings. As a result, hundreds of the birds were killed outright or survived with broken wings or legs. About 30 survivors were captured and placed in the Henry Doorly Zoo's Wildlife Safari Park near Omaha, where some of them can still be seen.

Like other birds with elongated heads and laterally located eyes, cranes appear to have limited forward binocular vision. As a result, they are highly vulnerable to collisions with elevated obstacles, such as electric transmission lines, often fatally, especially under foggy conditions or after dark. Interestingly, recent experiments involving the illumination of such lines with beams of near-ultraviolet light has drastically reduced the rate of collisions (Dwyer et al., 2019), indicating that, as for many birds, the spectral range of crane vision extends into the ultraviolet. Red is probably also an important part of the crane's color perception, given the apparent significance of red facial skin, and in some species, red eyes, as social signals.

Cranes obviously have very fine hearing, in part as attested to by their rich vocabulary of calls, which vary from soft purring sounds used between mothers and their young offspring to loud trumpetlike calls of *Grus* cranes that can be easily heard more than a mile away. The high-pitched piping calls of juveniles are not very loud but, surprisingly, can be easily heard when they are uttered in flight within a large flock of calling adults. Among *Grus* species this "baby voice" gradually shifts to one that is more adultlike during their first year of life.

The legs of cranes are very long, allowing for rapid running during takeoffs and jumping during social activities. On each foot they have three forward-facing toes that, unlike most waterfowl, are not webbed and one elevated hind toe that is too short to provide any perching ability. However, the two African crowned cranes have hind toes that are long enough to enable tree perching, and they even (although rarely) nest in trees (Steyn and Ellman-Brown, 1974).

The long legs of cranes would seemingly make extended standing periods tiring and difficult, but often the birds roost for many hours while standing in shallow water. They also stand for long periods while remaining perfectly balanced on a single leg, with the other leg partly lifted, or while scratching or stretching with the lifted leg. Cranes typically doze or sleep while standing erect, but their forelegs (anatomically, the tarsometatarsals, or fused ankle and foot bones) have to be fully folded forward when the birds are incubating or crouching.

Some behaviors, such as copulation, are more difficult because of the cranes' long legs. Copulation requires a good sense of balance when the male stands precariously on the female's back. The increasingly expanded hunting of sandhill cranes in many states has led to the presence of many wild birds with broken legs. These birds have great

difficulty landing, taking flight, and mating and probably have far greater risks from predation and limitations in foraging behavior than do intact birds.

Infrequently, as when the birds have just landed after completing a long migration flight or are resting in a safe location, cranes of all species will crouch and rest with their tarsi resting on the ground surface, as they do while incubating. However, this position seems awkward for them to achieve, and an immediate takeoff is impossible if the bird is suddenly frightened, which might be why the posture is so infrequently assumed.

2. Where do sandhill and whooping cranes occur in America?

The sandhill crane and whooping cranes are a study in great distributional contrasts. The sandhill crane (Maps 1 and 2) breeds from Florida and Mississippi north to the high Arctic on Banks and Baffin Islands, and from California and British Columbia east to western New York and southern Quebec. Its breeding habitats range through the tropical swamps and palm flats of Cuba, pine woodlands of Mississippi, wet prairie and marshes of the Great Plains, beaver ponds in eastern deciduous woods and western coniferous forests, muskeg bogs in northern taiga, permafrost-lined Arctic tundra ponds near sea level, and sandy slopes far beyond the Arctic Circle in northernmost Canada.

Its winter range is similarly widespread, from California to northern Texas and southern Georgia at the northern edge, with wintering occasionally extending to Nebraska. Its southern limits reach northern Mexico and the southern Gulf Coast from Texas to Florida. In Florida, greater sandhill crane migrants from the Great Lakes region winter together with a large residential population. There are also small, isolated, endangered resident populations in Mississippi, Cuba, and on Cuba's nearby offshore islands.

Over this vast range, several populations have been taxonomically recognized as distinct, and they breed in widely different regions and

habitats. Breeding habitats of the Arctic-nesting lesser sandhill crane are mostly lowland tundra and associated marshes; shorelines of rivers, lakes, and coastal areas; and grassy or sandy slopes up to about 3,000 feet in elevation as far north as Banks and Victoria Islands.

On the lowlands of the Yukon-Kuskokwim delta of western Alaska, the birds nest in two general habitat types: heath-marsh mosaic tundra areas and sedge-grass meadows. Most nesting occurs in wet marshes of the mosaic-patterned tundra areas and in the sedge meadows but also extends onto dry heath tundra. In some areas, such as on high-Arctic Banks Island, the birds nest on grass-covered sand dunes. They also often nest in muskeg areas of Canada and Alaska where there are open or sedge- or moss-covered areas surrounded by spruces and with scattered bushes.

The ill-defined Canadian sandhill crane race *rowani* breeds geographically between the larger greater sandhill crane of southern Canada and the northern United States, and the smaller and more tundra-adapted lesser sandhill crane. It nests in inaccessible bulrush marshes or muskeg areas vegetated with dwarf birches (*Betula pumila*) and tamaracks (*Larix laricina*). In central Canada the birds appear to prefer extensive bulrush cover and associated shallow marshes, while in the James Bay area of Ontario they have been observed nesting in sphagnum bogs among tamaracks and associated heather vegetation. This general sort of coniferous forest vegetation is scattered but widespread across western and central Canada.

This intermediate-sized population morphologically and genetically grades imperceptibly into the lesser and greater sandhill cranes (Krapu et al., 2011), and a still-uncertain percentage of the Mid-Continent Population of sandhill cranes consists of this race. The population of sandhill cranes wintering in western Oregon and northern California is also probably *rowani* from nesting areas in coastal British Columbia and southeastern Alaska (Ivey, Herzinger, and Hoffmann, 2005).

The greater sandhill crane's breeding habitats in the western states consist of open mountain parks

Opposite: Whooping cranes, Nebraska

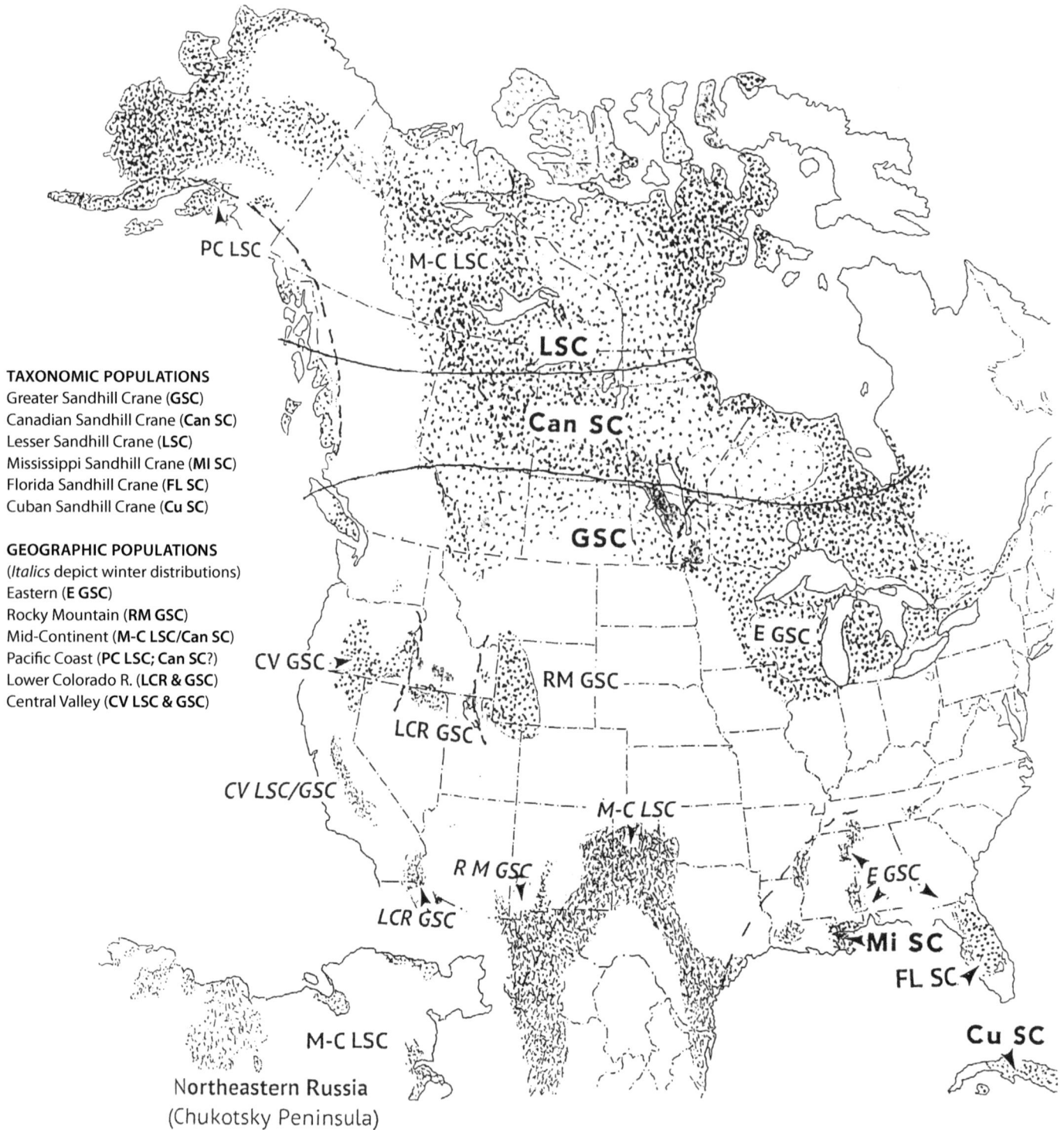

TAXONOMIC POPULATIONS
Greater Sandhill Crane (**GSC**)
Canadian Sandhill Crane (**Can SC**)
Lesser Sandhill Crane (**LSC**)
Mississippi Sandhill Crane (**MI SC**)
Florida Sandhill Crane (**FL SC**)
Cuban Sandhill Crane (**Cu SC**)

GEOGRAPHIC POPULATIONS
(*Italics* depict winter distributions)
Eastern (**E GSC**)
Rocky Mountain (**RM GSC**)
Mid-Continent (**M-C LSC/Can SC**)
Pacific Coast (**PC LSC; Can SC?**)
Lower Colorado R. (**LCR & GSC**)
Central Valley (**CV LSC & GSC**)

Map. 1. Current distribution of sandhill crane breeding and wintering areas and populations. The density of stippling approximates relative known breeding density. Abbreviations for wintering populations are in *italics*; the Pacific Coast breeding population (*PC*) may include both lesser and Canadian sandhill cranes and is part of the wintering Central Valley (*CV*) population, which also includes some greater sandhill cranes from California and Oregon (*CV GSC*).

Grand Island

Kearney

North Platte

Platte
River

Presumptive
breeding limits
of Canadian
Sandhill Crane

Probable breeding
limits of Greater
Sandhill Crane

Northern
Wintering
Limits
(all races)

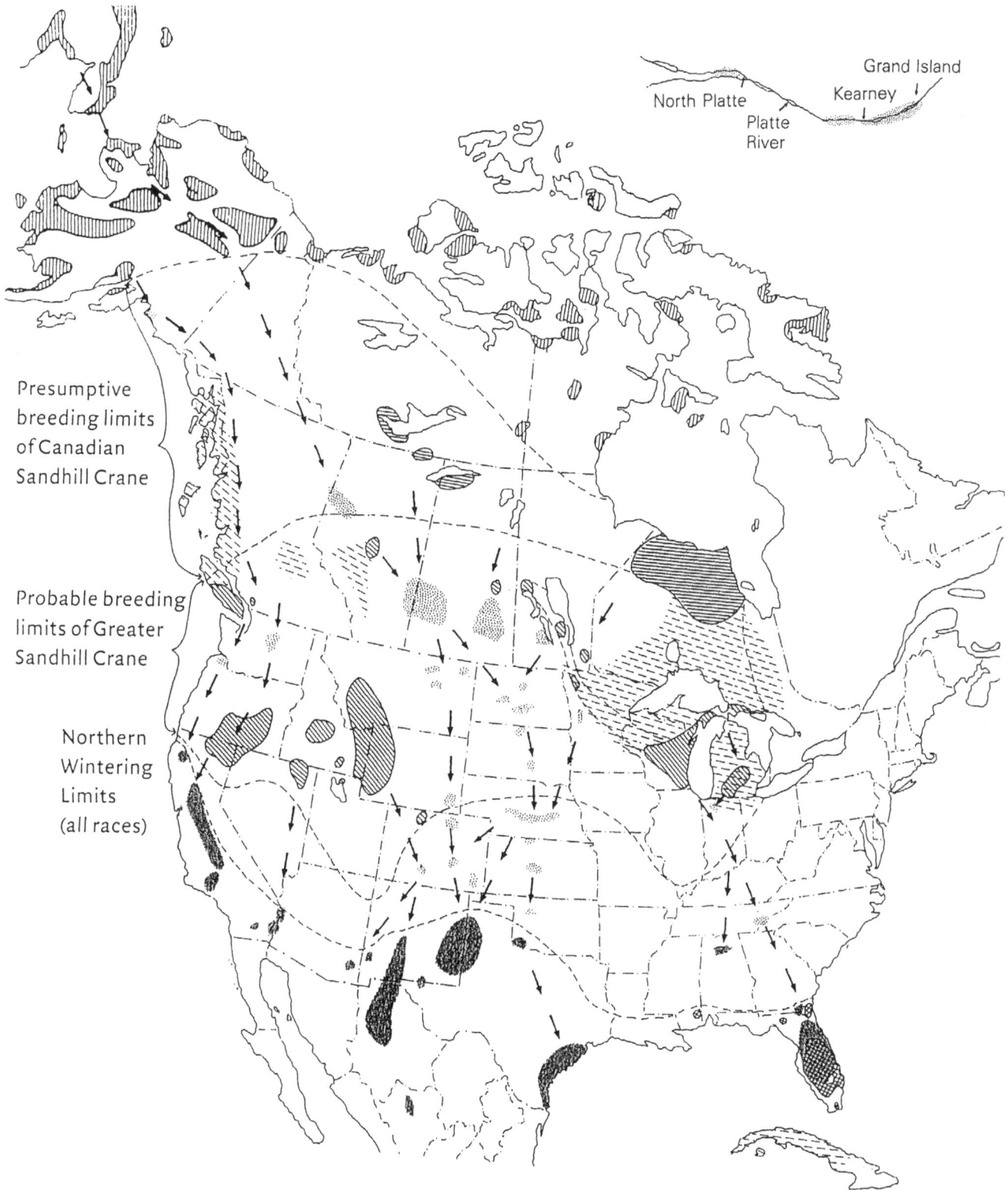

Map 2. Known migration routes, staging areas (light stippling), wintering areas (heavy stippling), and breeding areas (hatched) of sandhill cranes as of the late 1900s. Broken stippling indicates uncertain or low-density breeding areas. The inset shows crane distribution along the central Platte River (stippled).

Following pages: Sandhill cranes, males calling, Nebraska

in coniferous forests, beaver ponds, willow-dotted streams in sagebrush areas, and extensive shallow freshwater marshes in sagebrush or arid grasslands with associated wetlands. An essential breeding component is fresh water, with preferred depths of from a few inches to two or three feet near the nesting site.

In southern Michigan and Wisconsin, the plant cover use by breeding greater sandhill cranes usually consists of sedges, grasses, cattails, rushes, and reeds. However, in northern Michigan the typical breeding habitat consists of bogs, with associated heath vegetation, and such trees as tamaracks, pines, and black spruce (*Picea mariana*).

The Florida sandhill crane nests in pond areas associated with prairies dominated by saw palmettos (*Serenoa*) and scattered wooded hammocks that support cabbage palms (*Sabal*), pines, oaks, and wetland trees such as magnolias and cypress (*Taxodium*). Most nesting apparently occurs on shallow-water ponds grown up thickly to emergent vegetation such as cattails, rushes, arrowleaf (*Sagittaria*), sawgrass (*Cladium*), and spikerush (*Eleocharis*).

The Mississippi sandhill crane's nesting habitats consist of swamps and prairielike savannas surrounded by natural pine forests or pine plantations. The planting of trees on most of the native savanna has restricted this subspecies' breeding range, as has a natural succession of brush, cypress, and pines, which tends to eliminate the swamp-savanna vegetation.

In Cuba, the birds nest in relatively dry habitats that are typically parklike and sparingly grown to shrubs and trees, although some open prairie habitat does occur. Nests have been found on dry ground in palm flats along grass-covered arroyos, and in dry and sandy lowland situations with an abundance of dead grasses and scattered trees, such as tropical pines, palmettos, and various shrubs.

The whooping crane's historic breeding range covered parts of four glacially shaped and historically prairie-dominated states and four provinces from Indiana to Alberta. As a result of hunting and habitat losses incurred as farming of the rich soils of the northern Great Plains was developed, associated drainage of the region's once numerous glaciated wetlands occurred. However, the remaining wetlands of Alberta and Saskatchewan still serve as important stopover sites that the cranes use during spring and fall migrations.

The species' current breeding range (Map 3) is now confined to Canada's Wood Buffalo National Park, located along the Alberta–Northwest Territories boundary. The park covers 17,300 square miles, an area somewhat greater than twice the size of New Hampshire. Wood Buffalo National Park is a subarctic muskeglike area of glaciated potholes with innumerable ponds and small lakes varying in size from less than an acre to about 60 acres. All of these are quite shallow and are separated by low sandy ridges that support a dense growth of birches, willows, black spruce, and tamaracks. The ponds have borders that are densely covered with bulrushes, cattails, sedges, and many other shoreline plants typical of this subarctic region.

This remote park lies at the southern boundary of the Precambrian Shield, a vast area of scoured-off, billion-year-old rock substrate that covers much of northern Canada. Because of the fairly recent glacial action, the surface clay soils have limestone-derived glacial materials that are quite high in calcium and provide favorable environments for crustaceans, mollusks, and insects. The cranes choose ponds for breeding that are slightly alkaline, ignoring or avoiding nearby ponds that are somewhat more acidic and less rich in invertebrates. Additionally, the birds use only those breeding sites that are shallow enough to allow for easy foraging by wading, so wetlands up to about a foot in depth.

The whooping crane's winter range is now almost entirely centered at Aransas National Wildlife Refuge (NWR), a 115,000-acre federal sanctuary on the Texas coast, although recent reintroductions have resulted in small resident populations in Louisiana and Florida. Aransas NWR contains 22,500 acres of salt flats and estuarine marshes, the latter habitat being the cranes' primary foraging

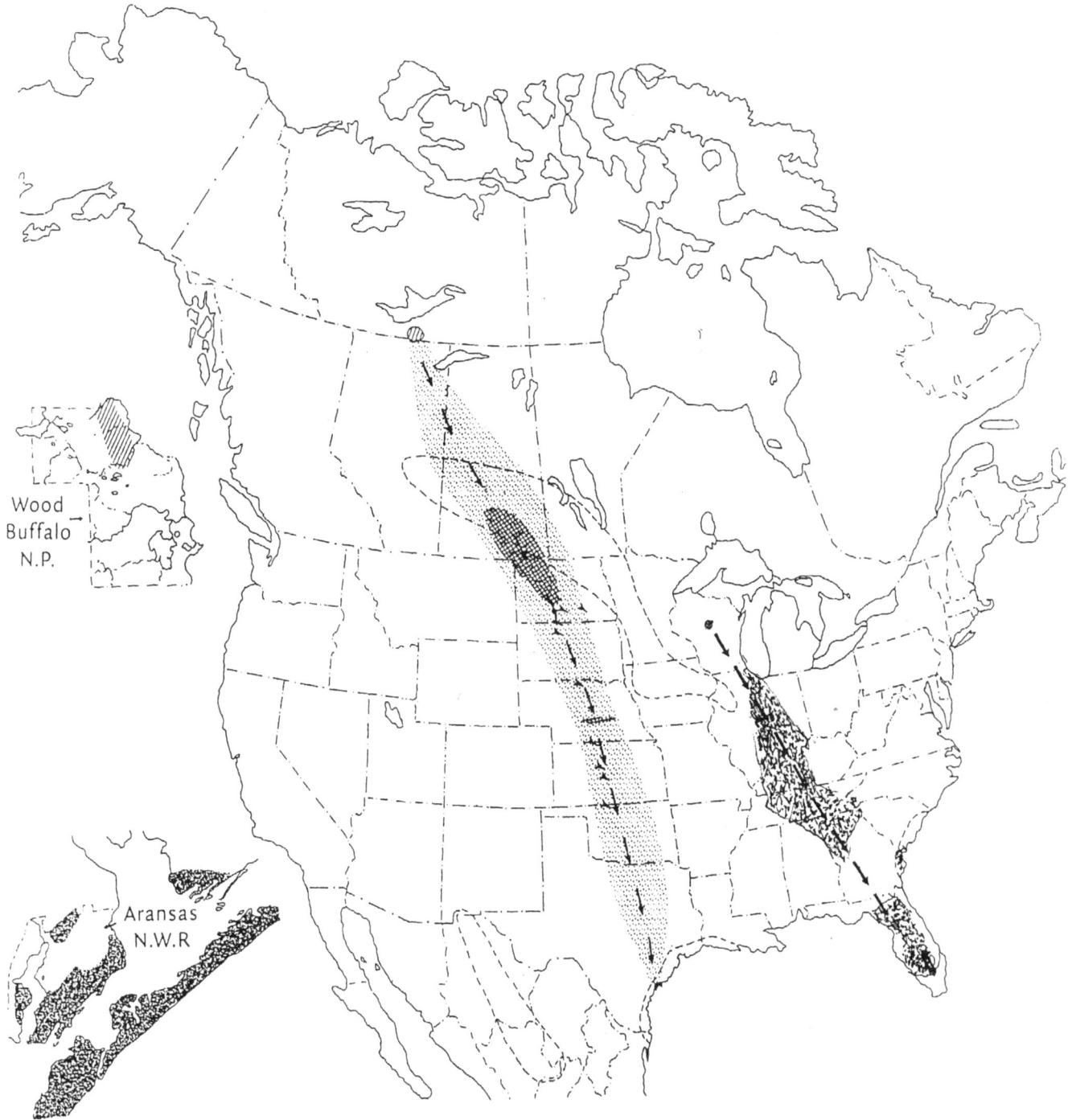

Map 3. Current breeding (hatched) and wintering (inked) areas of whooping cranes. Light stippling shows the width of the migration route of the Aransas–Wood Buffalo flock, crosshatching indicates a major staging area. Heavy stippling shows the migration path width of the reintroduced Eastern flock as well as the wintering range in Florida. Insets show the primary breeding area in Wood Buffalo National Park and areas of major winter use in Aransas National Wildlife Refuge. Historic breeding and wintering ranges are indicated by dashed lines.

grounds. Behind the marshes are areas of wet coastal prairie and woody subtropical vegetation.

Near the outer edge of the marshes a wide channel, the Gulf International Waterway, is a heavily used route for barges that often carry petrochemical materials that pose a constant threat to the cranes and their environment. However, in spite of this and other sources of danger, such as periodic hurricanes and invasive species of plants and animals, the cranes have prospered. Since the establishment of the refuge in 1937, the wintering population has increased from a low point of fewer then 20 birds in 1941 to more than 500 in 2020.

As a result of reintroduction programs, small flocks of whooping cranes now also occur in areas where they have never bred, at least for the past century or more. A few exist on the prairies of central Florida, the survivors of a large-scale reintroduction program that ultimately failed, leaving only nine birds remaining as of 2020.

Another and much more recent reintroduction has been taking place in southwestern Louisiana near White Lake, where until the late 1940s a few whooping cranes survived in coastal wetlands. Storms evidently eliminated all these birds by the early 1950s. It wasn't until 2010 that an effort was initiated to try to restore whooping cranes in Louisiana at the state's Rockefeller Refuge. In 2016, the first wild chicks since 1939 hatched in Louisiana. As of 2020 about 70 birds were survivors of repeated annual introductions of more than 100 young captive-raised birds that had been released over the previous decade, and a limited degree of breeding success has been obtained. (A similar degree of success in establishing a new population of migratory whooping cranes was achieved by the project Operation Migration, described in section 4.)

The ultimate fate of these reintroduction efforts is not yet predictable, but the goal in Louisiana is to establish a self-sustaining population of nonmigratory whooping cranes, namely a flock of approximately 120 individuals and 30 productive pairs whose levels are maintained for 10 years without additional restocking. A broader international restoration goal is to maintain a minimum of 40 productive whooping crane pairs in the Aransas–Wood Buffalo population and have two additional self-sustaining populations consisting of 25 productive pairs each. An alternate goal is to maintain 100 productive pairs in the Aransas–Wood Buffalo population and one additional self-sustaining population consisting of at least 30 breeding pairs.

3. How do the American cranes differ in their general behavior?

Sandhill Crane

Information on relative sociality in sandhill cranes can be deduced from average flock sizes under various conditions. Among daytime flock sizes in spring during the birds' stopover period in the Platte River valley, nearly one-fourth of the social units of foraging birds reported in one Nebraska study were groups of two and three birds, supporting the belief that the pair and family groups are probably the nuclear units of crane flocks. Similarly, Andrew Caven et al. (2020) reported that, while in Nebraska, the average number of birds in whooping crane social groups was 3.6 individuals with a mean maximum of 9.3 birds in spring and 9.9 birds in fall.

The daily flights of cranes between their daytime foraging areas and nocturnal roosts are closely tied to light levels. Almost certainly light levels, rather than specific sunrise or sunset times, are the critical timing factor. In the Platte River area, the cranes always begin returning to the river before sunset on cloudy days but often wait to return until a half hour or later beyond sunset on sunny days with extended periods of twilight. This pattern of behavior assures them of relatively safe roosts throughout the nighttime hours, at least from visually hunting predators such as eagles.

Predators of juvenile and adult sandhill cranes include wolves, foxes, dogs, bobcats, hawks, eagles, and possibly great horned owls. Crows and ravens are no doubt significant egg predators in most regions, and in the Arctic jaegers might be

Opposite: Adult whooping crane, Aransas National Wildlife Refuge, Texas

the most significant avian egg predator of lesser sandhill cranes. Among Florida sandhill cranes, raccoons are probably the most common predator of nesting birds, although various snakes and crocodiles might also pose dangers.

Although in Nebraska coyotes are often present near crane roosts, I have never seen an attempted attack on roosting birds. In many parts of the West and South bobcats are common and are known to be significant predators on both adult and juvenile sandhill cranes.

Golden eagles are also significant avian predators in the western states, and sandhill cranes are much warier of adult bald eagles than of immatures. I watched sandhill cranes that were standing on a sandbar respond to an immature bald eagle that landed on the bar some distance away by forming a small party of about a half-dozen birds and slowly advancing toward the eagle until it flew away. However, an adult bald eagle has been observed drowning a sandhill crane (Caven et al., 2018), and Stan Tekiela once showed me a photo he had taken of an adult bald eagle attacking a sandhill crane in flight.

There is little reason to believe that any significant differences exist in the sandhill crane races as to their preferred foods. It is evident that sandhill cranes are able to adjust their diets to the local sources of abundant vegetable foods, especially grain crops when they are available. It is also clear that corn provides the single most important source of food energy among lesser sandhill cranes during their spring stopover in Nebraska, probably contributing about 90 to 95 percent of the total daily food intake per bird.

Sandhill cranes forage primarily on land and do a great deal of digging with their bills, when necessary, to extract materials from under the soil. More often, they feed on visible food from the soil's surface. Large pieces of food, including live prey, are broken into smaller bits by piercing them or threshing them against the ground. Smaller pieces of food are delicately picked up from the ground with the tip of the beak and then tossed into the air and caught farther back in the beak.

Because corn contains only about 10 percent protein, the birds apparently supplement their protein intake somewhat by foraging on various invertebrates, which comprise nearly all of the remaining food materials that the birds consume during the spring period. J. C. Lewis (1979) commented that corn has a high net energy value, as much as 80 percent nitrogen-free extract. He suggested that this high corn diet in spring may be an important factor in the substantial weight gain that the birds put on while in the Platte valley. Likewise, G. C. Iverson, T. C. Tacha, and P. A. Vohs (1982) also concluded that the high energy values of cereal grains are an important aspect of crane survival strategies in winter and spring. None of the several food-analysis studies done on migrating or wintering sandhill cranes has reported any age-associated food intake variations.

L. H. Walkinshaw (1949) summarized information on the food of dependent young wild cranes, suggesting that earthworms are probably an important source of food under natural conditions, and that grasshoppers and other insects are also probably eaten regularly.

Walkinshaw (1949) described the food of a chick that he raised as including earthworms and beetles by the time it was three weeks old. It also ate mosquitos, spiders, grubs, moths, millers, and some houseflies. By about a month of age it was very fond of earthworms and would eat as many as 400 in a single day. By then it was also eating crickets, katydids, and short-horned grasshoppers on a daily basis as well as other foods. When over three months old it began to eat sweet corn, and within a week was eating an ear per day. Later in the fall it consumed mainly scratch food, such as wheat and cracked corn.

By the time the young are migrating during the fall, they appear to be eating essentially the same foods as adult birds. Protein sources are also important foods for adults during the breeding season; I have seen greater sandhill cranes depredating the eggs and young they removed from red-winged blackbird nests, and piercing and eating the contents of a clutch of eggs from

Opposite: Adult whooping crane, foraging, Aransas National Wildlife Refuge, Texas

a cinnamon teal's nest. It has also been reported that snakes, mice, and lemmings are also sometimes killed and eaten (Gerber et al., 2014).

Whooping Crane

Early studies by R. P. Allen (1952) effectively summarized what was known at that time about the foods of whooping cranes. He concluded that the animal foods of the whooping crane included mainly aquatic animals such as crayfish, blue crabs, aquatic insects, and freshwater minnows, plus some vegetation, and also such crops as sweet potatoes and sprouting corn. Allen was able to establish that at least 28 types of animal materials and 17 kinds of plants are consumed on the wintering grounds. He also determined that the seven major foods were blue crabs, polychaete worms, pistol shrimp, mud shrimp, crayfish, short razor clams, and green razor clams. Of these, blue crabs, mud shrimps, and other decapod crustaceans are preferred, as they are abundant and tend to be easily obtained.

Clams and smaller blue crabs are swallowed whole, while large crabs are carried to shore where the claws are broken off and the body then swallowed, followed by the claws. Clams are often swallowed whole. Fish, insects, and reptiles are apparently chance prey, as are frogs and birds, at least at Aransas NWR. On migration the birds feed on the egg masses of frogs and toads, adult frogs, and various insects as well as on catfish and probably other freshwater fishes (Caven et al., 2019).

On the wintering grounds, young birds feed within their parents' territories and are regularly fed by them. Usually the young bird remains within a few yards of its mother and utters a series of soft but penetrating calls, especially when the female has captured a food item and the juvenile begins begging. About half of the food caught by the female is passed on to the young during fall and winter months. As spring approaches, the young birds show more independence and sometimes move up to about 300 feet away from their mothers, periodically returning. Males occasionally also feed the young, but this task is seemingly done primarily by the female.

There is relatively little information on whooping crane predators, but predation on adult birds is apparently extremely rare because of their large size. Golden eagles are probably their greatest avian predator, and juvenile birds are very probably the most at risk from them. It is the juvenile segment of the population that is also most susceptible to general mortality during their first spring migration, especially when they become isolated from their parents and must face long migration routes, unfamiliar foods, and unknown dangers.

Mortality rates of juvenile whooping cranes appear to be very high in the first year of life, at least as compared to that of adults. D. G. Bergeson, B. W. Johns, and G. Holroyd (2001) monitored 22 pairs of whooping cranes with transmitters on 18 of their young. Of these 18, 28 percent fledged, 28 percent died of various known causes, and 22 percent were lost from unknown causes. A total of 16 young were fledged by the 22 pairs, of which 2 (10.1 percent) were the younger siblings. Three of the young were lost to fox and raven predation. Probably many of the post-fledging losses of young cranes can be attributed to accidents, illegal hunting, and similar diverse factors, in addition to predation dangers.

Besides foraging and roosting, wintering and migrating birds spend some time in social interactions such as fighting and dancing. Dancing occurs throughout the time that the birds are in the Aransas area, but the greatest amount of such activity is observed just after fall arrival and again prior to departure in the spring (Blankinship, 1976). When departing the area to migrate, whooping and sandhill cranes often leave in the middle of the day, rising and circling on air currents under favorable weather conditions that are associated with clear skies and tailwinds.

4. Where do cranes migrate and how do they navigate?

Lesser Sandhill Crane

Crane migrations are among the longest migrations of North America's largest birds and range from a few hundred miles to nearly 3,500 miles. The longest North American routes are those of lesser sandhill cranes that breed in northeastern Siberia (Yakutia) and winter in southeastern Arizona.

The migration of lesser sandhill cranes from Siberia and the northernmost portions of Canada begins in late August, reaches a peak during the third week of August, and after the middle of September begins to decline, until the last birds leave after mid-October. At about the same time, large numbers of birds build up in northwestern North Dakota, with smaller numbers in various staging points in eastern Montana.

Lesser sandhill cranes move southward from North Dakota and Montana across eastern Wyoming and western South Dakota and Nebraska to eastern Colorado and central Kansas, with birds arriving in the Arkansas River valley by mid-September to mid-October, and to various Kansas national wildlife refuges (Kirwin NWR, Quivira NWR) between mid-October and late November. A few areas in Oklahoma (Salt Plains and Washita NWRs) are major stopping points before the birds arrive in their wintering areas of New Mexico, Texas, and northern Chihuahua by late December.

The spring migration has historically taken a rather different form, with the vast majority, if not virtually all, of the lesser sandhill cranes wintering east of the Rocky Mountains stopping in the Platte River valley of Nebraska for approximately six weeks from late February or early March until the second week of April, with numbers peaking during the last week in March. In recent years, this pattern has shifted by about 10 to 15 days, so that in 2020 the peak numbers in the Platte valley occurred about March 12, and nearly all had left by the first week in April.

During this period, perhaps all—except the approximately 20,000 to 30,000 lesser sandhill cranes that winter in California—or at least 90 percent of the entire North American lesser sandhill crane population is concentrated into a stretch of about 80 miles of river, where there is a combination of a broad, shallow, braided stream; numerous sandy islands and bars; and fairly undisturbed stretches, with highway bridges averaging about six to eight miles apart. Nighttime roosts are generally located on broad stretches of the river that are 600 to 1,000 feet wide, with sandbars and islands having little vegetation, far from bridges, and well away from areas of human activity.

Regular spring crane surveys along the Platte River began about 1960, as legal hunting seasons began to be established in the Great Plains states. Surveys between 1959 and 1978 indicated peak populations from about 80,000 to 225,000 birds, averaging nearly 160,000 birds. More recent estimates of the midcontinental sandhill crane population over the same stretch of river indicate that the number of birds in the entire midcontinental flock (the Central Flyway) had reached at least 800,000 birds by 2019. This total includes both lesser and Canadian sandhill cranes, plus a small percentage of greater sandhill cranes probably headed for northwestern Minnesota, eastern Manitoba, and western Ontario.

Over time, the center of the Platte's sandhill population has gradually shifted downstream, from locations west of Kearney (such as where I first encountered them in the early 1960s) to river stretches closer to Grand Island, where the sandy islands and bars have been variably cleared of woody vegetation to make them more attractive to cranes, and where land and wetland acquisition by conservation agencies has been most active.

Furthermore, the birds have gradually moved farther away from the river to suffice their foraging needs, as corn-harvesting efficiency has improved, as soybeans have increasingly replaced corn as the primary crop in the central Platte valley, and as the exploding snow goose population has increasingly competed with the cranes for food. The cranes are

Following pages: Sandhill cranes, foraging at dawn, Bosque del Apache National Wildlife Refuge, New Mexico

now also leaving their roosts to forage earlier in the morning and staying out later in the afternoon, sometimes returning to their roosts well after sunset.

Most of the lesser sandhill cranes that stage in the Platte valley must still fly an additional 1,000 to 3,000 miles to reach their nesting area (Map 2), and thus the degree of fattening that they undergo in the Platte River valley may be of great importance to their physical condition at the critical time of reproduction.

After the lesser sandhill cranes leave Nebraska in late March and early April and head north, they begin to spread out, and there is no comparable staging area along the remaining spring migration route that has an abundant and easily available food supply. In recent years many of the cranes have made a brief stop in northern South Dakota for a final fat accumulation before departing the corn-rich plains.

Greater sandhill cranes utilize several migration routes (Map 2). A major eastern route, probably followed by all of the greater sandhill cranes nesting from Minnesota to Michigan and adjoining Great Lakes areas, funnels initially into the Jasper-Pulaski Fish and Wildlife Area near Medaryville, Indiana, and then continues more or less directly southeastward across Kentucky, Tennessee, and Georgia into peninsular Florida. Their return route in spring is probably very similar to the fall route, although less extensive use of the Jasper-Pulaski area occurs at that time of year.

A relatively minor second route includes those greater sandhill cranes that breed in northwestern Minnesota and adjacent Canada, which join the midcontinent lesser and Canadian sandhill cranes that winter along the Texas coast (Krapu et al., 2014).

Several migratory routes are known for the greater sandhill cranes of western North America (Map 2). The most important route extends from the northern Rocky Mountain breeding population that is concentrated in eastern Idaho, western Montana, and Wyoming and migrates to wintering areas in the central Rio Grande valley of New Mexico, with a stopover in the San Luis Valley of southern Colorado, on the eastern slope of Colorado's Front Range.

A second relatively minor route extends from the highlands of northern Nevada and adjacent parts of Utah and Idaho to the Lower Colorado River valley. A third minor fall route leads from nesting areas in Oregon and California south to relatively nearby wintering areas in northern California.

Spring and fall crane migrations often involve some long nonstop flights. Studies by J. E. Toepler and R. A. Crete (1979) of radio-tagged greater sandhill cranes indicated that five birds flew nonstop 362 miles (from Chattanooga, Tennessee, to Impassible Bay, Florida) in 9.5 hours. During spring migration, one pair migrated 538 miles in 55 hours, making two overnight stops en route from the Jasper-Pulaski Area to its breeding marsh in central Minnesota. These birds migrated mainly during clear to partly cloudy weather, flew from 170 to 300 miles per day, and landed before sundown. Only a few birds migrated into headwinds or crosswinds, and most apparently migrated at altitudes of about 160 to 3,300 feet.

Once, when I was on St. Paul Island (one of the Pribilof Islands) in early June, I heard a flock of sandhill cranes calling from high above me, beyond my eyesight. These remote and tiny volcanic islands in the Bering Sea are located 200 miles from the nearest Alaskan landmass (Unalaska Island in the Aleutian Islands) and about 500 miles from the nearest Russian mainland. There are only a few other sight records of sandhill cranes from the Pribilofs, mostly of single birds and nearly all from early June. It seems impossible that the birds could have made landfall anywhere except on the Pribilofs, unless they turned around and flew 200 miles back to the Aleutians, a 400-mile round trip. I still wonder what became of them.

Whooping Crane

R. P. Allen (1952) analyzed the migrations of whooping cranes in great detail. S. R. Derrickson (1980) and Pearse et al. (2018, 2020) have supplemented his early records with more recent data.

Opposite: Whooping crane adult pair, Saskatchewan, Canada

In general, the migration follows a narrow and direct corridor between Wood Buffalo National Park and Aransas National Wildlife Refuge. Nebraska provides the largest number of historical records of migrating cranes, primarily because the Platte River was apparently their most important spring and fall staging area. Like the sandhill cranes, which use the same general area, the whooping crane historically roosted on the river bars at night and came to buffalo wallows early in the morning, where they fed on various aquatic life. The birds also foraged on the prairie uplands, often turning over cattle chips and feeding on the beetles under them. More recent research indicates that wetland habitats are preferred over all others in the Great Plains (A. Caven, pers. comm.).

The Wood Buffalo National Park and Aransas NWR migration corridor is widest in the Canadian provinces and North Dakota, and generally narrowest in the area from the Platte River valley of Nebraska southward (Map 3). Pearse et al. (2018) compared long-term Wood Buffalo–Aransas migration route data (1942–2016) with more recent (2010–2016) data and found that the 95 percent confidence limits of the overall core corridor width has averaged 294 kilometers (182 miles), but the corridor has gradually shifted eastward at an average rate of 1.2 kilometers (0.7 mile) per year, in association with a modest narrowing of the corridor's width.

S. Derrickson (1980) reported that spring departure from Aransas NWR usually falls between April 1 and April 15, with the last birds leaving by May 1, but with occasional stragglers remaining until mid-May, and rarely staying all summer. Spring departure from Aransas may extend over a period of as long as 44 days, or as short a period as 13 days. R. P. Allen (1952) estimated the spring migration to require from 9 to 23 days, averaging about 15 to 16 days. The first birds generally arrive on the Wood Buffalo National Park breeding grounds in late April.

The southward migration from Wood Buffalo National Park falls between September 12 and 26, and normally all the birds have arrived at Aransas NWR by mid-November. Nonbreeding birds evidently migrate earlier or faster than do breeders, since the earliest arrivals rarely have any immatures with them. Some stragglers arrive as late as the latter part of December. The normal fall migration, from late September to early November, is a more protected movement than is the spring migration. With recent strong indications of climate change, these dates are likely to shift backward in spring and forward in fall, as they have done with sandhill cranes and probably the great majority of other migratory birds in North America (Møller, Fiedler, and Berthold, 2004; Johnsgard, 2009b).

Daily movements are so far rather little studied, but by using radio-telemetric methods biologists were able to track one whooping crane family all the way from Wood Buffalo National Park to Aransas in 1981. It completed a 2,271-mile journey in less than a month, from October 4 to November 3. During that journey the birds made a series of nine flights, which ranged in distance from 18 to 470 miles and averaged about 175 miles per day (Emanuel, 1982).

Similar aerial tracking results were reported by Kuyt (1990), who listed 11 cases of long-distance nonstop flights in excess of 600 kilometers (372 miles) per flight, the longest of which was 1,809 kilometers (1,124 miles) and lasted more than 17 hours. It was aided by strong tail winds, and the birds reached a maximum ground speed of 105.9 kilometers (65.8 miles) per hour. Calculated air speeds ranged from 23.4 to 70.4 kilometers per hour (14.5 to 43.7 miles per hour).

Crane Navigation

All of the evidence on crane migration indicates that navigation between nesting and wintering areas occurs as a result of learning the routes by association with older and more experienced flock mates, usually the parents. Proof of this statement may be found in the results of two major experiments with whooping cranes.

The first occurred from 1975 to 1989, when the US Fish and Wildlife Service and Canadian

Wildlife Service transported 289 whooping crane eggs from Wood Buffalo National Park and inserted them into the nests of greater sandhill cranes at Grays Lake NWR in Idaho. The eggs were incubated, and the 209 that hatched were reared by the sandhills. The 90 that fledged accompanied their foster parents to the sandhill cranes' traditional wintering grounds at Bosque del Apache NWR in southern New Mexico, with 85 successfully reaching the refuge. This process, repeated over a several-year period, gradually established a flock of nearly 40 whooping cranes that used this new migration route. Although this aspect of the experiment was a success, the whooping crane chicks imprinted on sandhill cranes, and when they matured they either failed to obtain mates or, in at least one case, mated with a sandhill crane and produced a hybrid.

A different approach to the attempted establishment of a new migratory flock of whooping cranes began in 1997 when captive-hatched chicks at Necedah NWR in Wisconsin were not exposed to adult whooping cranes but were tended and fed by keepers dressed in costumes resembling whooping cranes. During their fledging period the young birds were introduced to and imprinted upon ultralight aircraft, which they learned to follow while the craft taxied about.

Later, as they fledged, they were taken on local training flights and eventually undertook the 1,220-mile migration to a wintering site in Florida. The first cohort of eight young made the trip successfully to Florida in 50 days. During the winter, two of the birds died, but the remaining six independently made the return flight to Necedah in Wisconsin, four of them arriving in less than ten days, averaging more than 100 miles per day.

Succeeding years of the Operation Migration project eventually brought the flock of whooping cranes up to about 100 birds. One of the findings from the experiment is that the cranes return to the same general area where they were hatched after a single route-learning experience. However, the birds don't follow the exact route that they had first experienced but use the same general corridor, indicating that they do not have to rely on specific learned landmarks in achieving the trip back to their natal home. Because of very poor reproductive success by the experimental birds, and the extremely high costs of training and leading them on their initial migration, Operation Migration was terminated in 2020, when 85 birds were still surviving.

The lesson from both of these experiments is that young cranes learn migration routes from their parents and experienced flock mates rather than instinctively acquiring them, and that a migratory "tradition" is thereby developed and transmitted from generation to generation in a cultural-like fashion. Only by having strong social bonds can this process work, and the loss of a local migratory tradition can destroy the migration route of a local population permanently.

5. How do cranes communicate?

Cranes are among the most vocal of all of the birds classified as nonpasserines (those species generally known as songbirds) and have voices of amazing carrying capability and nuance. This trait is understandable given their high degree of territoriality and the large sizes of territories that cranes occupy. Another factor influencing the number and complexity of crane vocalizations is the importance of pair- and family-bonding in maintaining migratory traditions and establishing social structure in flocks, such as providing effective group-warning systems in times of danger or group decisions on when to begin or terminate long migratory flights.

G. Carlson and C. H. Trost (1992) found that 98 percent of adult whooping crane males' guard calls were significantly lower in pitch than those of females, providing for reliable sex identification in the field. Other research (Klenova, Volodin, and Volodina, 2008) has indicated that cranes can recognize their mate by vocal characteristics alone, which is not surprising, considering the remarkable acoustic complexity of crane vocalizations. An extensive comparative review of

Following pages: Sandhill cranes, pair displaying, Platte River

the behavior and vocalizations of the cranes of the world was provided by D. H. Ellis et al. (1998). The basic vocabulary of sandhill cranes was described by Nesbitt and Bradley (1997) and summarized by Gerber et al. (2014).

Nearly a dozen rather quiet calls are used by young birds and adults for close-range communication. They include trills and peeps of chicks and several "purring" calls of low amplitude used by older birds. Among the purring calls are flight-intention purrs, feeding purrs uttered while foraging, growling purrs produced during aggressive situations, precopulatory purrs, and in-flight purrs. Other minor adult calls include snoring sounds that trigger alerts in other birds, distress calls by restrained birds, and loud yelps by birds separated from pair or family members (Gerber et al., 2014).

Several especially loud calls are important to adult sandhill cranes, all of which are rattling-like vocalizations ("rattles"). When uttered in flight ("flight calls"), they might be heard for more than two miles. When uttered on the ground, they include the "guard" and "unison" calls (Nesbitt and Bradley, 1997; Gerber et al. 2014).

Flight calls are a series of 7 to 20 loud, rattling notes uttered at the rate of about 15 per second. Those of males average 0.73 kilohertz (kHz) and those of females 1.0 kHz, and they might last a second or more. Flight calls are often used by flying cranes or by cranes on the ground in response to others flying out of sight or at night.

Guard calls are a similar or identical series of very loud rattling notes used by dominant territorial pairs or individuals in aggressive situations that might serve to intimidate and deter intruders. They also might be uttered when flying above a nesting territory. The guard call is also uttered when one or more birds mob a potential predator. It is repeated as long as the disturbance is present.

Unison calls are often uttered by pairs on foraging, roosting, or loafing sites. The unison call (Figs. 6, 13, and 19) is uttered by paired birds and is a duet that might be initiated by either pair member as a threat display toward other adults or as a triumph ceremony following an agonistic encounter. As such it serves as a pair-bonding and pair-maintenance function.

Both guard calls and unison calls are additionally used to advertise a pair's territory and to avoid conflict with other territorial adults. They may be uttered as a duet by pairs or by family groups, including juveniles at least nine weeks old (Gerber et al., 2014).

L. H. Walkinshaw (1965a) reported that little was known of the process of pair formation in sandhill cranes, but he judged that it occurred when the birds were about three years old. Thereafter, the newly mated pairs probably spend a summer or more on their territories, usually in marshes unoccupied by resident birds. The sandhill cranes he studied returned to Michigan in pairs, and these immediately dispersed to breeding territories after their spring arrival. Thus, pair-bonding must occur on wintering areas, or during the rather brief spring migration.

Pair-bonding in sandhill cranes is now known to be similar to that of most or all other cranes, with the unison-call ceremony (Fig. 6c) playing a vital role in the establishment and maintenance of pairs. In the sandhill crane, both sexes keep their wings completely folded during unison-calling, and the only significant movements are vertical head-lifting movements of the male, performed each time he utters a call-note. The female typically begins the display with a long, pulsed call that sounds something like machine-gun fire, followed by a prolonged series of short calls uttered in synchrony with slightly longer calls by the male. Occasionally a male will raise his back feathers and also lift his inner wing feathers while calling during high-intensity threat situations. Both birds typically remain stationary during the entire ceremony (Archibald, 1975).

The unison-call ceremony of the whooping crane (Fig. 6d) closely resembles those of several other *Grus* species that appear to be close relatives, according to G. Archibald. The female usually utters one long call followed by a short call for each male call but sometimes also utters two or three short calls for each male call. The female does not

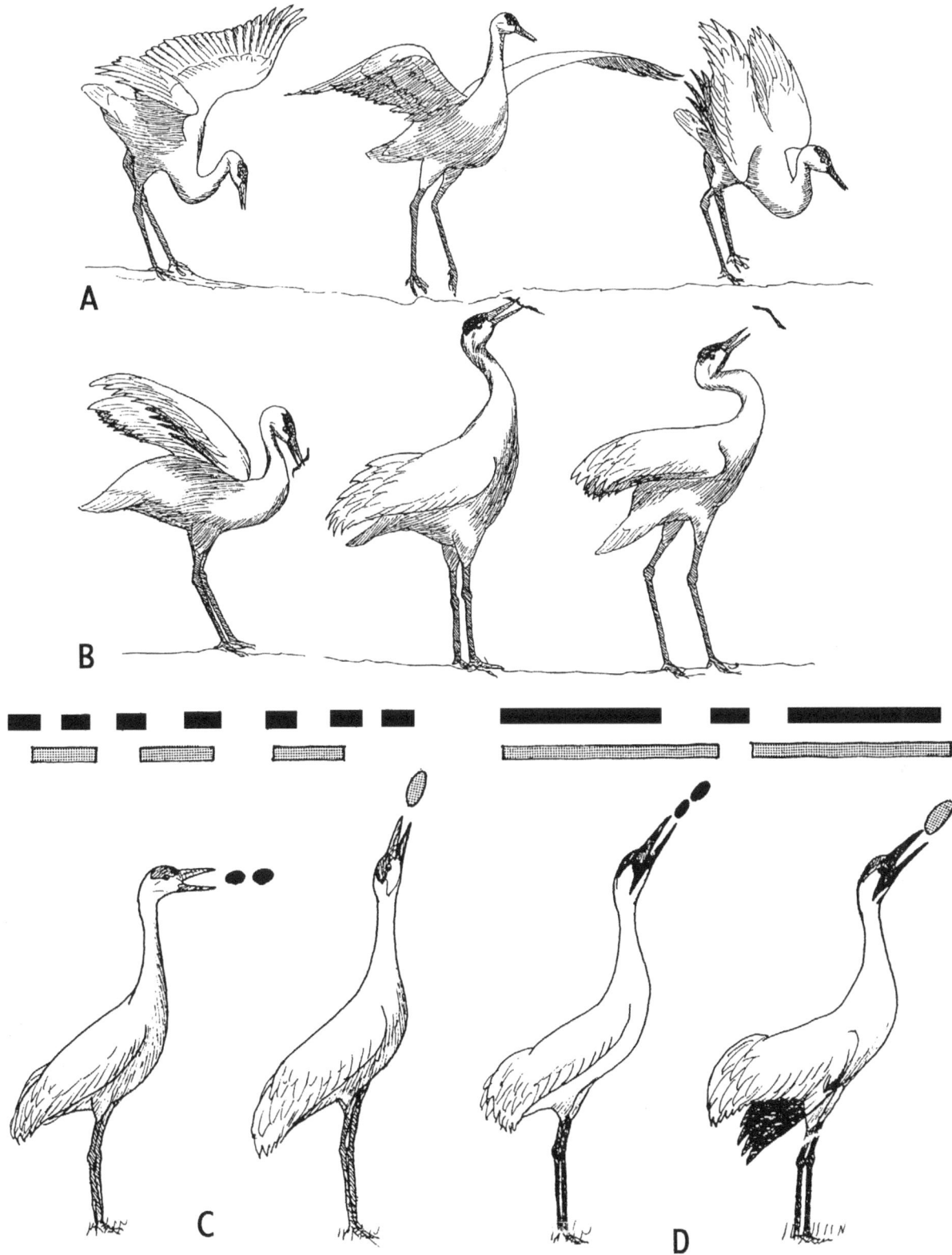

Fig. 6. Crane dancing, including bowing (A) and tossing (B) (after Voss 1976). Also unison-calling by sandhill crane (C) and whooping crane (D). Female calls are shown in ink, male calls by shading; overhead bar lengths and sound "bubbles" indicate call durations. After Archibald (1976).

usually lower her wrists during the unison-call ceremony, but the male strongly lowers his, exposing the black primary feathers. In both sexes the curved tertial feathers are held upward, forming a distinct plume.

Probably the most fascinating aspect of individualized crane communication behavior is "dancing," which is performed by all the species of cranes. Although dancing is also generally believed to be associated with courtship, it is clearly much more complex than having that single function, and indeed may occur in birds less than two days old. The dancing display of cranes is common to all species and is clearly an ancient type of behavior, which might be as closely related to redirected aggression or even to play behavior as it is to courtship (Dinets, 2013).

K. S. Voss (1976) described the major components of dancing in lesser sandhill cranes, while C. Y. Happ and G. Happ (2017) photographically illustrated the comparable and probably identical behavior in greater sandhill cranes. The several display elements of dancing consist of tossing objects into the air ("toss" of Happ and Happ) (Fig. 6b), "bowing" (Fig. 6a, left), which is often followed by jumping with wing-spreading (the "jump" of Happ and Happ) (Fig. 6a, middle), and prolonged wing-spreading (the "spread-hold" of Happ and Happ).

Other display elements described by Happ and Happ include head-bobbing (Fig. 6a, right) with the neck retracted ("tuck-bob"), arching the neck upward with the beak also uptilted and the wings spread ("arch"), a rotational jumping with the wings spread ("tour-jete"), a graceful synchronous turning of the pair ("minuet"), and turning on the run while holding one wing outstretched ("single-wing spin"), and tilting the body downward while gaping and holding both wings spread downward ("wing-spread-forward-bowtilt"). They also recorded an infrequent display in which one bird breaks away from a dancing pair and then rushes back while flapping and gliding ("run-flap-glide").

K. S. Voss (1976) observed dancing in sandhill crane chicks from 82 days of age onward and reported that it occurred in many situations thereafter. She divided dancing behavior into several component parts, which may occur in varying combinations. Still-flightless chicks dance by alternate wing-flapping, jumping or bouncing, and running movements. These are often performed with their parents and might both strengthen parent-offspring bonds and help the chick gain physical strength and coordination.

As the juveniles grow older, bowing and stick-tossing also become a part of the activity. During bowing, the neck is retracted as the legs are bent, and the bird bends forward and extends or lifts its wings (Fig. 6a, left). It then quickly extends its neck and legs, followed by a return to the retracted position. Bowing is often interspersed with jumping, or each bow may end with a jump. This display, as described and named by Voss, is not what Happ and Happ named the bow but rather is a brief part of the highly complex jumping sequence.

In the stick-tossing display, the bird bends forward, quickly grabs an object in its bill, extends it neck and legs, and then flings its bill upward, throwing the object up into the air. The neck is then quickly retracted, and the bird bows forward once again (Fig. 6b). This is the only display of cranes that uses an object as an integral part of its display; incorporating environment object-use into a display is rare among birds, generally.

Archibald stated that unpaired cranes two to three years old often dance with one another while on staging areas and that dancing probably serves to thwart aggression and facilitate pair formation, but it also occurs in very young birds as a normal part of motor development prior to fledging.

Dancing behavior also occurs in situations of limited danger, such as when humans are approaching from a distance or are in the general vicinity of a nesting site. It thus often occurs during periods of mild fear, as when the birds are placed in a situation of uncertain response to a possibly dangerous situation.

V. Dinets (2013) observed that although dancing often occurs among unpaired subadults, birds in well-established flocks dance more often than those in recently formed flocks, where needs for

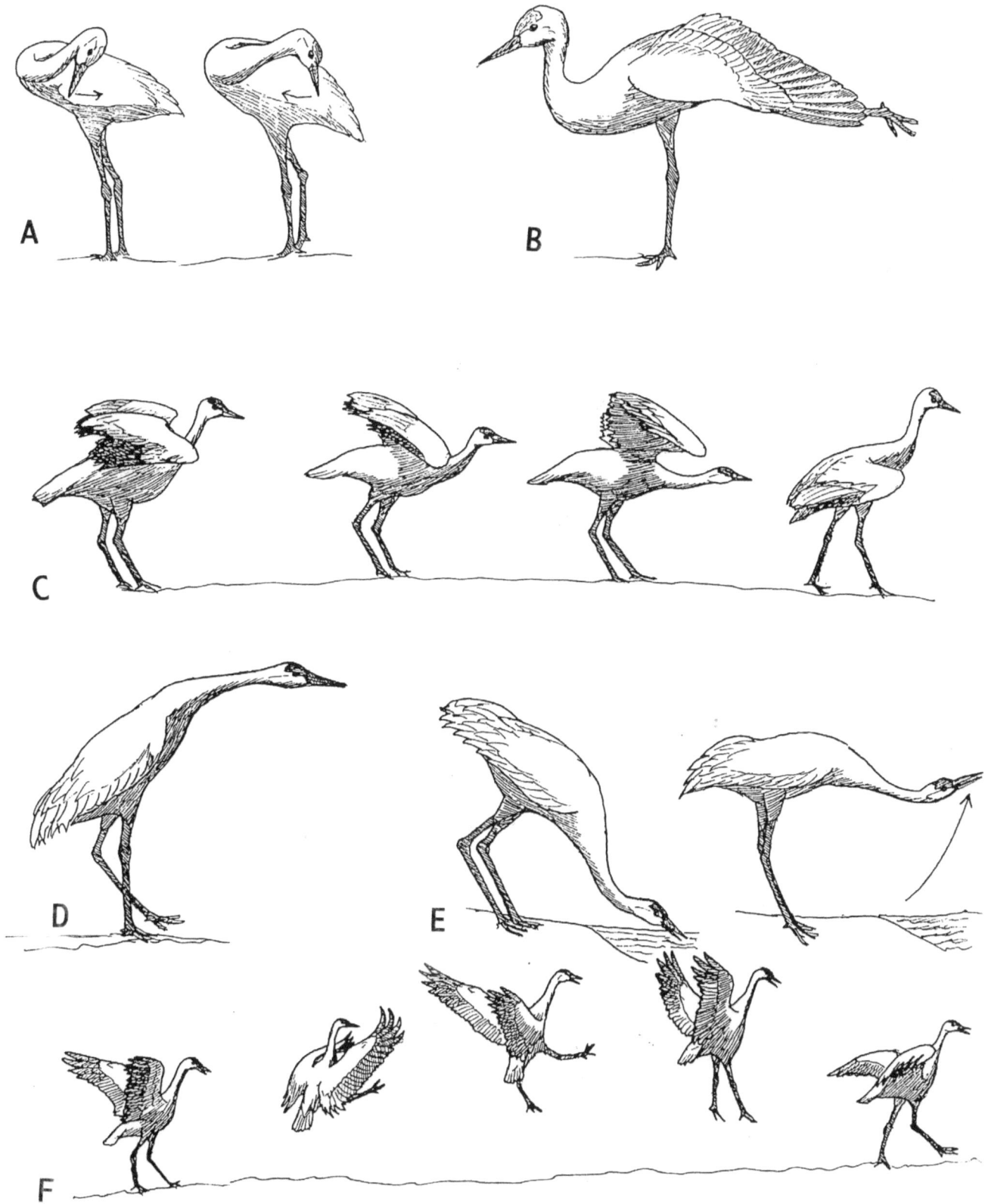

Fig. 7. Crane general (A–E) and agonistic (F) behavior, including body preening or back-slicking (A), wing-stretching (B), bow-stretching (C), flight-intention (D), drinking (E), and attack (F). After Voss (1976).

socialization would be higher. Adults of established pairs dance infrequently, as do yearlings that are not in flocks, but dancing may occur in prefledged chicks in company with their parents, and two-year-old birds dance frequently while they are at least a year before they are fully sexually mature. Dinets listed five criteria for behavior that constitutes true "play" activity and noted that all five criteria were met by crane dancing.

D. R. Blankinship (1976) also observed that dancing sometimes occurs in a noncourtship context among wild whooping cranes, such as between males of two nearby pairs. Although social dancing and fighting appear to have very similar behaviors—such as mutual jumping—fighting is recognizable by its associated bill-sparring and other actions obviously intended to inflict harm on the other bird. Chasing, bill-sparring, jump-raking with the toes' blunt claws while kicking an opponent, and beak-stabbing another bird are the highest levels of agonistic behavior. Fighting often occurs when a male of one pair encroaches into the personal space of another pair or the female of a pair is closely approached by a male other than her mate. Fighting is frequently followed by unison-calling by one or both participating pairs or potential pairs.

Threat-preening (Fig. 7a) is a common low-intensity threat posture that seems identical to normal preening but is prolonged, and the beak and head are oriented to the side of the body that is toward the threatened individual. Other generalized agonistic displays involve an expansion and brightening of the red crown skin; tertial-raising (Fig. 8a); and preening of the shoulder, lower breast, or belly feathers, which is sometimes performed while slowly strutting forward (Fig. 8e). A ruffle-shaking of the body feathers with the neck partly retracted (Fig. 8b) is an appeasement or submissive signal.

A display frequently used in threat situations is a prolonged downward bow of the head and neck with the crown skin greatly expanded and colorful (the "bill down" of Happ and Happ, Fig. 8a). The display ends with a soft growl and is better considered an agonistic display rather than a part of the dance repertoire.

Nesbitt and Archibald (1981) illustrated the more common agonistic displays of Florida sandhill cranes, including bill-stabbing, bill-sparring during fighting, a directed walking threat toward an opponent with the bill angled down and the crown skin conspicuously expanded (called "adornment walking" by Masatomi and Kitagawa, 1974/1975), a head-lowered charge, a prolonged low bow with the bill pointed directly downward (the "bill down" of Happ and Happ), and a generalized body- and wing-shaking that begins with a less intense bow and ends with breast or belly preening. Aggressive charging of another crane is performed by rapidly or methodically approaching and making flying jumps at the opponent (Fig. 7f).

Lastly, there is a submissive posture, in which the bird assumes a neck-retracted submissive posture with its bill directed somewhat downward and the bare crown skin retracted forward and dull in color. During agonistic situations a bird might also sink to the ground into a crouching posture (Fig. 8d). This posture has been called the "crouch-threat" (Happ and Happ, 2017) and the "cower-crouch" (Urbanek and Lewis, 2015). These are evidently two outwardly similar but functionally different displays that might indicate imminent attack (the crouch-threat) or submission and hiding from danger (the cower-crouch).

Nest or chick defense often involves a drooped-wing threat (the spread-wing display of Voss). The bird stands erect and spreads both wings outwardly (Fig. 8c, left). It is performed when facing a potentially intimidated predator, such as a fox, while remaining in place or slowly walking toward the animal. "Distraction behavior" is common and involves a crane reacting and attempting to lure a mammalian predator away from a chick or nest by lowering its wings and acting as if it were disabled and unable to fly (Fig. 8c, right). However, I have seen a sandhill crane with a young chick attack a female moose by flying into her face and sending her into quick retreat. Reports have also been made of cranes chasing caribou from the vicinity of their nests or young.

Opposite: Whooping crane, adult calling, Grays Lake National Wildlife Refuge, Idaho

Fig. 8. Crane agonistic behavior, including tertial-raising (A), appeasement (B), nest-defense (C), crouch-threat (D), ruffle-preening (E), and charge (F). After Voss (1976).

Pair-bonds can evidently be formed fairly quickly in whooping cranes, and in the apparent absence of elaborate display behavior such as dancing. This rapid bonding can happen in spite of the importance of making a good mate choice—considering the long-term implications of the permanent pair-bonding typical of all cranes.

Blankinship (1976) observed an interesting case of mating in which one of the parents (probably a female) of a whooping crane family was lost to an unknown cause. The remaining bird and its offspring stayed in the same area without obvious change in behavior, but only three weeks later the adult had taken a new mate. This was evidently done rather rapidly, and Blankinship made no mention of the process other than that the new male would not tolerate the juvenile and repeatedly drove it away.

Similarly, G. Maroldo (1980) described a notable mating history of a crippled wild whooping crane (named Crip), which had first been observed at Aransas NWR in the winter of 1945–46. After his first wild mate was shot in March 1948, Crip was observed with a new mate within a month, indicating that mate replacement under wild conditions can occur fairly rapidly.

During his remarkably long lifetime of at least 35 years (a record or near-record for longevity in wild whooping cranes), Crip had a total of five different mates (probably also a record). In 2017 Karine Gil and I observed a color-banded whooping crane at Aransas NWR that was 33 years old, and there is a record of a 50-year-old captive whooping crane at the International Crane Foundation.

Sandhill crane longevity records are generally somewhat shorter, although a sandhill crane at the National Zoo in Washington, DC, lived for 61 years, and there are several cases of wild birds surviving into their thirties. For wild Rocky Mountain sandhill cranes, the longevity record is at least 40 years (Drewien, Brown, and Clegg, 2010), a remarkable record in view of the fact that this population is legally hunted. In the more heavily hunted Mid-Continent Population, the reported survival record is 19 years (Gerber et al., 2014).

Evidently, fertility in very old cranes remains remarkably high; a captive male Siberian crane at the International Crane Trust was still fathering offspring (via artificial insemination) until he died in his late seventies. Copulation in the sandhill crane takes the same general form found in other *Grus* species and probably all cranes. C. D. Littlefield and R. A. Ryder (1968) observed copulation by Rocky Mountain greater sandhill cranes on 25 occasions. They noted that it occurred at various times throughout the day and that on only two occasions was any dancing behavior associated with copulation.

L. H. Walkinshaw (1973) observed copulation by eastern greater sandhill cranes on five occasions and commented that it was typically performed at the birds' breeding territories, and in all five instances it occurred during morning hours. In every observed case the female approached the male and assumed a receptive posture with her neck extended forward at a 45-degree angle and her wings somewhat extended. The male swiftly approached and copulated with his wings beating slowly. Essentially the same behavior sequence occurs in the Eurasian crane (Fig. 9).

Following a successful copulation, there is a postcopulatory display that in sandhill cranes may last up to 20 seconds. The birds typically stand side by side with their crowns expanded and their necks stretched vertically upward. They also typically simultaneously perform a "charge" display and then stand with their beaks horizontal and their crowns expanded for several seconds. The postcopulatory (and unison-call) display of the Siberian crane is notable for the symmetry of its vertical neck- and head-posturing by the pair (Fig. 10a).

Many less elaborate or less conspicuous behavioral activities also have social-signaling function (Voss, 1976). Prior to taking flight—if sudden flight is not caused by a dangerous stimulus—cranes bend their necks progressively forward into a distinctive leaning posture (Fig. 7d). The display probably serves to make certain that all of a group's members are alert and ready to take flight together. This "flight-intention" behavior is

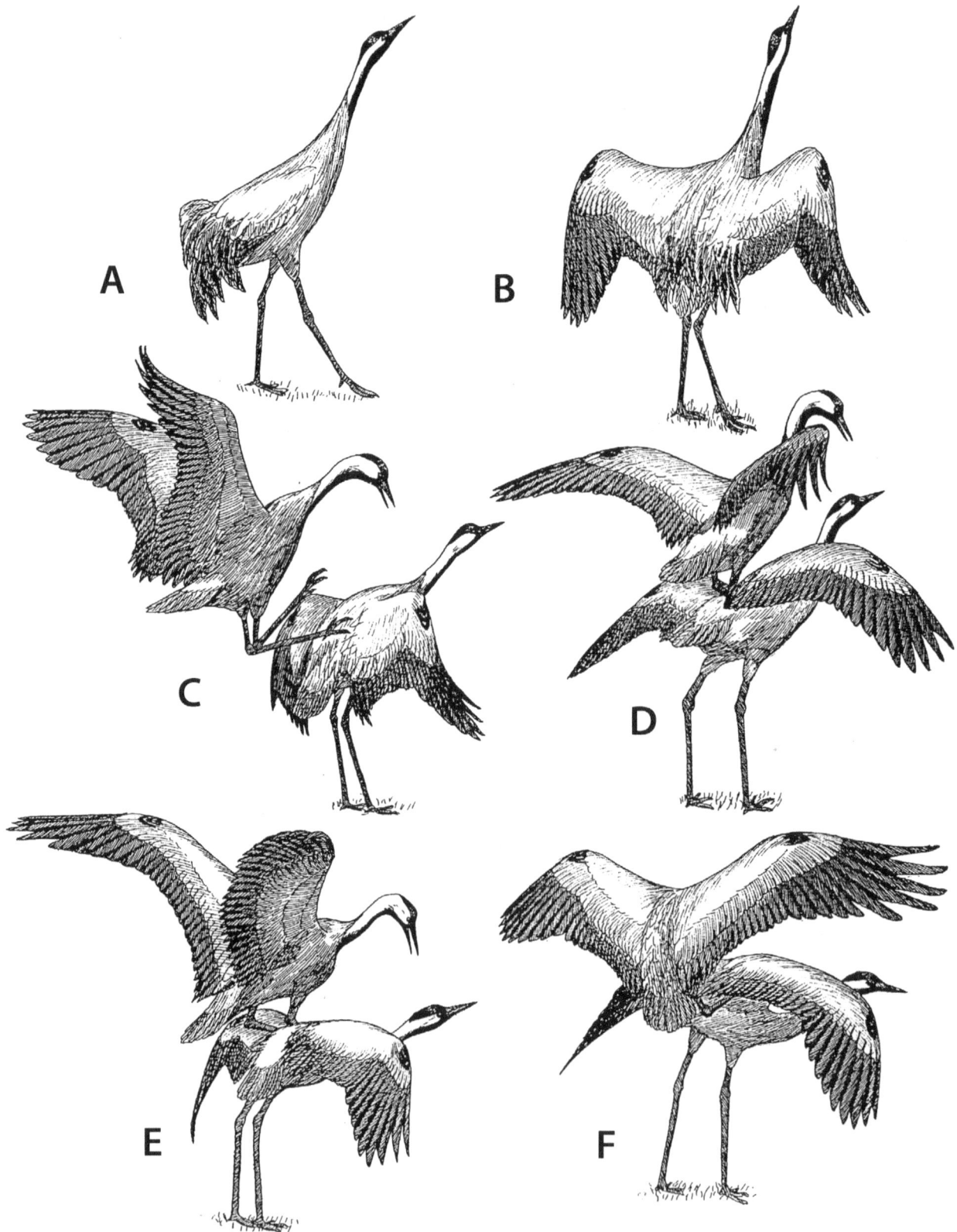

Fig. 9. Copulatory behavior of the Eurasian crane, including male approach (A), female receptive posture (B), and copulation sequence (C–F). After Glutz von Blotzheim (1973).

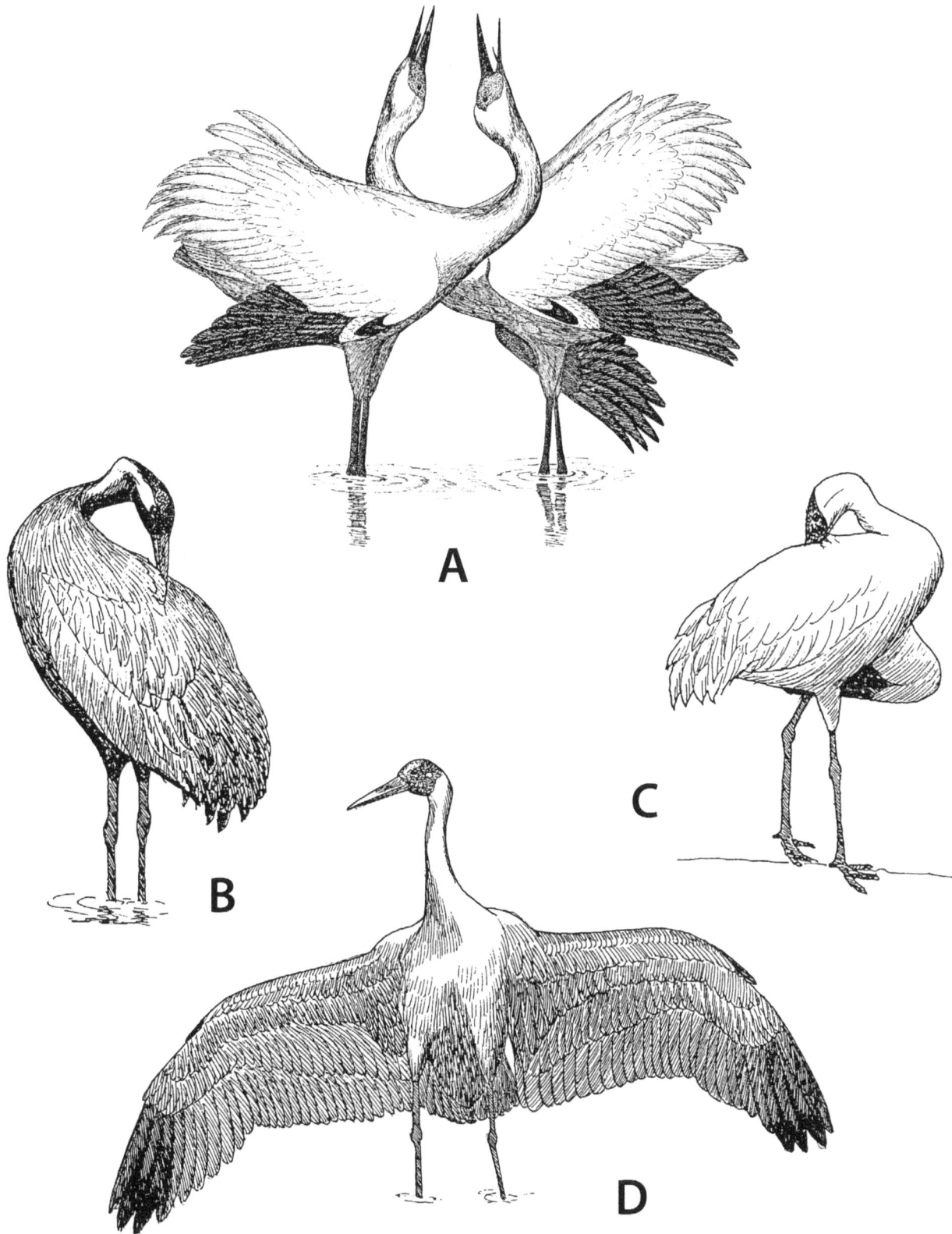

Fig. 10. Crane social behavior, including unison-calling of Siberian crane (A), threat-preening by Eurasian crane (B) and Siberian crane (C), and nest defense wing-spreading by brolga (D). Various sources.

especially evident among families, and when one member begins it, the posture is likely to be assumed by others until takeoff occurs. However, if it is initiated by a young family member, it is often ignored by the adults, whereas its performance by one or both adults greatly increases the probability of the group taking flight.

Many crane behaviors have no apparent social significance but are important as apparent "comfort," self-maintenance activities or have generalized survival benefits (Masatomi, 2004). Self-preening by cranes is a time-consuming activity that begins shortly after hatching and continues throughout life, especially during molting periods. Typically cranes preen a single feather area for up to about 20 seconds, then move to another area. Frequently each feather is intially nibbled at its base and then gently drawn through the beak between the upper and lower mandibles. This is the process especially for the longer body and wing feathers, the vanes of which must be kept in fine repair if they are to provide an efficient airfoil. During molting periods the larger feathers are often extracted in the course of preening.

An activity that is apparently derived from normal preening behavior (Fig. 7a) is "back-slicking." In this behavior, the head and bill are usually directed toward the uropygial gland at the base of the tail, apparently to obtain oil, and then the head and beak are vigorously rubbed over the surface of the back and wing as well as over the underparts and rest of the body that can be reached by the bill.

The sandhill and Eurasian cranes perform a nearly identical behavior, after first digging in mud or a mixture of mud and decayed vegetation and grabbing some with the bill. The crane then performs back-slicking, spreading the material over most of the body feathers and producing a stain that is often a bright rusty brown, somewhat similar in color to that of the juveniles' plumage. This "feather-painting" is characteristic of only adult cranes on nesting territories. It seems probable that the added coloration has functional significance as a camouflaging device for nesting birds.

Several other commonly performed behaviors are also self-directed and apparently serve as "comfort movements" or body maintenance activities, or are associated with basic physiological functions, such as eating, drinking, and defecation. Drinking is performed by dipping the bill in the water and quickly raising it upward and forward (Fig. 7e). A single drinking sequence requires about five seconds, and it may be repeated up to about seven times in succession.

Stretching activities by cranes are "comfort movements" that occur in three major forms. Frequently a single wing and the corresponding leg are stretched simultaneously (Fig. 7b). At other times, both wings are stretched simultaneously as the back is held horizontally and the neck is extended and held nearly vertically. Finally, during "bow-stretching," (sometimes called a "two-wing stretch") (Fig. 7c) a bird raises both wings simultaneously while extending the neck horizontally forward. The wings may be held in an extended position for several seconds before the head is raised and the wings are folded. A yawnlike "jaw-stretching" also sometimes occurs in cranes, especially during periods of relative inactivity. None of these postures seems to serve any obvious social communication function.

Lastly, walking and running (Fig 11a) are performed in a humanlike manner, at rates of from less than one to more than three steps per second. When running fast, cranes achieve a bouncing gait, and occasionally a running crane will extend its wings and flap them to some extent, apparently to gain additional speed or maintain balance.

Takeoffs (Fig. 11a) are done into the wind, and the speed of the wind affects the distance needed to attain flight. In flight, the legs typically are held back in direct line with the body (Fig. 11b), but it is not uncommon to see cranes flying in cold weather with one or both legs tucked invisibly forward in the flank feathers, producing a gooselike flight profile. Local foraging flights are done at much lower altitudes than during migration and with little or no formation flying, so that at any great distance a large crane flock typically has an amorphous, changing shape.

Fig. 11. Flight behavior of red-necked crane, including takeoff (A), flight (B), and landing (C). After Masatomi and Kitagawa (1974/1975).

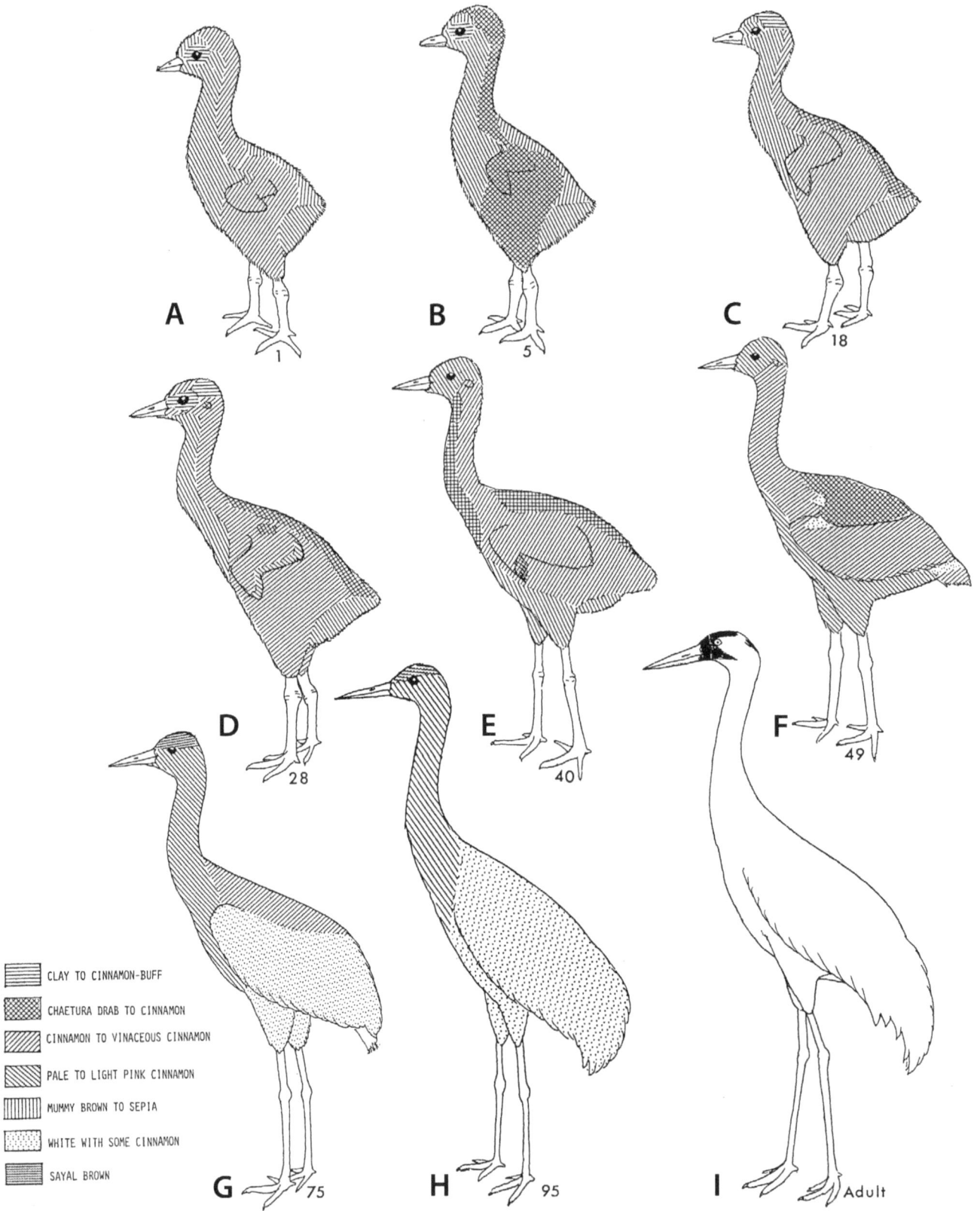

CLAY TO CINNAMON-BUFF

CHAETURA DRAB TO CINNAMON

CINNAMON TO VINACEOUS CINNAMON

PALE TO LIGHT PINK CINNAMON

MUMMY BROWN TO SEPIA

WHITE WITH SOME CINNAMON

SAYAL BROWN

Fig. 12. Stages of whooping crane plumage development during first 95 days after hatching (A–H) and adult plumage (I). Numbers indicate days after hatching. After Stephenson (1971).

Flying crane flocks have no "leader," but vocal contact among pairs and family members while in flight no doubt prevents them from becoming separated. Prior to striking out on long-distance flights, whooping cranes typically attain an altitude of several thousand feet above land while group-soaring ("kettling") in thermal updrafts. They then begin a long glide with their wings rigidly held out in a slightly streamlined profile. They then also assume coordinated, often V-shaped, formations that reduce air turbulence and increase flight speed (Kuyt, 1992). Long-distance migratory flights consist of repeated altitude gains by soaring, alternated with long, gliding descents.

Landing is done by lowering the legs and "setting" the wings in a decurved umbrellalike profile; leg-lowering perhaps improves aerial stability during the bird's landing approach by lowering its center of gravity (Fig. 11c). Usually sandhill cranes take quick drinks of water immediately after landing at an evening roost and then gradually wade out into shallow water and settle a short distance away from the nearest neighbors.

6. How do cranes nest and rear their young?

Sandhill Crane

The normal age of maturity among wild sandhill cranes probably varies among races, where climatic and ecological differences might result in differing rates of growth and maturity. D. H. Johnson (1979) assumed that both sexes of sandhill cranes begin to breed in the wild at 4 years of age, but in the Florida race of sandhill cranes, males may attempt to breed at 2 years and females at 3. The modal age for first successful breeding in Florida is 3 years in males and 4.7 years in females (Nesbitt and Tacha, 1997). Although males may be able to breed at 3 years, several more years might be needed before all the birds are successful at mating and establishing territories because of competition for mates and favorable territories.

In a study of pair-bonding in greater and Florida sandhill cranes, Nesbitt and Tacha (1997) monitored birds for 426 pair-years. Forty-four percent of 72 Florida sandhill crane pair-bonds were broken during the study, of which 68 percent was due to death and 32 percent to divorce. Among both Florida and greater sandhill cranes, the incidence of divorce was related to a failure to reproduce; 52.6 percent of pairs that failed to produce young divorced, and only 10 percent of pairs that divorced had a history of successful reproduction. Pair longevity was not correlated with pair productivity among pairs that had existed more than three years. The overall divorce rate in the Florida race was 3.9 percent. The annual mortality rate for adults of this race in Georgia was 11 percent (Bennett and Bennett, 1990), so the probability of one or both members of a pair dying within a year would be roughly 22 percent.

Mate loss in the Florida sandhill crane was studied by Nesbitt (1989). Following mate loss,

Fig. 13. Unison call of greater sandhill crane (male on right).

Following pages: Greater sandhill cranes, adult and young, Grays Lake National Wildlife Refuge, Idaho

established males usually retained their territories, remated, and attempted nesting, often successfully, the following season. Six of ten surviving females left their territory, and two to three years passed before four of them re-paired and attempted to nest again. The females that retained their territories usually paired with younger, often inexperienced males, but divorced males that retained their territories re-paired with females that were as old or older than themselves.

A substantial amount of information is available on the timing of breeding in the various races of sandhill cranes. The Florida Population of sandhill cranes not only begins nesting earlier but also has a much more prolonged egg-laying period, with eggs seen as early as December and as late as August. This perhaps reflects a considerable incidence of renesting behavior, which in the Florida race might occur as many as three times. Three probable cases of renesting were reported by J. M. Valentine, Jr. and R. E. Noble (1970) for the Mississippi race.

In migratory populations nest initiation dates range from early April to mid-June. Renesting in the greater sandhill crane has been found only in those pairs that lost their clutches during the first half of the incubation period (Gerber et al., 2014). L. H. Walkinshaw (1965a) reported that in Michigan 82 nests were found in April, 37 in May, and one each in June and July. This would suggest that less than 5 percent of the nests located there were likely to have resulted from renesting. Studies of the lesser sandhill crane have offered no firm evidence of renesting, which would seem unlikely within the constraints of a short breeding season.

In a dense concentration of birds at Michigan's Phyllis Haehnle Sanctuary, seven pairs usually nested each year of Walkinshaw's study, and he determined the average territory size over a five-year period to be about 43.5 acres, although he estimated that some birds occupied territories as small as 8 acres. In that sanctuary the birds not only defended the wet marsh area but also used adjacent dry marsh areas after their young were

Fig.14. Sandhill crane incubating. First-hatched chicks often climb onto the back of their parent while the second-laid egg is still being incubated.

hatched. At times, paired cranes will utter the unison call in early morning or near sundown, apparently as a kind of an announcement of territorial occupancy (Fig. 13).

C. D. Littlefield and R. A. Ryder (1968) estimated that the smallest territory in their study area in central Oregon was 3 acres and the largest 168 acres, with eight averaging 62 acres. This is somewhat similar to the fairly dense territories reported by R. C. Drewien (1973) in the Grays Lake area of Idaho, where 10 territories averaged about 42 acres.

Of 26 lesser sandhill crane nests studied by C. M. Boise (1977) in Alaska, most were on slightly raised mounds in wet marshes, although the whole range also included shallow-water sites and some on dry tundra. Overall, they were generally in drier situations than those typical of other races. Walkinshaw found that 120 greater sandhill crane nests in Michigan were built in shallow-water marshes, typically among cattails and sedges. Twelve of 13 nests built in bogs mostly consisted of sticks and clumps of mosses. Forty-nine nests were surrounded by water, and all were well isolated from humans.

In Michigan, the period of nest construction requires approximately a week, and the nest is constructed by both birds working a few hours each day. Nests in bogs tend to be smaller than those built in marshes, and some nests built on dry land tend to be very small. The size of the nest is evidently largely a reflection of the amount of water and associated vegetation immediately around the nest, and this is highly variable.

In his Michigan studies, L. H. Walkinshaw (1965a) found that the eggs were laid from two to three days apart. As soon as the first egg is laid, incubation begins and is performed alternately by both members of the pair. As in nearly all other cranes, the great majority of clutches are of two eggs (average clutch size of 207 nests was 1.9 eggs). The attentive period of the cranes is to some extent regulated by the behavior of the nonincubating bird, since the incubating bird seldom leaves the nest until it is relieved by its mate (Fig. 14). Walkinshaw found that male attentive periods averaged

215 minutes for 41 periods, and females averaged 195 minutes for 33 periods. The eggs were always found to be incubated during the night, and in four observed cases this was performed by the male. The average nighttime attentiveness period for the five nests was 938 minutes (15.6 hours).

During the daytime hours the nests were found to be incubated for 98 percent of the observed time, and slightly over half of this daytime incubation was observed to be performed by the male. Daytime changeovers in incubation duties were found to range from one to seven times, and during 29 observation days the average number of changeovers was 3.6. Evidently, no changeovers take place during nightime hours.

In Walkinshaw's (1965a) Michigan studies, he stated that 74 percent of 107 nests were successful, and that 68 percent of 201 associated eggs hatched. If deserted nests are discounted, young hatched in 81 percent of 96 nests, and 74.4 percent of eggs hatched from a total of 180. In Michigan, raccoons were found to be the most serious predators of eggs. Raccoons were also reported to be serious egg predators in Oregon by Littlefield

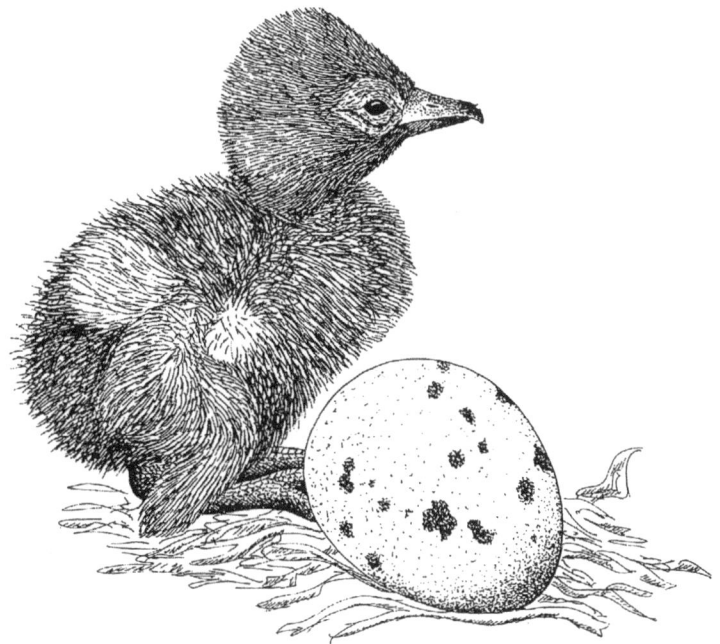

Fig 15. Sandhill crane chick and egg.

and Ryder (1968). Coyotes were also present there and were found to be minor egg predators but serious sources of mortality for young birds. Boise (1977) estimated that predators such as gulls, jaegers, foxes, and native human residents were responsible for the loss of 27 percent of the eggs of lesser sandhill cranes in western Alaska, where overall nesting success was estimated at 67 percent and hatching success was 64 percent.

The incubation of greater sandhill cranes has been found to average 30 days under natural conditions, with a range of 28 to 32 days. No evidence exists of significant variations in incubation among the various subspecies. Typically, a single day separates the time of hatching of the young in two-egg clutches (Fig. 15). Newly hatched young are usually fed the eggshell from which it hatched by the parent attending the nest, who breaks it up into very small pieces and feeds it to the young bill to bill. However, very little, if any, food is usually given to them on the first day. Yet by the time they are about six hours old they often leave the nest a short distance, sometimes even swimming short distances. Often the male will take the first-hatched chick on short exercise walks while the female is still incubating the remaining unhatched egg (Fig. 16).

By the day after hatching the young are eating small items, and if the two eggs hatch on separate days the older chick often follows one of its parents away from the nest while the second one is still

Fig. 16. Sandhill crane with downy chick.

Fig. 17. Sandhill crane uttering guard call.

being brooded. When both chicks are fairly strong, they are generally taken away from the nest site by both their parents, often into dry fields or drier marshy areas where insect foods are abundant.

Fledging in the lesser sandhill crane occurs at about 50 days of age, in the Florida race at about 56 days, and in greater sandhill cranes at 65 to 75 days. The rate of survival of young birds until autumn is probably fairly high in most areas but seems to be lower in the Arctic. Walkinshaw (1965a) reported that 284 juveniles fledged out of 294 hatched young among Michigan nests, suggesting a 96.5 percent fledging rate. By comparison, Boise (1977) reported that 57 percent and 71 percent of the lesser sandhill crane chicks she observed during two successive breeding seasons survived to fledging.

Whooping Crane

Whooping cranes begin pair-bonding at two to three years of age; initial averge first breeding is at four years (Urbanek and Lewis, 2015). Nesting behavior studies at Wood Buffalo National Park have been carried out since 1966. E. Kuyt (1981a) has summarized much of the resulting information on territoriality and nest use. He found that of 192 nest sites studied, at no time did the birds use the same nest in successive years, although they often nested in the same marsh. Territorial defense and unison-calling (Fig. 19) occur in these areas, but the breeding range is lightly populated, and the birds have contact with only a few other birds each year. Since the cranes are both very long-lived and have high fidelity to old territories, there is

Fig. 18. Whooping crane wading.

Fig. 19. Whooping crane unison-calling.

probably only a small amount of territorial inter-action each year, so much time is spent in forag-ing and body maintenance or "comfort" behavior such as preening (Fig. 20).

Kuyt observed that territorial birds attacked and chased off both single and paired cranes. He believed that the territorial bond is sufficiently strong for a bird to return to its territory even in the event of the death of its mate. Thus, territo-ries are likely to be reused for many years and may become vacant only in the event that both adults die during the same year.

The composite nesting areas (probably entire home ranges) in the Sass River and Klewi River vi-cinity of Wood Buffalo National Park range from 0.4 to 4.3 square miles, with 15 averaging 1.5 square

Fig. 20. Whooping crane preening.

miles. Two territories in the Nyarling River area av-eraged 13.4 square miles, and one in Alberta only 0.15 square mile. The grand average from all areas is 1.8 square miles. These generally large areas in-clude some habitats not used for nesting, although much of the area eventually becomes used by the pairs or families during foraging in shallow water (Fig. 18) or other daily activities.

Most historical records of crane nests indi-cate that they are located along lake margins or among rushes or sedges in marshes with the wa-ter anywhere from 8 to 10 inches deep to as much as about 18 inches deep. The nests are often 2 to 5 feet in diameter and range in height from about 8 to 18 inches above the surrounding water level. Nesting has also been reported on muskrat houses and on damp prairie sites. A nest studied by R. P. Allen at Aransas NWR was constructed in cattails in water apparently initially about a foot deep. However, falling water levels eventually made this level much less.

Judging from various accounts, it is likely that eggs are normally laid two days apart and that in most cases two eggs are laid. E. Kuyt reported that of 203 clutches he observed between 1966 and 1980, 91 percent of them contained two eggs, 8 percent had a single egg, and 1.5 percent had three eggs. He also reported two apparent cases of renesting in wild birds.

Both sexes incubate (Fig. 21), and R. P. Allen (1952) provided detailed observations on incuba-tion behavior and nest-relief activities. He deter-mined that the male spent more time on the nest than did the female and that nest exchanges av-eraged 7.6 per day. Toward the end of the incuba-tion period, the female began to spend more time on the eggs and relieved the male more frequently.

L. H. Walkinshaw (1973), studying the same captive birds for seven days, made similar obser-vations. He found that the female did more night-time incubation than did the male, but that the male did 53 percent of the daytime incubation. During the entire seven-day period the eggs were incubated 93 percent of the time. W. G. Conway (1957) watched the same pair some years later and

Fig. 21. Whooping crane incubating.

found that the male did most of the nighttime incubation and the female undertook most of the daytime responsibility.

Whichever bird does the incubating, the other one serves as "guard." In particular, Allen found the male to be intolerant of intruders such as various wading birds, particularly herons and egrets. Walkinshaw observed cranes chasing herons, egrets, pelicans, ducks, and even swallows. Historical accounts by egg collectors indicate that injury-feigning, with wings drooped and spread and the head lowered, is a common response to human intrusion near the nest.

The incubation period is probably 33 to 34 days under wild conditions but has been found to be 30 to 31 days in incubators. Conway (1957) reported that the second chick hatched three days after the first one, and the second-hatched bird did not receive a higher level of protection from poaching of food by the older chick until about 30 hours after hatching. He also stated that the newly hatched chicks at the New Orleans Zoo were fed earthworms, dragonflies, and grasshoppers by their parents, and that the young birds were offered food almost constantly. A chick hatched at Aransas NWR in 1950 was quite active within 24 hours after hatching, and by the fourth day was being brooded more than 100 yards from the nest.

During the first 20 days after hatching, the families generally remain within a mile of the nesting site, with daily movements averaging about 0.5 mile, according to S. R. Derrickson (1980). The young birds fledge when they are about 80 to 90 days old. Until that time they are vulnerable to large predators such as wolves. Derrickson's data suggest that chick and juvenile losses tend to occur throughout the summer, rather than being concentrated during the first two weeks after

Fig 22. Whooping cranes dancing.

hatching. He judged that relatively dry conditions during his summers of fieldwork on the breeding grounds may have made the older young more vulnerable to large predators than would be the case when water supplies are adequate.

Whooping crane juveniles continue to be fed by their parents, especially by the female, for an extended time during their first fall and winter. They probably do not become truly independent until they are gradually abandoned by their parents the following spring. However, the young birds typically follow their parents northward in the spring, and it is likely that they are not forcefully separated from them until their arrival on the breeding grounds. Prior to their arrival on the breeding grounds the adult breeding pairs spend a good deal of time dancing (Figs. 22 and 23) and performing other pair-maintenance behaviors such as unison-calling. Most copulations seem to occur just prior to egg laying, although several instances have been seen during spring staging along the Platte River.

Fig. 23 Whooping cranes dancing.

7. What are the American crane populations and their trends?

Sandhill Crane

There is no simple way to summarize the numerical status of the sandhill crane in North America given the fact that there are four mainland races (greater, Canadian, lesser, and Mississippi) plus the insular Cuban race. Beyond that, the greater sandhill crane has three geographically isolated populations (Eastern, Rocky Mountain, and Lower Colorado River Valley) as well as three populations that winter in company with one or two other races, making overall counts of the separate races difficult.

One of these mixed-race populations is California's Pacific Coast Population (Collins et al., 2016). These cranes breed in the Pacific coast states, from California north through southern Washington, British Columbia's Vancouver Island, and southern Alaska. At least the northern part of this population consists of the Canadian race *rowani*, which evidently winters from western Oregon south into California's Sacramento River valley nearly to the Sacramento–San Joaquin delta (Pogson and Lindstedt, 1991; Ivey, Herzinger, and Hoffmann, 2005), in company with lesser sandhills and perhaps also some greaters. This population is reportedly increasing, with about 11,000 birds in 2016 (Collins et al., 2016). Additionally, hundreds of greater sandhills from eastern Oregon's Harney Basin and northeastern California also migrate south to winter in California's Central Valley, adding to the genetic and geographic diversity found there.

A more northerly breeding component of the Pacific Coast Population nests along the Alaska Peninsula and the southern coast of Alaska east through the Kenai Peninsula and winters in the southern parts of California's Central Valley. In 2007–8 the total Central Valley population was 20,000 to 27,000 birds, with about 6,800 in the delta region being greaters (Ivey et al., 2014a). A more recent (2012–14) estimate indicated an average population of 29,000 birds (Table 1) and was judged to be increasing by Collins et al. (2016).

The other mixed-race winter assemblage is relatively small numerically, with a 2012–14 average of about 3,000 birds (Collins et al., 2016), which winter along with a few lessers in the Lower Colorado River valley, mostly in Cibola NWR, and adjacent areas of southeastern Arizona, the Sonny Bono NWR of southern California, and along the Gila River in Arizona (see Map 2). The greaters in this population breed mostly in northeastern Nevada, plus some in Idaho and Utah. This population is apparently stable (Collins et al., 2016), so specific numerical estimates are probably not crucial, although because of its overall small size it deserves close monitoring.

Of the single-race populations of greater sandhill cranes, the Eastern Population is doing remarkably well, with a 2012–14 spring average of about 75,000 birds. During the mid-1900s the population was far smaller and largely limited to Wisconsin, Michigan, and southern Ontario. It has expanded markedly in both population size and geographic range during the last several decades (Maps 1 and 2).

The next largest single-race population of greater sandhill cranes is the Rocky Mountain Population, with an estimated stable population of 18,000 birds, based on a 2012–14 average (Collins et al., 2016). During the early 1990s the population was estimated at 20,000 to 21,500 birds by Drewien, Brown, and Kendall (1995) and was considered by them to be stable or slightly declining. This population breeds mainly in western Montana and Wyoming, eastern Idaho, northern Utah, and northwestern Colorado. It winters mostly in the middle Rio Grande River of New Mexico and to a lesser degree in southwestern New Mexico, southeastern Arizona, and the Northern Highlands of Mexico (Maps 1 and 2).

The largest population of lesser sandhill cranes is the Mid-Continent Population, which breeds from Yakutia in northeastern Russia east to Baffin Island in northeastern Canada and has a population that, because of its vast range, is impossible to measure accurately. Recent spring estimates in Nebraska's Platte/North Platte River valley, where nearly all of the populations stage for a few weeks in March, have generally ranged from about 600,000 to 800,000 birds. One recent (2019) spring count has suggested a population in excess of a million birds (Table 1), although the most recent three-year average would be closer to 700,000 to 800,000 birds.

The eastern end of the central Platte valley also supports some staging greater sandhill cranes en route to nesting grounds in Minnesota and Manitoba, and the entire valley probably includes much larger numbers of Canadian sandhill cranes headed for breeding grounds in Alberta, Saskatchewan, and Manitoba. The overall Mid-Continent Population makeup has been estimated as 65 percent lessers, 30 percent Canadians, and 5 percent greaters. It is impossible to judge the abundance of the Canadian race accurately, but if the Mid-Continent Population has 700,000 spring birds, and 30 percent consists of Canadians, the Canadian component might total at least 200,000

Table 1. American Crane Abundance, Population Trends, and Hunter Kill

Races and Geographic Subpopulations[a]	Approximate Population	Population Trend	Annual Hunter Kill[a]
Single-race populations			
Greater Sandhill Crane (GSC)			
Eastern Population (EP)	70,600[c]	Increasing	950
Rocky Mountain Population (RMP)	22,000	Stable	1,200[c]
Lower Colorado River Population (LCRP)	2,500	Stable	—
Lesser Sandhill Crane (LSC)[b]	ca. 700,000	Stable/Increasing	—
Canadian Sandhill Crane (CaSC)[b]	?	?	?[a]
Mixed-race populations			
Mid-Continent Population (MCP)[b]	660,000	Stable/Increasing	51,400
Pacific Coast (Flyway) Population (PCP)	29,000	Increasing	Few
Central Valley Population (CVP)[c]	11,000	Increasing	—
Resident populations			
Mississippi Sandhill Crane (MISC)[d]	133	Stable	—
Florida Sandhill Crane (FLSC)[e]	ca. 5,000	Stable	—
Cuban Sandhill Crane (CuSC)[f]	526	Declining locally	—
Whooping Crane[g]			
Aransas–Wood Buffalo flock (AWBF)	506	Increasing	—
Eastern migratory flock (EMF)	83	Stable	—
Louisiana nonmigratory flock (LNF)[h]	76	Uncertain	—
Florida nonmigratory flock (FNF)	9	Declining	—

[a] Sandhill crane population estimates are mostly from Mirande and Harris (2019) and Collins et al. (2016). Hunter kill estimates are based mostly on Dubovsky (2018) for the 2017 hunting season. Additionally, the Mexican kill has been judged as less than 10 percent of the overall midcontinent kill, and the Native subsistence kill in Alaska is negligible.

[b] The 2016–18 Platte River survey estimate of 660,000 is a three-year average, but the 2019 estimate was more than 1 million.

[c] The winter CVP population is about 75 percent lesser sandhill cranes and 25 percent greater. Some Canadian sandhill cranes from coastal British Columbia and probably southeast Alaska are also present in the PCP. See Ivey, Herzinger, and Hoffmann (2005).

[d] See Hereford and Bilodeaux, 2010.

[e] See Nesbitt and Hatchitt, 2008.

[f] See Galvez-Aguilera and Chavez-Ramirez, 2010.

[g] Based mostly on estimates in *The Bugle* (ICF Newsletter), November 2019, with updates to spring 2020. The 2020 total excludes an estimated 29 birds wintering outside the primary Aransas survey area. The total population has remained stable over the past three winters, owing to low fledging rates in Canada and associated low (8.4 percent) annual recruitment rates.

[h] As of early 2020, the 83 greater sandhill cranes in the eastern migratory flock included 14 wild-hatched and 69 captive-raised birds. Of 158 juvenile whoopers released in Louisiana, 76 were surviving, including 3 wild-hatched birds (*Eastern Crane Bulletin*, June 2020).

birds, and the lesser component close to 500,000. The Mid-Continent Population has been slowly increasing at the rate of a few percent annually since at least the 1960s, when spring estimates in the Platte valley averaged about 160,000 birds. In spite of heavy hunting pressure, it has thus only quadrupled in six decades, whereas the protected whooping crane population has increased by at least 25-fold during that period. However, current data suggest that the increase in the rate of "sport" killing in the Mid-Continent Population is increasing faster than the rate of growth in crane abundance (Dubovsky, 2018).

Among the residential races of sandhill crane, the Florida race (which is barely separable morphologically from the greater race) has long had a population totaling about 4,000 birds (Table 1). Nearly all of them are limited to Florida, but about 500 occur in and near Georgia's Okefenokee Swamp. The Florida cranes are an unhunted population, and the best data on survival and mortality rates, pair-bond lengths, and other important

Following pages: Whooping cranes, Platte River valley, Nebraska

demographic and social parameters have come from studies of this protected population (Nesbitt, 1989, 1996, 1997; Nesbitt and Hatchitt, 2008; Nesbitt and Wenner, 1987).

In contrast, the Mississippi sandhill crane is surviving by a figurative thread. It is federally endangered, and the race's entire population is limited to a 20,000-acre refuge that is constrained and threatened by development. The Mississippi Sandhill Crane National Wildlife Refuge was established in 1975 when the population of the race was fewer than 30 birds. In spite of numerous setbacks, the population has slowly increased. By 2010 it had reached about 130 birds, largely through the release of captive-bred birds (Table 1). Since then the population has remained stable.

Finally, the Cuban race of the sandhill crane is in only slightly better numerical condition than the Mississippi race. Recent counts have indicated a population of about 500 birds (Table 1), as compared with somewhat earlier estimates of 550 to 650 individuals (Galvez-Aguilera and Chavez-Ramirez, 2010). The birds are scattered over about 13 locations in Cuba, and there are also some on offshore islands, including the Isla de la Juventud (previously known as the Isle of Pines). Studies there have indicated only moderate nesting success, with losses resulting from such factors as predation, flooding, and human disturbance.

Whooping Crane

In contrast to the critical population status of the Mississippi sandhill crane, the whooping crane has been one of the great success stories in the history of American conservation. Like the Mississippi sandhill crane, the whooping crane's population once dropped to as few as about 20 individuals in Texas and Louisiana. This occurred in Texas about 1939–40, and the population then may have included no more than three or four breeding pairs, with the remaining birds unpaired owing to immaturity or the lack of any available sexual partners.

In spite of the 1937 establishment of a 115,000-acre national wildlife refuge (Aransas NWR) that protected their wintering population, the whooping cranes also had to survive a long and arduous migration route to and from their northern breeding grounds, which at that time were still unknown. After many years of searching across subarctic Canada, the breeding grounds of this population were finally discovered in 1954 to be about 2,500 miles north of their wintering area. They fortunately turned out to be in an already established Canadian national park, Wood Buffalo National Park, in the boundary region of northern Alberta and the Northwest Territories. Nevertheless, it required eight decades of intensive protection and close monitoring to bring the historic nuclear population up to slightly more than 500 birds, which occurred in 2019 (Map 3, Table 1).

From its pitifully small population in the 1940s, the Aransas NWR–Wood Buffalo National Park flock grew painfully slowly, often increasing at a rate of only one or two birds per year. However, as the breeding pool increased, the number of young cranes arriving at Aransas NWR increased substantially, especially recently, with as many as 30 or more juveniles sometimes arriving at Aransas with their parents in the past few years. However, the flock is still highly vulnerable to potential catastrophic events, such as hurricanes on their wintering grounds and forest fires on their breeding grounds.

Simultaneously with this brightening state of affairs for the historic Aransas–Wood Buffalo flock, efforts were being made to establish a second, nonmigratory flock somewhere within the overall historic range of the species, especially after the failure of the egg-switching experiment in Idaho. In central Florida, the Kissimmee Prairie had been used by whooping cranes as a wintering range until possibly into the late 1930s, and it was decided that this area could be used as a release point for hand-reared juveniles in a reintroduction experiment.

In 1993 a cohort of 14 juveniles was released there, followed by 19 in 1994, 19 more in 1995, and additional birds in later years until a total of more than 300 had been released. Bobcats killed a large number of them during the first two years of the project, after which the release enclosures were moved away from bobcat habitats and the survival rates were improved. By 1996 a few birds were seen forming pair-bonds, mating, and even building nests, but it was not until 2000 that the first chick was successfully hatched, seven years after the start of the project. In 2002 two chicks from the same clutch hatched, but one was taken by a bald eagle not long after hatching.

By 2003 the population of adult-plumaged birds had risen to 87, and in the spring of 2005 a total of 12 pairs nested, hatching nine chicks, of which five survived at least to the following summer. However, by 2006 only 50 birds were still present, and of 47 nesting attempts only four chicks had survived long enough to reach independence.

At the end of 2007, 41 birds were present in the flock, with only one chick having survived to the end of the year. Thirty were present in the summer of 2008, with no chicks having hatched that year. The project officially ended in 2008, although in 2009, one chick hatched and apparently fledged. As of 2019, only 9 survivors remained in the flock out of the 300-plus birds that had been released during the project. The experiment provided a powerful example of the difficulties inherent in trying to establish a flock of captive-raised birds that are able to adapt, survive, and reproduce under natural conditions.

8. What are the present status and future prospects for cranes?

Unfortunately, the basic needs of cranes and those of humans are almost diametrically opposed. Cranes need wild places and open spaces, whereas humans gather in crowds, partly to be able to enjoy the comforts and conveniences of city life. Ironically, we very probably would live longer and happier lives if we would emulate cranes and adopt some of the spacing behavior that would reduce some of the stresses of crowding, to say nothing of the mental and physical health benefits of a more active cranelike lifestyle.

Not surprisingly, the fortunes of cranes have inversely diminished as human populations have increased. Of the 15 currently recognized species of cranes, one is critically endangered, four are endangered, and seven are classified as vulnerable (Table 2, which excludes the endangered whooping crane). In an earlier summary (Johnsgard, 2015) that listed the world crane taxa by subspecies, three species and four additional subspecies

Table 2. The Cranes of the World and Their Population Status

Species (IUCN Population Status)	Approximate Population	Major Breeding Areas	Population Trend
Black Crowned Crane (Vulnerable)	43,000–70,000	W & E Africa	Decreasing
Gray Crowned Crane (Endangered)	26,500–33,500	S & E Africa	Decreasing
Siberian Crane (Critically Endangered)	3,600–4,000	NE Russia	Stable?
Wattled Crane (Vulnerable)	Over 9,600	S Africa	Decreasing?
Blue Crane (Vulnerable)	25,000–30,000	South Africa	Mixed trends
Demoiselle Crane (Least Concern)	170,000-220,000	Russia	Decreasing
Brolga (Least Concern)	15,000–20,000	Australia	Uncertain
Sarus Crane (Vulnerable)	15,000–20,000	Asia, Australia	Stable?
White-naped Crane (Vulnerable)	6,700–7,700	E Russia	Mixed trends
Red-crowned Crane (Endangered)	2,800–3,430	China, Japan	Endangered
Hooded Crane (Vulnerable)	14,000–16,000	E Russia	Increasing
Black-necked Crane (Vulnerable)	12,000	Tibetan plateau	Increasing
Eurasian Crane (Least Concern)	Over 700,000	Europe, Russia	Mixed trends

Note: Mostly based on Mirande and Harris (2019)
IUCN = International Union for Conservation of Nature

were classified as endangered, and six were considered vulnerable. The IUCN (in Winkler, Billerman, and Lovette, 2020) lists the 15 species' conservation statuses as 26.7 percent of least concern, 46.7 percent vulnerable, 20 percent endangered, and 6.7 percent critically endangered. No other group of birds with representatives in mainland North America has such a high percentage of their world taxa with a more ominous population outlook.

Of the many causes of these population declines, habitat losses—especially breeding habitat destruction, degradation, and disturbance—are prime causes and are largely responsible for the near extinction of North America's whooping crane. The species was also hunted mercilessly for its feathers (the longer wing feathers were highly valued as writing quills) as well as being shot for skins, meat, and eggs until it was finally protected with the passage of the international Migratory Bird Treaty Act of 1918. Since then mortality causes have shifted, although purposeful killing has not entirely ceased and together with collisions is still a significant cause of mortality.

Between 1950 and 2011, 101 whooping cranes were known to have died or disappeared on the Aransas wintering grounds (Stehn and Haralson-Strobel, 2014). Of 50 carcasses that were recovered between 1950 and 2009, the deaths of 24 of the birds were from unknown causes. Among the other deceased birds, 20 percent had been shot, 20 percent had collided with overhead power lines, 16 percent had died from predation, 14 percent had died of trauma, and 6 percent had died from other causes and/or disease. About 20 percent of the total known losses occurred in the wintering area; the most significant losses seem to occur during migration and so far are from unknown causes.

Based on their data, Stehn and Haralson-Strobel believed that deaths during migration might make up more than 80 percent of the annual mortality, including some probable illegal shooting. However, Pearse et al. (2019) determined that, of 19 confirmed and suspected deaths of whooping cranes from the Aransas–Wood Buffalo flock,

about 45 percent occurred in winter, about 40 percent during summer, and only about 15 percent during migration. Of the determined causes of death, predation was the most common. Among 24 whooping crane deaths from the Rocky Mountain cross-fostering experiment, 11 were caused by power line and fence collisions, 4 were from disease, 2 from predation, and the rest were from various other causes.

Windingstad (1988) reported that the major nonhunting causes of death among 170 sandhill crane carcasses included avian cholera, avian botulism, and mycotoxins. Other miscellaneous causes included hailstorms, lightning, lead poisoning, predation, avian tuberculosis, and collisions with power lines. Many studies have pointed out the widespread problem of crane mortality associated with power line collisions, including mortality along the Platte River (Wright et al., 2010). Power lines have also been reported as a significant cause of death in South African blue cranes (Shaw et al., 2010), 12 percent of which might die annually from collisions. Forty-three million miles of such lines criss-cross the world, and large, nonagile birds such as storks, pelicans, swans, and cranes are especially vulnerable to such accidents. Cranes have a notably narrow frontal binocular field of view that renders them especially vulnerable to such collisions (Martin and Shaw, 2010).

In the heavily hunted Mid-Continent Population of about 700,000 lesser and Canadian sandhill cranes, it has been estimated that at least 51,000 were legally killed in 2017 in the United States and Canada (Dubovsky, 2018). At least 7.3 percent of the total population was thus eradicated by people grouped in the US Fish and Wildlife Service's oxymoronic category of "recreational hunters," making it by far the most rapidly increasing, most significant, and most senseless source of mortality in the lesser sandhill crane's population, which has a long-term average annual recruitment rate of less than 10 percent, leaving little room for other mortality factors if the population is to maintain itself.

Elsewhere in the world, Siberian cranes are already being adversely affected by climate change, as their Arctic habitat is losing its upper permafrost layers, causing the lakes to expand and flood nesting islands. On the other hand, black-necked cranes are thriving, a change at least partly affected by reduced mortality on both the breeding and wintering grounds as a result of warmer weather (Harris, 2009). The recent high degree of breeding success in those Arctic-breeding birds that need a breeding season long enough to accommodate their extended fledging periods, such as lesser sandhill cranes, swans, snow geese, and other high-Arctic geese, may likewise be benefiting from longer and milder nesting seasons, but the changes might also prove to be equally beneficial to predators and blood-sucking insects.

Butler, Metzger, and Harris (2017) predicted that future climate change on the breeding grounds—with fewer days below freezing during winter and more precipitation during breeding—would result in less recruitment among whooping cranes. They also predicted that whooping crane recruitment and population growth may fall below long-term averages when atmospheric carbon dioxide concentration increases, as expected, to 500 ppm by 2050.

The effects of climate change are and are going to be so varied by latitude, weather, and geographic factors that no single positive or negative overall effect on any species can be postulated in advance. Some species, such as the Eurasian crane, will probably be both positively affected in the short term by improved breeding season conditions and negatively affected in the long term by such things as increased variability in rainfall, increased extreme weather events, and changes in farming planting practices (Hansbauer, Vegvri, and Harris, n.d.). Other undesirable changes can be expected worldwide, such as increased sea levels causing extensive lowland flooding, generally decreased water availability, and correspondingly reduced agricultural productivity.

Following pages: Sandhill cranes at a snowy roost, Platte River, Nebraska

II Observing and Enjoying Cranes

Where to Observe Cranes in the United States and Canada

Wildlife Refuges and Sanctuaries

United States

Note: A more complete and detailed list of locations in the United States and Canada where wild sandhill and whooping cranes might be seen, with descriptions of more than 100 locations, can be found in one of my earlier books on sandhill and whooping cranes (Johnsgard, 2011). Lundin (2005) provided information on finding cranes in Europe, and von Treuenfels (2007) described similar crane-rich locations in Europe, Africa, and Asia.

Alabama

Wheeler National Wildlife Refuge. 35,000 acres. This refuge is just east of Decatur and is a major wintering ground for both waterfowl and cranes. After first appearing at the refuge during the 1990s, wintering greater sandhill cranes have increased in number, reaching 20,000 birds in 2018. The cranes begin arriving in late November, and numbers peak in early January. For information, contact Wheeler NWR, 3121 Visitor Center Road, Decatur, AL 35603; phone 256-350-6639. See also Festival of the Cranes in the list of winter crane festivals. https://www.fws.gov/refuge/wheeler/

Alaska

Creamer's Field Migratory Waterfowl Refuge. 12 acres. The Creamer's Field refuge on the outskirts of Fairbanks is a major fall stopping point for up to about 2,000 lesser sandhill cranes returning with newly fledged young from breeding areas in the Yukon-Kuskokwim delta during late August and early September. For more information contact Creamer's Field Migratory Waterfowl Refuge, 1399 College Road, Fairbanks, AK 99701; phone 907-452-5162. See also Tanana Valley Sandhill Crane Festival in the list of summer crane festivals and https://friendsofcreamersfield.org/.

Arizona

Willcox Playa region. Roughly 35,000 lesser sandhill cranes winter from November through February on the state-owned **Willcox Playa** (about eight miles south of Willcox), **Whitewater Draw** (between Bisbee and Elfrida), and other playa wetlands and agricultural fields of Cochise County in southeastern Arizona. These cranes are the most southwestern flock of the Mid-Continent Population of lesser sandhill cranes, and they breed up to 3,500 miles away in northeastern Russia (Yakutia). For more information, see the Wings Over Willcox Birding and Nature Festival in the list of winter crane festivals.

California

Carrizo Plain Preserve. 18,000 acres. This Nature Conservancy preserve about 75 miles west of San Luis Obispo includes a large alkaline lake that supports up to about 6,000 wintering cranes in January. Address: PO Box 15810, San Luis Obispo, CA, 93401; phone 805-536-8378. The remote **Carrizo Plains National Monument** (204,000 acres) consists of grasslands and alkali flats surrounded by mountains. Within it the area around the usually dry Soda Lake attracts large numbers of wintering sandhill cranes. The monument's visitor center is located on Soda Lake Road, Santa Margarita, CA 93453; phone 805-475-2131.

Cosumnes River Preserve. 4,600 acres. California's Central Valley and the Sacramento–San Joaquin delta is the heart of the wintering grounds for the Pacific Flyway population of greater and lesser sandhill cranes. Heavy use by the cranes is seemingly centered in a broad zone between Folsom Lake and the western end of San Francisco Bay. Cosumnes River Preserve is located 20 miles south of Sacramento and north of Thornton on Bureau of Land Management land and managed by Ducks Unlimited and the Nature Conservancy. More than 30,000 lesser sandhill cranes from Alaska and perhaps Russia winter on the region's agricultural lands from September through February. They also roost in other local preserves, including **Woodbridge Ecological Reserve** (also known as Isenberg Crane Refuge) near Galt. The Woodbridge site consists of some properties along Woodbridge Road designated as protected crane roosts. A third site is the Nature Conservancy's **Staten Island** preserve (9,000 acres). Staten Island is an island in the Sacramento–San Joaquin delta that is a working farm but serves as a wildlife preserve in winter, attracting up to 5,600 roosting cranes by October. All three sites are within 15 miles of one another. Address: Bureau of Land Management, Cosumnes River Preserve, 13501 Franklin Blvd., Galt, CA 92632; phone 916-684-2816. See also the Sandhill Crane Festival at Lodi in the list of fall crane festivals.

Lower Klamath and Tule Lake National Wildlife Refuges. Lower Klamath and Tule Lake are two of the six refuges in northern California and southern Oregon that compose the Klamath Basin National Wildlife Refuge complex. Tule Lake NWR covers 39,000 acres, and Lower Klamath occupies 51,000 acres. Greater sandhill cranes breed on both of these refuges, and Lower Klamath NWR is a staging area for 20 to 30 percent of the sandhill crane's winter Central Valley population. Shared address: Tule Lake National Wildlife Refuge, 4009 Hill Road, Tulelake, CA 96134; phone 530-677-2231. https://www.fws.gov/refuge/tule_lake/

Merced National Wildlife Refuge. 10,200 acres. This refuge near Los Banos in the San Joaquin Valley has the largest concentration of lesser sandhill cranes in the Pacific Flyway, which arrive in November, peak at about 25,000 birds in January, and leave by March. Up to 60,000 Arctic-nesting geese also winter here. Address: San Luis NWR Complex, PO Box 2176, Los Banos, CA 93635; phone 209-826-3508. **Pixley National Wildlife Refuge.** 6,400 acres. This refuge is located near Delano in the San Joaquin Valley. Up to about 6,000 sandhill cranes winter here from November through March, and it may be one of the best places for seeing cranes in the Central Valley. It is part of the Kern NWR complex. Address: Pixley National Wildlife Refuge, PO Box 670, Delano, CA 93216; phone 661-725-2767. https://www.fws.gov/refuge/pixley/. Other refuges in Merced County's central San Joaquin Valley that support wintering sandhill cranes are **San Luis NWR** (7,400 acres, near Banos; phone 209-826-3508) and **Kesterson NWR** (5,900 acres, near Gustine; phone 918-839-1869). Kern complex address: Kern National Wildlife Refuge Complex, 10811 Corcoran Road, Delano, CA 93215; phone 661-725-2767.

Sacramento National Wildlife Refuge Complex. 35,000 acres. Five national wildlife refuges are included in this complex of refuges in the Sacramento River region. They are **Sacramento NWR** (10,700 acres), **Delevan NWR** (5,600 acres), **Colusa NWR** (4,000 acres), **Sutter NWR** (2,600 acres), and **Sacramento River NWR** (10,100 acres). Collectively they winter 3 million waterfowl and moderate numbers of sandhill cranes. Address for complex: Sacramento National Wildlife Refuge, 752 County Road 99W, Willows, CA 95988; shared phone 530-934-2801. Just ten miles south of Sacramento is **Stone Lakes National Wildlife Refuge**, a suburban refuge where sandhill cranes are common during fall and winter. Address: 1624 Hood-Franklin Road, Elk Grove, CA 95748.

Colorado

Fruitgrowers Reservoir. This privately operated irrigation reservoir on the western slope of the Front Range is the best place in western Colorado for seeing sandhill cranes in western Colorado, with 20,000 stopping during March and April. Directions: From Delta drive east six miles on Hwy. 50 and then turn left (toward Grand Mesa) on Hwy. 65. After five miles, turn right on 21 Road and then take an immediate left on Fruitgrowers Road. After a mile the road turns right, crosses the dam, and leads to a parking lot on the west side. The cranes feed in the wetlands across the causeway at the north end of the reservoir. North Road provides the best viewing (Kingery, 2007).

San Luis Valley National Wildlife Refuge Complex. About 25,000 Rocky Mountain greater sandhill cranes pass through the San Luis Valley from mid-February to mid-April, stopping at **Monte Vista National Wildlife Refuge**. The fall migration peak is in mid-October. Monte Vista NWR is reached by driving south from Monte Vista on State Hwy. 15 (Gunbarrel Road) for six miles to the entrance of the auto tour route. **Alamosa National Wildlife Refuge** is an 11,168-acre refuge located about seven miles southeast of Alamosa and is a fine birding location but attracts few cranes. Both refuges are at about 7,800 feet of elevation. Address: PO Box 1148, Alamosa, CO 81101; phone 719-589-4021. Monte Vista NWR address: 6120 Hwy. 15, Monte Vista, CO 81144; phone 719-589-4021. The refuge complex headquarters are at 8248 Emperious Road, Alamosa, CO 81101. A checklist that includes the birds of both Alamosa and Monte Vista refuges is available online, or contact the Colorado Division of Wildlife, 6060 Broadway, Denver, CO 80216; phone 303-297-1192. For more information, see also the Monte Vista Crane Festival in the list of winter crane festivals. https://www.fws.gov/refuge/monte_vista/

Florida

Paynes Prairie Preserve State Park. 21,000 acres. This state park is located 10 miles south of Gainesville. It supports up to 5,000 wintering greater sandhill cranes and about 50 pairs of resident Florida sandhill cranes. A few reintroduced whooping cranes were surviving here in 2020. Guided tours are offered from November to April. Address: 100 Savannah Blvd., Micanopy, FL 32667; phone 352-329-4100. Another good place to visit is **Myakka River State Park** (29,000 acres). It is Florida's largest state park and supports a population of nesting Florida sandhill cranes and 250 other bird species. Address: 13208 State Road 72, Sarasota, FL 34241; phone 941-361-6751. A third good crane-watching location is **Circle B Bar Reserve** (1,267 acres). Owned by the Polk County Board of County Commissioners, the nature preserve is free, including a nature discovery center. The entrance is on the south side of SR 540 (Winter Lake Road) between US 98 and Thornhill Road, Lakeland. Address: 4299 Winter Lake Road, Lakeland FL 33803; phone 863-668-4673. Lastly, the drive on County Road 225 along Orange Lake in unincorporated Evinston may reveal sightings of cranes from the road.

Idaho

Grays Lake National Wildlife Refuge. 22,000 acres. Grays Lake NWR is north of Soda Springs, off Hwy. 34. The turnoff is about 27 miles north of Soda Springs and 21 miles from Freedom, Wyoming. From the intersection it is about 3 miles north to the refuge office, visitor center, and overlook. This refuge hosts the largest nesting population of greater sandhill cranes in the world; more than 200 nesting pairs have been counted in some years. Sandhills begin arriving in early April from their wintering areas. During the fall staging period in late September and early October, as many as 3,000 cranes have been observed at one time. Trumpeter swans also nest here. Address: 74 Grays Lake Road, Wayne, ID 83285; phone 208-574-2755.

Indiana

Goose Pond Fish and Wildlife Area. 7,200 acres. This small state-owned area is located in Greene County, southwestern Indiana, just south of Linton. As many as 26,000 greater sandhill cranes have been seen during migration at this Indiana Department of Natural Resources area. Address: 13540 W. County Road 400 S., Linton, IN 47441; phone 812-512-9185. For more information see also the Marsh Madness Sandhill Crane Festival in the list of winter crane festivals.

Jasper Pulaski Fish and Wildlife Area. 8,062 acres. This state-owned area is located in northeastern Indiana, in northwest Pulaski and southwestern Starke Counties. Its acreage is a mixture of state and privately owned lands. The peak numbers occur in mid- to late November when up to 35,000 birds might be present, probably representing the highest concentrations of Eastern Population greater sandhill cranes that can be seen anywhere. For information contact the Indiana Department of Natural Resources, 5822 Fish and Wildlife Lane, Medaryville, IN 47957; phone 219-843-4841 or 877-463-6367.

Kansas

Cheyenne Bottoms Waterfowl Management Area. 18,000 acres. This famous state-owned wildlife area is about five miles north of Great Bend, in Barton County. The site is recognized as being of international importance for migratory shorebirds and is also an important stopover point for midcontinent sandhill cranes, with occasional use by whooping cranes. A bird list is not available online but can be obtained from the area manager at Route 1, Great Bend, KS 67530; phone 620-793-3066. http://www.cheyennebottoms.net/

Kirwin National Wildlife Refuge. 10,800 acres. This refuge is about ten miles southeast of Phillipsburg, in Phillips County. Large flocks of migrating sandhill cranes regularly stop here, and whooping cranes have also been rarely reported. A checklist of 234 total species is available from the refuge manager at Route 1, Box 103, Kirwin, KS 67644; phone 785-543-6673. https://www.fws.gov/refuge/kirwin/

Quivira National Wildlife Refuge. 21,800 acres. This outstanding marshland refuge is located 12 miles northeast of Stafford, in Stafford County. It contains 14,700 acres of marsh and is notable for its diverse wetland birds, including consistent spring and fall use by up to 180,000 sandhill cranes and a few whooping cranes during spring (mid-March to mid-April) and fall (October to November). A checklist of 340 species (one of the largest refuge bird lists in the entire inland Great Plains region) is available from the refuge manager at RR3, Box 48A, Stafford, KS 67578; phone 620-486-2393. https://www.fws.gov/refuge/quivira/

Minnesota

Agassiz National Wildlife Refuge. 61,500 acres. Agassiz NWR is situated in the eastern transition zone between tallgrass prairie and northern forest 11 miles east of Holt in Marshall County. Sandhill cranes are common from spring to fall and nest here. A checklist of 287 species reported on the refuge is available from the refuge manager in Middle River, MN 56737; phone 218-449-4115. The list is also available online (in Wildlife & Habitat): https://www.fws.gov/refuge/agassiz/

Roseau River Wildlife Management Area. 62,025 acres. Located 20 miles northwest of Roseau, this state-owned area is one of Minnesota's most important waterfowl migration and breeding areas, and is an important migratory stopover area for sandhill cranes. For information, contact DNR Wildlife Area Office, HCT 5 Box 103, Roseau MN 56751; phone 218-463-1557.

Following pages: Sandhill cranes, adult and young, Grand Teton National Park, Wyoming

Mississippi

Mississippi Sandhill Crane National Wildlife Refuge. 19,000 acres. This refuge about seven miles north of Biloxi protects the highly endangered race of Mississippi sandhill crane. As of 2020, it had about 130 birds present on the refuge. Nature trails are available, and free refuge tours are provided throughout the year. Address: 7200 Crane Lane, Gautier, MS 19553; phone 228-497-6322. https://www.fws.gov/refuge/mississippi_sandhill_crane/

Montana

Charles M. Russell National Wildlife Refuge. 1,094,300 acres. Charles M. Russell NWR is an enormous refuge of shortgrass plains that adjoins the impounded Fort Peck Lake. Sandhill cranes are common migrants in spring and fall. A bird checklist of 240 species is available from the refuge manager at PO Box 110, Lewistown, MT 59457; phone 406-538-8706. https://www.fws.gov/refuge/charles_m_russell/

Freezout Lake Wildlife Management Area. 12,000 acres. This state-owned shallow sink-type lake in northern Montana is managed for waterfowl and wetland birds. Sandhill cranes are common in spring and fall. Spring migration begins in early March. Up to 10,000 trumpeter and tundra swans, and 300,000 snow and Ross's geese are present during fall migration, which begins in early November and continues until the lake freezes over. The area is located 60 miles west of Great Falls, off US Hwy. 89, near Fairfield. Address: US 89, Choteau, MT 59411; phone 406-467-2646.

Medicine Lake National Wildlife Refuge. 31,457 acres. Located one mile south of Medicine Lake. Migrants that regularly visit this grassland and shallow lake refuge include sandhill cranes (common in spring, abundant in fall) and whooping cranes (rare in spring and fall). A bird checklist of 228 species is available from the refuge manager. Address: HC 51, Box 2, Medicine Lake, MT 59247; phone 406-789-2305. https://www.fws.gov/refuge/medicine_lake/

Nebraska

Central Platte Valley. This approximately 80-mile stretch (the "Big Bend") of the Platte River in central Nebraska, roughly between Overton and Chapman, hosts one of the world's great bird spectacles in early spring, when millions of waterfowl and more than a half-million sandhill cranes descend into the Platte valley and the adjoining Rainwater Basin immediately to the south. The birds of this 10,000-square-mile region, which total more than 390 species, have been documented by Brown and Johnsgard (2013). Cranes are also locally abundant along the **North Platte River** west of this stretch, such as between North Platte and Sutherland, near Lewellen, and near Scotts Bluff, totaling possibly 220,000 birds in 2020 (Andrew Caven, pers. comm.)

The Crane Trust. This educational and research organization controls and manages more than 2,000 acres of riparian wetlands along the Platte River, where up to 200,000 sandhill cranes have been seen between Grand Island and Alda. The Crane Trust's Visitor and Nature Center (5325 S. Alda Road, Wood River, NE 68883; phone 308-382-1820) is located six miles west of Grand Island on the south side of I-80 at Alda exit 305. It is open daily through the spring migration season (see website for hours). The visitor center provides birding information to tourists and, like Lillian Annette Rowe Sanctuary, provides morning and evening excursions to crane-viewing blinds along the Platte River. More extended tours with a professional photographer are also available. To reach the Crane Trust's headquarters (phone 308-384-4633) drive about a mile south from I-80 exit 305 and turn east on Whooping Crane Drive. Continue east through a (sometimes chained) metal gate at the junction of Whooping Crane and Sandhill Crane Drives and continue for about another mile east on Sandhill Crane Drive to the Trust's building complex. https://cranetrust.org/

Lillian Annette Rowe Sanctuary. This 2,500-acre Audubon sanctuary is located about two miles south and two miles west of Gibbon. Riverside blinds at Rowe Sanctuary provide the primary festival-based crane viewing opportunities; up to 200,000 cranes have been seen along this stretch of the Platte River between Minden and Gibbon. The refuge and its plant and animal life have been described by Johnsgard (2020). For information, contact Rowe Sanctuary, 44450 Elm Island Road, Gibbon, NE; phone 308-468-5282. See also Nebraska Crane Festival, held at Kearney, in the list of spring festivals.

North Platte National Wildlife Refuge. 5,047 acres. This refuge is located four miles north and eight miles east of Scottsbluff. It is part of the Crescent Lake/North Platte NWR complex and includes Lake Minatare (430 acres), Winters Creek (700 acres), and Lake Alice (1,377 acres when full but currently dry). The best wetland bird habitat is at Winters Creek, which seasonally supports up to about 1,000 sandhill cranes. The refuge bird list totals 228 species and is available online or from the refuge manager at 10630 Road 181, Ellsworth, NE 69340; phone 308-762-4893 or 308-635-7851. https://www.fws.gov/refuge/north_platte/

Rainwater Basin Wetland Management District. This multicounty region south of the central Platte River contains hundreds of temporary to semipermanent playa wetlands that extend from Phelps County east to Butler and Saline Counties. The Rainwater Basin attracts millions of migrating geese during March in wet springs (Brown and Johnsgard, 2013). Whooping cranes often use the more remote wetlands for foraging, but sandhill cranes generally forage in corn stubble or wet meadows near the Platte River. A collective bird list for the Rainwater Basin and adjacent central Platte valley has more than 300 species, including 120 wetland species, and is available from the US Fish and Wildlife Service, PO Box 8, Fink, NE 68940; phone 308-263-3000.

New Mexico

Bitter Lake National Wildlife Refuge. 23,310 acres. Located ten miles northeast of Roswell, this refuge is a major wintering area for lesser sandhill cranes of the midcontinent group, although numbers have declined in recent years as local agricultural practices have changed. A bird checklist of 285 species recorded on the refuge is available from the refuge manager at PO Box 7, Roswell, NM 88201; phone 575-622-6755. It is also available online (under Wildlife & Habitat). https://www.fws.gov/refuge/bitter_lake

Bosque del Apache National Wildlife Refuge. 57,191 acres. From 20,000 to 30,000 greater sandhill cranes of the Rocky Mountain Population winter in and around the refuge, as do thousands of snow geese, Ross's geese, and other waterfowl. The refuge is known for its splendid opportunities for photographing cranes, and its long-running fall Festival of the Cranes has a variety of photography classes, guided birding and nature tours, and an extensive speaker program. Address: 1001 N-1, San Antonio, NM 87832, phone 575-835-1828. https://www.fws.gov/refuge/Bosque_del_Apache/. For information on the Festival of the Cranes, see the separate list of autumn crane festivals or https://www.friendsofbosquedelapache.org.

Grulla National Wildlife Refuge. 3,235 acres. This small refuge is located a few miles east of Arch. Most of it consists of a salt lake and the rest is grassland. It is largely managed to provide winter habitat for sandhill cranes (grulla is the Spanish word for cranes), and 100,000 or more might be present from December to March. A checklist of 85 species recorded on the refuge is available from the refuge manager at c/o Muleshoe NWR, PO Box 549, Muleshoe, TX 79347; phone 806-946-3341. It is also available online. https://www.fws.gov/refuge/grulla/

North Dakota

Note: North Dakota has the largest total number of national wildlife refuges (20) and wetland management districts (10) of any state as well as a unique national game preserve and national wildlife management area. Given its geographic position in the middle of the Central Flyway, the flyway with probably the greatest number of migratory waterfowl (Johnsgard, 2012b), North Dakota is also directly in the middle of the migratory routes of both the Aransas–Wood Buffalo flock of whooping cranes and the Mid-Continent Population of sandhill cranes. In spite of all its wildlife refuges, North Dakota is also the state that in recent years has had (after Texas) the second-highest number of sandhill cranes killed annually by "sportsmen." Hunting is allowed at 14 of North Dakota's 20 national wildlife refuges.

Audubon National Wildlife Refuge. 24,700 acres. Situated at the east end of Lake Sakakawea between Minot and Bismarck, this refuge contains about 13,500 acres administered by the federal government and 11,200 acres supervised by the state. It mostly consists of shortgrass prairie and reservoir shoreline along with some prairie potholes and marshes. Sandhill cranes are abundant during spring and fall. A checklist of 239 species is available from the refuge manager at RR1, Coleharbor, ND 58531; phone 701-442-5474. It is also available online (under Wildlife & Habitat). https://www.fws.gov/refuge/audubon/

Des Lacs National Wildlife Refuge. 18,000 acres. This refuge is located one mile west of Kenmare, where sandhill cranes are common to abundant during spring and fall. A collective bird checklist of 308 species reported from all three refuges in the "Souris loop" (Des Lacs, J. Clark Salyer, and Upper Souris) is available from the manager at Des Lacs Refuge Complex, PO Box 578, Crosby, ND 58730; phone 701-385-4046. (See J. Clark Salyer NWR in this section for an online version.) https://www.fws.gov/refuge/des_lacs/

Devils Lake Wetland Management District. 221,989 acres. This enormous WMD near Devils Lake has 187 waterfowl production areas totaling 40,113 acres, ten easement refuges totaling 15,891 acres, and 2,521 conservation easements totaling 149,124 acres. It also includes **Lake Alice National Wildlife Refuge** (12,1794 acres) about 30 miles northwest of Devils Lake and **Kelly's Slough National Wildlife Refuge** (1,300 acres) about 12 miles northwest of Grand Forks. Sandhill cranes are common to abundant at these locations during spring and fall. Bird lists are available from the district office at 218 SW 4th St., PO Box 908, Devils Lake, ND 58301; phone 701-662-8611. https://www.fws.gov/refuge/devils_lake_wmd/

J. Clark Salyer National Wildlife Refuge (formerly Lower Souris NWR). 58,700 acres. Located three miles north of Upham, this refuge commonly hosts sandhill cranes in spring and fall, and more than 250,000 ducks and 300,000 snow geese visit annually. A bird checklist of 308 species collectively reported from all three "Souris loop" refuges (Des Lacs, J. Clark Salyer and Upper Souris) is available from the J. Clark Salyer NWR manager, Box 66, Upham, ND 58799; phone 701-768-2548. It is also available online (under Wildlife & Habitat). https://www.fws.gov/refuge/j_clark_salyer/

Lake Ilo National Wildlife Refuge. 4,043 acres. Located one mile east of Dunn Center, this small refuge commonly has sandhill cranes during spring and fall. A checklist of 226 species is available from the refuge manager at PO Box 127, Dunn Center, ND 58626; phone 701-548-8110. https://www.fws.gov/refuge/lake_ilo/

Long Lake National Wildlife Refuge. 22,300 acres. Situated about four miles southeast of Moffitt, this refuge is mostly prairie grasslands, ravines, fields, trees and shrub plants, and marshy or shallow lake wetlands. It is one of North Dakota's most important stopover sites for sandhill cranes and waterfowl migrants, the more common species including tundra swans, Canada geese, and greater white-fronted geese. A checklist of 289 species is available from the refuge manager at RR1, Moffitt, ND 58560; phone 701-387-4397. https://www.fws.gov/refuge/long_lake/

Lostwood National Wildlife Refuge. 27,647 acres. Located 16 miles southwest of Kenmare, this refuge is a mixture of rolling hills; pristine mixed-grass prairie; and many small, shallow "pothole" wetlands, some of which are alkaline. The spring and fall migrations include sandhill cranes, tundra swans, snow geese and greater white-fronted geese, and dozens of duck species. A checklist of 234 species is available from the refuge manager at RR2, Box 93, Kenmare, ND 58746; phone 701-848-2722. https://www.fws.gov/refuge/lostwood/

Upper Souris National Wildlife Refuge. 32,000 acres. Upper Souris NWR is located seven miles north of Foxholm. Sandhill cranes are abundant during spring and fall in all of the three refuges of the "Souris loop" (Des Lacs, J. Clark Salyer, and Upper Souris). A collective bird checklist of 308 species is available from any of the three (or online at the J. Clark Slayer NWR website). Address: RR1, Foxholm, ND 58738; phone 701-468-5467. https://www.fws.gov/refuge/upper_souris/

Oklahoma

Salt Plains National Wildlife Refuge. 31,997 acres. This refuge is three miles southeast of Jet, in Alfalfa County, on the Salt Fork of the Arkansas River. Most of the area is covered by the Salt Plains Reservoir, but upland forest, rangeland, and extensive salt flats provide a unique habitat. Sandhill cranes are common during spring and fall, and whooping cranes are regular transients. A checklist of 296 species is available from the refuge manager at Route 1, Box 76, Jet, OK 73749; phone 580-626-4793. It is also available online (under Wildlife & Habitat). https://www.fws.gov/refuge/salt_plains/

Oregon

Malheur National Wildlife Refuge. 185,000 acres. This refuge is located about 40 miles south of Burns and is a breeding site for about 200 pairs of greater sandhill cranes as well as an important staging area for cranes migrating to and from California. About 6,000 migrant cranes are often present in late March and April, with a maximum of about 14,000 birds. During autumn, 2,000 to 3,000 greater sandhills are often present, with their numbers peaking in mid-October. Address: PO Box 235, Princeton, OR 97721; phone 541-493-2612. https://www.fws.gov/refuge/malheur/

Sauvie Island Wildlife Area. 13,000 acres. This state-owned bottomland site in the lower Columbia River valley on the outskirts of Portland is a major stopover and wintering site for thousands of sandhill cranes from September to March. The largest number are present in late October, and hundreds remain to overwinter. Address: 18330 NW Sauvie Island Road, Portland, OR 97231; phone 503-621-3488.

South Dakota

Pocasse National Wildlife Refuge. 2,540 acres. Pocasse NWR is located along the east side of the Missouri River just north of Pollock, in Brown County, off US Hwy. 83. Mostly marshes and open water (1,045 acres of wetlands), this refuge is an important stopover area for migrating sandhill and whooping cranes as well as for waterfowl. Administered from Sand Lake National Wildlife Refuge, general information may be obtained from the refuge manager at Sand Lake NWR, RR1, Box 253, Columbia, SD 57433; phone 605-885-6320.

Tennessee

Hiwassee Wildlife Refuge. 6,000 acres. About 20,000 greater sandhill cranes that breed around Lakes Michigan and Superior are typically present during the winter at this small island state-owned refuge in Chickamauga Lake at the confluence of the Tennessee and Hiwassee Rivers. It is the largest wintering site for the Eastern Population of greater sandhill cranes. For more information, contact refuge staff at 545 Priddy Road, Birchwood, TN 37308; phone 423-614-3018. See also the Tennessee Sandhill Crane Festival in the list of winter festivals.

Texas

Aransas National Wildlife Refuge. 54,829 acres. Located seven miles south of Austwell. Nearly all the whooping cranes that breed in Alberta's Wood Buffalo National Park winter at Aransas NWR, the early arrivals usually appearing by late October and all leaving by early April. As of the winter of 2019–20, this slowly recovering population numbered slightly more than 500 birds. A checklist of 392 bird species is available from the refuge manager at PO Box 100, Austwell, TX 77950; phone 361-349-1181. It is also available online (under Wildlife & Habitat). https://www.fws.gov/refuge/aransas/ See also the Whooping Crane Festival in the list of winter festivals.

Brazoria National Wildlife Refuge. 10,407 acres. Brazoria NWR is located about ten miles northeast of Freeport; sandhill cranes are common here during fall and winter. Wintering birds also include large numbers of snow, Ross's, Canada, and greater white-fronted geese, totaling up to 100,000 geese and 80,000 ducks of 24 species. A recent Brazoria NWR bird checklist with 301 species is available from the refuge manager at 24907 FM 2004 Road, Lake Jackson, TX 77566; phone 979-964-4011. It is also available online (under Wildlife & Habitat). https://www.fws.gov/refuge/brazoria/

Buffalo Lake National Wildlife Refuge. 7,700 acres. Situated 30 miles southwest of Amarillo, this refuge includes about 1,000 acres of surface water resulting from the impoundment of Tierra Blanca Creek and the adjoining grasslands. The refuge's alkaline wetlands are a major wintering area for lesser sandhill cranes. A bird checklist contains 344 species and is available from the refuge manager at PO Box 228, Umbarger, TX 79091; phone 806-499-3382. It is also available online (under Wildlife & Habitat). https://www.fws.gov/refuge/buffalo_lake/

Laguna Atascosa National Wildlife Refuge. 45,187 acres. Laguna Atascosa NWR is located 25 miles east of Harlingen. Sandhill cranes are common during fall and winter, as are many waterfowl and shorebirds. A bird checklist containing 369 species is available from the refuge manager at PO Box 450, Rio Hondo, TX 78583; phone 956-748-3607. It is also available online (under Wildlife & Habitat). https://www.fws.gov/refuge/laguna_atascosa/

Muleshoe National Wildlife Refuge. 5,809 acres. Situated 20 miles south of Muleshoe, the refuge contains lakes, marshes, shortgrass plains, and other terrestrial habitats. The alkaline sink-type lakes provide the single most important wintering habitat in North America for lesser sandhill cranes, which often number more than 100,000 birds and during some winters have reached 250,000. The bird checklist includes 282 species and is available from the refuge manager at PO Box 549, Muleshoe, TX 79347; phone 806-946-3341. It is also available online (under Wildlife & Habitat). https://www.fws.gov/refuge/muleshoe/ About 100 miles northeast of Muleshoe NWR, and 1.5 miles south of Umbarger, is **Buffalo Lake National Wildlife Refuge** (7,664 acres), and it also seasonally holds very large numbers of migrating and wintering sandhill cranes. Address: PO Box 179, Umbarger, TX 79091; phone 806-499-3382. https://www.fws.gov/refuge/buffalo_lake/

San Bernard National Wildlife Refuge. 27,414 acres. Located about 10 miles south of Lake Jackson and 12 miles west of Freeport, San Bernard NWR is home to sandhill cranes during fall and winter. The San Bernard, Brazoria, and Big Boggy NWRs make up a coastal group of refuges that collectively winter many cranes and migratory waterfowl, especially snow, greater white-fronted, Canada, and Ross's geese. A checklist for the three-refuge complex contains 301 species and is available from the Brazoria refuge manager at 6801 County Road 306, Brazoria, TX 77422; phone 979-964-3639. It is also available online (under Wildlife & Habitat). https://www.fws.gov/refuge/san_bernard/

Utah

Bear River Migratory Bird Refuge National Wildlife Refuge. 81,000 acres. Sandhill cranes are very common in the Bear River NWR and adjoining wetlands west to North Bay of Great Salt Lake. This refuge near Brigham City is also famous for its waterfowl and shorebird populations. During migrations it attracts up to 60,000 tundra swans; more than 90 percent of Utah's tundra swans use the freshwater wetland habitats of the refuge. A bird checklist is available online (under Wildlife & Habitat). Address: 2155 W. Forest St., Brigham City, UT 84302; phone 435-723-5887. https://www.fws.gov/refuge/bear_river_migratory_bird_refuge/

Washington

Columbia National Wildlife Refuge. 28,000 acres. Up to 25,000 Pacific Flyway sandhill cranes stage in the Columbia River basin during spring migration, among the eroded basalt channeled scablands of central Washington. Address: 51 S. Morgan Lake Road, Othello, WA 99344; phone 509-488-3140. Information is available at https://www.fws.gov/refuge/columbia/. See also Othello Sandhill Crane Festival in the list of spring festivals.

Wisconsin

Leopold–Pine Island Important Bird Area. 16,000 acres. This site near Baraboo (and close to the headquarters of the International Crane Foundation) straddles the Wisconsin River in Sauk and Columbia Counties west of Portage. A mosaic of marsh, grassland, deciduous forest, and farmland, this Important Bird Area includes five large tracts managed by federal and state agencies, nonprofit organizations, and private individuals. It attracts thousands of sandhill cranes each fall. The Aldo Leopold Foundation provides guided tours to view the crane roost. For information, contact the Leopold Center, E13701 Levee Road, Baraboo, WI 53913; phone 608-355-0279.

Necedah National Wildlife Refuge. 44,000 acres. This wildlife refuge is located three miles west of the town of Necedah (produced na-see'-dah). Whooping cranes that were raised here in captivity and trained to follow ultralight planes were escorted to wintering areas in Florida to establish a new migration route tradition. Now they return here and have begun to nest independently in and near the refuge. Greater sandhill cranes also nest at the refuge and stage here during spring and fall migrations. Address: N11385 Headquarters Road, Necedah, WI 54646; phone 608-565-2551. https://www.fws.gov/refuge/necedah/

Wyoming

Greater sandhill cranes are common and widespread throughout the Greater Yellowstone region and breed commonly in **Yellowstone National Park**, such as around Bechler and Fountain Flats. They breed throughout **Grand Teton National Park**, where they often nest at shallow wetlands that are in open woods or close to woods, such as the willow flats and wetlands near Rockefeller Lodge (Johnsgard, 2015). They also breed commonly on wetlands in the **National Elk Refuge** near Jackson, on the Flat Creek wetlands just north of Jackson, and at **Seedskadee National Wildlife Refuge**, a 14,500-acre federal refuge in the Green River valley (Johnsgard, 2019). They breed along both slopes of the Bighorn Mountains, especially in Johnson and Sheridan Counties, and throughout the **Bighorn National Forest** (Canterbury, Johnsgard, and Downing, 2013).

About 10,000 or more lesser sandhill cranes stage from the second half of March through early April at **Table Mountain Wildlife Habitat Management Area**, a 1,700-acre state-owned wildlife area near Torrington.

Canada

Note: For general information on Canadian sites, contact Environment Canada–Canadian Wildlife Service, Twin Atria Building, 2nd floor, 4999 98th Ave., Edmonton, AB, Canada T6B 2X3; phone 401-468-8075. National Wildlife Areas are federally owned areas that may have limited access. Visiting a Migratory Bird Sanctuary may require advance permission from the Canadian Wildlife Service and up to 45 days of advance notice. Ramsar Convention sites are designated as wetlands of international importance for migratory and breeding wetland birds.

Alberta

Note: For Alberta tourism information contact Travel Alberta, Department E, PO Box 2500, Edmonton, AB, Canada T5J 2Z4; phone (from Alberta) 800-222-6501 or (from US) 403-427-4321.

Beaverhill Lake. 71,781 acres. This provincial area is located near Tofield, about 40 miles southeast of Edmonton. Sandhill cranes stage here during spring migration, with up to 8,000 recorded in late April. It is also an important waterfowl staging area (spring and fall) with more than 200,000 birds regularly using the site each year. For information, contact the Fish and Wildlife Division, Department of Energy and Natural Resources, Main Floor, North Tower, Petroleum Plaza, 9945 108th St., Edmonton, AB, Canada T5K 2C9; phone 403-442-2605.

Wood Buffalo National Park. 4,266 square miles. This wetland complex is in the boreal forest biome of northern Alberta and southwestern Northwest Territories, and is the historic nesting location for the primary migratory flock of whooping cranes. It is owned by the Government of Canada and administered by Parks Canada with input from local aboriginal groups and communities. It is also classified as an Important Bird Area and has two Ramsar Convention wetlands. Access is highly restricted during the summer crane breeding season. For information contact Parks Canada. https://www.pc.gc.ca/en/pn-np/nt/woodbuffalo

Saskatchewan

Note: For general information on Saskatchewan's nature sites, contact the Department of Parks, Recreation and Culture, 3211 Albert St., Regina, SK, Canada S4S 5W6; phone 306-787-2700. For tourism information, contact Tourism Saskatchewan, 189-1621 Albert St., Regina, SK, Canada S4P 2S5; phone 306-787-9600 or 877-237-2273.

Last Mountain Lake National Wildlife Area. 18,850 acres. During fall up to 50,000 sandhill cranes stage at this jointly administered federal-provincial area, and whooping cranes are regular migrants. The north end of Last Mountain Lake is one of the Prairie Provinces' most important waterfowl staging areas, with up to 450,000 geese present as well as other water and land birds. It is a designated Important Bird Area and globally important wetland (Ramsar) site. For information, contact Last Mountain Lake National Wildlife Area Pavilion, 1 Wildlife Road, Wreford No. 280, SK S0G 4M0, Canada; phone 306-836-2022. https://www.canada.ca/en/environment-climate-change/services/national-wildlife-areas/locations/last-mountain-lake.html

Quill Lakes. 252,527 acres. The Quill Lakes are located immediately north of the town of Wynard in east-central Saskatchewan and are shallow saltwater lakes. Up to 12,000 sandhill cranes use the area during migration, and during fall migration whooping cranes have been regularly observed in this general area. This provincial and private area is a Ramsar wetland site of international

Opposite: Whooping crane family foraging, Saskatchewan, Canada

importance. For information, contact the Canadian Wildlife Service at the address for Redberry Lake Migratory Bird Sanctuary.

Redberry Lake Migratory Bird Sanctuary. 25,452 acres. Redberry Lake is a medium-sized saltwater lake near Hafford and is notable in an area characterized by mostly freshwater aquatic environments. The lake and provincial area is regularly used by whooping cranes and is an important staging ground for ducks and other waterfowl. For information, contact Environment and Climate Change Canada, Canadian Wildlife Service, Protected Areas—Prairie Region, 115 Perimeter Road, Saskatoon, SK S7N 0X4; phone 800-668-6767 (toll-free in Canada only). https://www.canada.ca/en/environment-climate-change/services/migratory-bird-sanctuaries/locations/redberry-lake.html

Zoos and Bird Parks

Calgary Zoo. Calgary, Alberta. This zoo is notable for its breeding success with whooping cranes, and it raises a few whooping cranes for release every year. Its breeding pair of whooping cranes nested and raised two chicks in 2019. Address: 1300 Zoo Road NE, Calgary, AB, Canada T2E 7V6; phone 403-232-9300. https://www.calgaryzoo.com/

International Crane Foundation, Baraboo, Wisconsin. The 300-acre headquarters of the ICF is the only place in the world that keeps and exhibits all of the world's crane species, many of which are in open-air and habitat-appropriate enclosures. Nonmembers may gain admission by buying gate tickets; members have unlimited admission and may also use the fine Ron Sauey Memorial Library and participate in a variety of special events. These might include a summer "Evening with the Cranes" and a "Cranes of the World Festival" as well as a "Member Appreciation Day" in early fall, with behind-the-scenes tours and special programs. Address: E11376 Shady Lane Road, PO Box 447, Baraboo WI 53913; phone 608-356-9462. https://www.savingcranes.org/ (See also the Leopold–Pine Island Important Bird Area in the Wisconsin section.)

Lee G. Simmons Conservation Park and Wildlife Safari, Ashland, Nebraska. This drive-through park between Omaha and Lincoln near Ashland has about 25 lesser sandhill cranes that were rescued during a severe winter storm in the Platte River valley. At least one offspring has been produced at the park. Address: 6406 N. 192 St., Ashland, NE 68003; phone 402-944-9453. http://www.wildlifesafaripark.com/

San Diego Zoo Safari Park, San Diego, California. As of 2020, San Diego's Zoo Safari Park was exhibiting examples of the West African black and East African gray crowned cranes, Indian sarus crane, white-naped crane, wattled crane, red-crowned crane, and demoiselle crane. The zoo is located near Escondido. Address: 15500 San Pasqual Valley Road, Escondido, CA 92027; phone 760-747-8702. https://www.sdzsafaripark.org/

Sylvan Heights Bird Park, Scotland Neck, North Carolina. This bird park has one of America's largest collections of waterfowl as well as several species of cranes and many other rarely exhibited birds, including about 25 wetland species and 60 or more other species. Members can participate in special programs, such as a spring "Duckling Day," with tours of the park's breeding center, and a spring North Carolina Science Festival. Address: 500 Sylvan Heights Park Way, PO Box 368, Scotland Neck, NC 27874; phone 252-826-3186. https://shwpark.com/

Woodland Park Zoo, Seattle, Washington. This fine zoo has an exhibit of the cranes of Russia's Amur River basin, including the rare white-naped crane and the even rarer red-crowned crane. Address: 5500 Phinney Ave. N., Seattle, WA 98103; phone 206-548-2500. https://www.zoo.org/

Opposite: Gray crowned crane pair, Maasai Mara National Reserve, Kenya

Note: Other major US zoos that typically have good exhibits of cranes include the **Bronx Zoo**, New York, NY; the **San Antonio Zoo**, San Antonio, TX, which usually has a few whooping cranes as part of a breeding program; the **Louisville Zoo**, Louisville, KY, with a red-crowned crane exhibit; and Smithsonian's **National Zoo**, in Washington, DC, with various cranes.

Seasonal List of North American Crane Festivals

Note: Within each season's section, the festivals are ordered chronologically rather than alphabetically by state.

Winter

Alabama

Festival of the Cranes, Wheeler National Wildlife Refuge. This two-day festival occurs in early January at Wheeler NWR, which is located on the Tennessee River near Huntsville. It is sponsored by the refuge and the Wheeler Wildlife Refuge Association (https://www.friendsofwheelerrefuge.com/). The cranes begin arriving in late November, and numbers peak in early January. For more information, see the festival webpage on the refuge association's website and also check the Events listings at Alabama Birding Trails (https://alabamabirdingtrails.com/).

Arizona

Wings Over Willcox Birding and Nature Festival, Willcox. This January event's highlights are the roughly 25,000 lesser sandhill cranes that winter in the nearby Willcox Playa and agricultural fields of Cochise County. This is the most southwestern flock of the Mid-Continent Population of lesser sandhill cranes, and they breed nearly 4,000 miles away in northeastern Russia. The festival is usually a four-day event, with bird tours, seminars, and exhibits of live raptors and reptiles.

For more information see http://wingsoverwillcox.com/index.asp.

Tennessee

Tennessee Sandhill Crane Festival, Birchwood. This free two-day festival is held in mid-January at the Hiwassee Wildlife Refuge and the Community Center in Birchwood (south of Dayton), and is sponsored by the Tennessee Wildlife Resources Agency. Typically, about 20,000 greater sandhill cranes that breed around Lakes Michigan and Superior are present during winter at this small (6,000-acre) refuge in Chickamauga Lake (at the confluence of the Tennessee and Hiwassee Rivers). It is the largest wintering site for sandhill cranes in the southeastern states except for Florida, which supports most of the wintering eastern sandhill crane population. For more information, see https://www.tn.gov/content/tn/twra/wildlife/birds/sandhill-crane-festival.html.

Texas

Whooping Crane Festival, Port Aransas. This four-day festival is held south of Aransas National Wildlife Refuge at Port Aransas and occurs near the end of February. It is centered on the refuge's famous flock of wintering whooping cranes, although thousands of greater sandhill cranes and more than a hundred other bird species are also then present along this amazingly bird-rich area of the Texas coast. The festival includes boat tours to Aransas NWR for viewing whooping cranes, workshops, seminars, and bus tours to a variety of birding locations. For more information, see https://www.whoopingcranefestival.org/.

Indiana

Marsh Madness Sandhill Crane Festival, Linton. This two-day event is held during late February or early March on the 9,000-acre Goose Pond Fish and Wildlife Area in Greene County, southwestern Indiana. As many as 26,000 greater sandhill cranes have been seen during migration on this Indiana Department of Natural Resources area just south of Linton. The event is sponsored by the Friends of Goose Pond. For more information, see https://friendsofgoosepond.org/.

Colorado

Monte Vista Crane Festival, Alamosa. This three-day festival occurs during the second weekend of March during spring migration when about 25,000 Rocky Mountain greater sandhill cranes pass through the San Luis Valley National Wildlife Refuge Complex of the San Luis Valley from mid-February to mid-April. In addition to a large speaker program, there are birding tours to Monte Vista and Alamosa National Wildlife Refuges, to local playa wetlands for shorebirds, and to upland habitats for raptor watching. For more information, see https://mvcranefest.org/.

Spring

Nebraska

Nebraska Crane Festival, Kearney. This two- to three-day Audubon Nebraska festival held in the central Platte River valley is the oldest of all crane-oriented festivals (celebrating 50 continuous years in 2020). It was previously known as the Rivers and Wildlife Festival, but it centers on sandhill and whooping cranes and other Platte valley wildlife. The festival occurs during the third weekend in March, when the largest migratory congregation of sandhill cranes (ca. 700,000) in the world passes through central Nebraska and the first whooping crane migrants of the Aransas–Wood Buffalo flock are also arriving in the Platte valley. Riverside blinds at Audubon's Lillian Annette Rowe Sanctuary provide the primary festival-based crane viewing opportunities from early March to early April; up to 70,000 cranes have been seen on this single Platte River roosting area. The Crane Trust, 25 miles east near Grand Island, also has similar riverside blinds and helps to

accommodate the thousands of birders who visit the region in March. For more information, see https://ne.audubon.org/crane-festival.

Washington

Othello Sandhill Crane Festival, Othello. This three-day event is held in late March when about 25,000 Pacific Flyway sandhill cranes stop over during spring migration among the partially impounded and scenic sage-covered basaltic scablands of Columbia National Wildlife Refuge. Information is available at https://www.othello-sandhillcranefestival.org/.

Yukon Territory (Canada)

Crane and Sheep Viewing Festival, Faro. This three-day festival is held in early May, when at least tens (perhaps hundreds) of thousands of lesser sandhill cranes pass through a deep montane valley (the Tintina Trench) between the Pelly and Selwyn Ranges during their migration to breeding grounds in Alaska's Yukon River valley and the Yukon-Kuskokwim delta. The region's sheep are Fannin bighorns, a rare genetic intergrade or hybrid population between the Dall's and Rocky Mountain bighorn sheep. For information contact the Town of Faro by phone at 807-994-2728 or by email at info@faroyukon.com.

Summer

Alaska

Tanana Valley Sandhill Crane Festival, Fairbanks. This (usually) three-day festival occurs in late August at the 2,000-acre Creamer's Field Migratory Waterfowl Refuge in Fairbanks. The 2,200-acre Creamer's Field refuge is a major fall stopping point for lesser sandhill cranes and their newly fledged young arriving from the Yukon-Kuskokwim delta. After only a few weeks at the refuge, they make their way east across Alaska and undertake the rest of the 3,000-mile flight to winter quarters in the southern Great Plains. Often up to 2,000 sandhill cranes are present as well as similar numbers of lesser Canada geese and other waterfowl, plus coyotes, foxes, and occasional moose. The cranes are remarkably tame while in the refuge; they have become accustomed to people walking nearby on the three miles of refuge trails and offer great photographic opportunities. For information see https://friendsofcreamersfield.org/.

Colorado

Yampa Valley Crane Festival, Steamboat Springs and Hayden. This four-day festival of the Colorado Crane Conservation Coalition occurs in early September. There are many workshops, nature walks, educational displays, raptor exhibits, and talks by biologists as well as sunrise and sunset crane-viewing sessions. The cranes are part of the Rocky Mountain Population of the greater sandhill crane; about 600 to 1,200 summer and breed in wetland areas of Routt and Moffatt Counties, such as around Steamboat Lake State Park. For more information, see https://coloradocranes.org/.

Fall

Idaho

Greater Yellowstone Crane Festival, Driggs. This one-day festival at the Driggs City Center Plaza is organized by the Greater Yellowstone Crane Initiative and hosted by the Teton Regional Land Trust. The event occurs in September at the start of the fall migration of Greater Yellowstone's component of the Rocky Mountain Population of greater sandhill cranes, which in total number about 22,000 birds. Although there are no organized crane-viewing events, family-oriented activities and educational booths that involve the wildlife and ecology of the Greater Yellowstone region are available. For more information, see https://tetonlandtrust.org or email info@tetonlandtrust.org.

Wisconsin

Whooping Crane Festival, Princeton. This free three-day festival is located along the Fox River in central Wisconsin's prime sandhill crane habitat, such as the state-owned White River Marsh Wildlife Area, where a few captive-reared whooping cranes have nested recently. The event is sponsored by the City of Princeton and occurs in mid-September, when sandhill and whooping cranes are approaching their fall migration. Speakers, crafts, games, vendors, and other family-oriented activities fill the festival's agenda. For more information, click Bird City Wisconsin in the left panel at https://www.cityofprincetonwi.com/.

Michigan

CraneFest, Bellevue. This free two-day festival sponsored by Michigan Audubon (https://www.michiganaudubon.org/) and the Battle Creek Kiwanis Club occurs in October at Big Marsh Lake near Bellevue in Calhoun County. Up to about 2,500 sandhill cranes might be seen roosting in the lake during fall migration. The event is held in Bellevue at the Kiwanis Youth Conservation Area, which overlooks Big Marsh Lake. For more information, visit https://www.michiganaudubon.org/news-events/signature-events/cranefest/.

California

Sandhill Crane Festival, Lodi. This three-day festival is organized by the Lodi Sandhill Crane Association and occurs in early November. Lodi is in California's Central Valley wintering grounds of the Pacific Flyway population of greater and lesser sandhill cranes. More than 8,000 sandhill cranes from Alaska and perhaps Russia winter on the region's agricultural lands and various local wildlife refuges, including the Cosumnes River Preserve. Tours include bird walks, crane-viewing on the Sacramento–San Joaquin delta, and observing the cranes' return to roosting sites on the Cosumnes

River Preserve, the Woodbridge Ecological Reserve South, and Staten Island. For information see https://www.cranefestival.com/index.php or email info@cranefestival.com.

New Mexico

Festival of the Cranes, Bosque del Apache National Wildlife Refuge. This famous long-running four-day event occurs in mid-November at the Bosque del Apache NWR, a scenic mountain-rimmed refuge located along the Rio Grande River about 20 miles south of Socorro. From 20,000 to 30,000 greater sandhill cranes of the Rocky Mountain Population winter in and around the refuge, as do thousands of snow geese, Ross's geese, and other waterfowl. The refuge is widely known for its splendid opportunities for photographing cranes, and the festival has a large number of photography classes, guided birding and nature tours, and an extensive speaker program. It is sponsored by the Friends of the Bosque del Apache National Wildlife Refuge. For more information, see https://www.friendsofbosquedelapache.org.

Gray crowned cranes in flight.

Following pages: Gray crowned crane flock, Lake Manyara National Park, Tanzania

III The Old World Cranes:
Their Populations and Conservation Status

Note: The following species are listed here in the taxonomic sequence that was suggested by the mitrochondrial analysis of Krajewski, Sipiorski, and Anderson (2010) and takes into account their return to *Grus* several species of cranes recently placed in *Antigone*. Recent population estimates are mostly based on Mirande and Harris (2019).

Gray Crowned Crane (*Balearica regulorum*)

This species and the related black crowned crane are members of a group of four nonoverlapping populations that are now confined to Africa south of the Sahara. They are the only living descendants of a group of cranes that once ranged

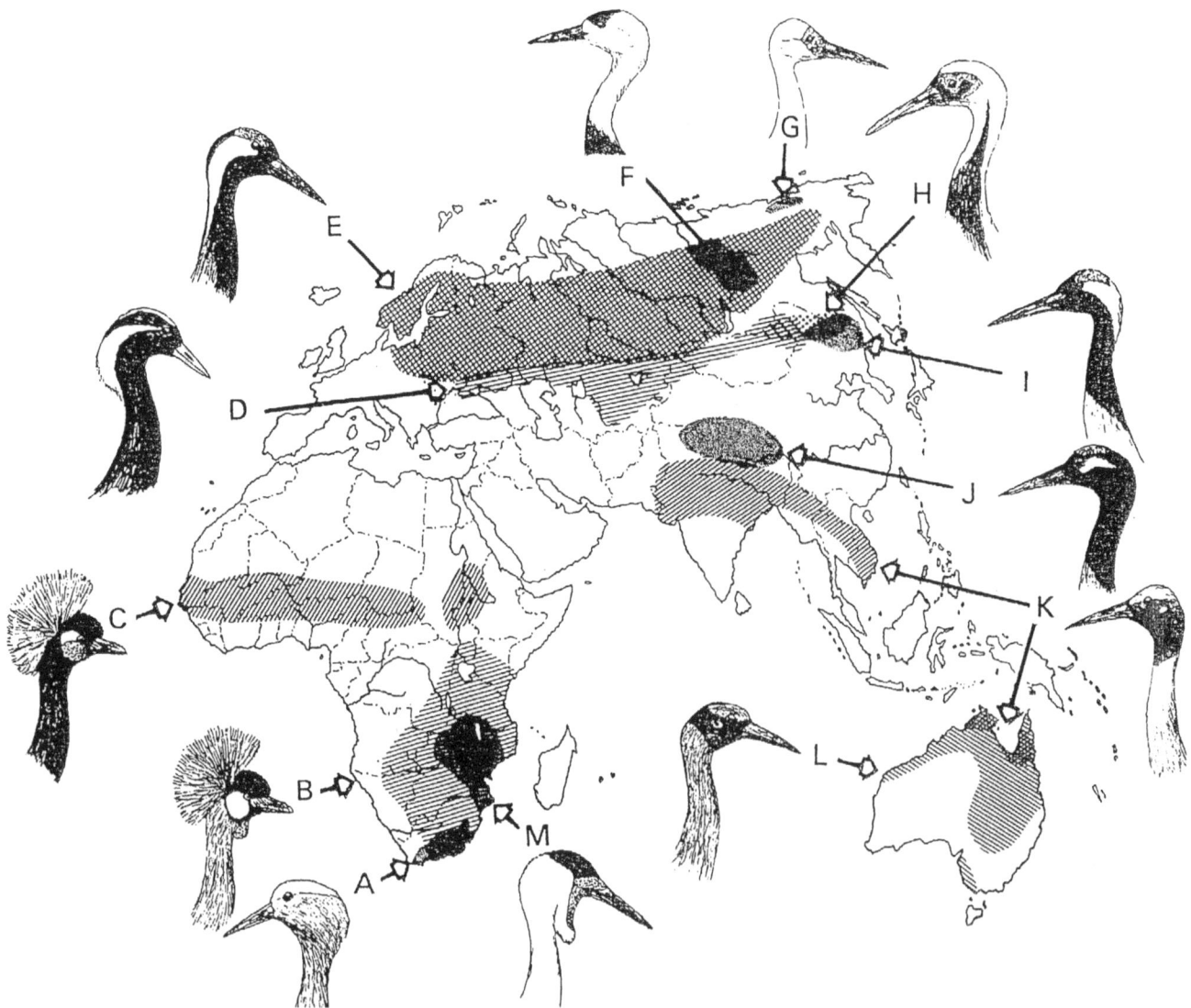

crane (C), demoiselle crane (D), Eurasian crane (E), hooded crane (F), Siberian crane (G), white-naped crane (H), red-crowned crane (I), black-necked crane (J), sarus crane (K), brolga (L), and wattled crane (M).

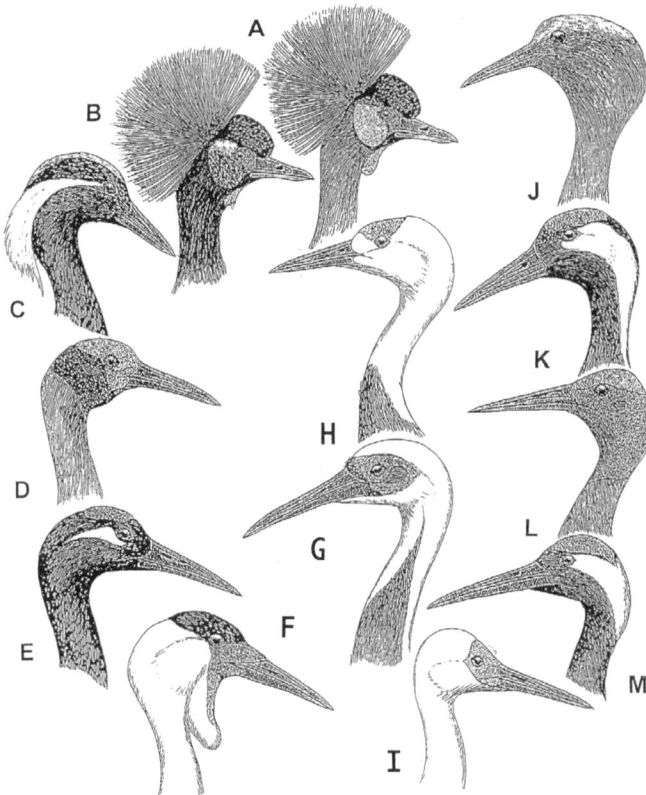

Fig. 25. Head profiles of gray crowned crane (A), black crowned crane (B), demoiselle crane (C), sarus crane (D), black-necked crane (E), wattled crane (F), white-naped crane (G), hooded crane (H), Siberian crane (I), blue crane (J), Eurasian crane (K), brolga (L), and red-crowned crane (M).

widely over the world, including North America, but were eventually replaced by more advanced types of cranes. Crowned cranes have relatively short stout bills; lack elongated, decurved inner wing feathers; and also lack the highly elongated tracheal (windpipe) structure that is so characteristic of more advanced cranes. They are an extremely attractive group of birds with distinctive golden yellow crowns, white to golden wing coverts, and grayish white to pale blue eyes. Like all other cranes, crowned cranes "dance," and these dances include lively leaps and bows as well as a ruffling of the long and ornamental feathers of the lower neck and breast. The wings are also often spread, exposing the beautiful contrasting upper wing coverts.

Both of the crowned cranes are associated with open country, especially favoring grasslands in the vicinity of water. Unlike the other types of cranes, they prefer to roost in elevated locations, especially large trees. However, they also at times roost in shallow water in the manner of more typical cranes. They are quite social and outside of the breeding season often occur in flocks of from a few dozen to as many as 150 birds. Like other cranes, they are strongly monogamous, and probably even during the nonbreeding season the nuclear social unit consists of the pair or family. Families remain intact for nine or ten months, after which time the adults drive the young from their territory and prepare to nest again. The young birds from the same general area then tend to associate in flocks, spending much of their time foraging in fields. Crowned cranes consume a wide variety of foods, ranging from grass and grain seeds to insects, earthworms, and even crustaceans.

Fig. 26. Gray crowned crane, adult.

Gray crowned cranes range from South Africa north to extreme eastern Zaire, Uganda, and Kenya, with the northernmost birds separated by only a few hundred miles in northern Kenya from the eastern race of the black crowned crane. At least until recently, these birds were still relatively common in many areas, such as in Kenya and southern Uganda, where the population has been judged to be as dense as two to three birds per square mile.

As recently as 2008 the gray crowned crane was regarded as of least concern by the International Union for Conservation of Nature (IUCN), but in 2009 it was uplisted to vulnerable, and by 2013 it had again been reclassified, as endangered. Based on information published in 2014, the gray crowned crane East African population was 19,500 to 26,000 birds, with the largest numbers in Kenya (10,000–12,500) and Uganda (6,500–8,000). The South African race was estimated at 7,000 to 7,500, with 6,500 of the birds in South Africa, 200 to 700 in Zimbabwe, more than 250 in Mozambique, and less than 20 each in Botswana and Namibia (Mirande and Harris, 2019).

Black Crowned Crane (*Balearica pavonina*)

Early literature often treated the gray crowned crane of southern Africa as only racially distinct from the black crowned crane, but the most recent taxonomies regard them as a separate species, and they are so treated here. Black crowned cranes occur in sub-Saharan Africa from Senegal, Sierra Leone, Nigeria, and northern Cameroon on the west eastward to the upper Nile River valley. The more western populations (the "West African black crowned crane," *B. pavonina*) differ slightly from those of the upper Nile valley (the "Sudan black crowned crane," *B. ceciliae*). The eastern gray-necked species extends from about Khartoum south to Lake Turkana and east to the Ethiopian lakes. This population appears to have declined markedly, from 65,000 to 90,000 individuals in 1985 to 28,000 to 55,000 individuals in 2004, with the great majority now occurring in Sudan and South Sudan (IUCN, 2013).

The western species *pavonina* is declining rapidly, with an estimated maximum loss of 30 to 49 percent of the population between 1985 and 2004, but it still occurs through the sub-Saharan Sahel (semidesert zone) and the Sudan-Guinea savannas, with records from as far south as the Democratic Republic of Congo. The western subpopulation was estimated to number about 15,000 birds in 2004. The major remaining concentrations of the western race apparently are in the Lake Chad basin, Mauritania, and Senegambia. This crane has become very rare in Mali, and it has been extirpated from Sierra Leone and perhaps also from Nigeria, where, ironically, it is designated as the national bird.

Black crowned cranes differ only slightly from their gray-necked and more southerly relatives. Besides their generally darker body coloration, birds of the eastern race of black crowned crane also tend to be somewhat smaller and darker than those from farther west, and they exhibit a smaller white area on the upper cheek than do most western birds. In both races the lower portion of the cheek is tinged with red.

Adult vocalizations of the West African black ("Nigerian"), East African gray ("Kenyan"), and South African gray ("Southern") crowned cranes were studied by G. Archibald (1975, 1976). He observed rather marked differences between the West African species and the two populations of gray crowned studied. Thus, the guard call of *Balearica* is a hollow-sounding honklike vocalization that is relatively low in pitch and rich in harmonic development. However, although the guard call of the West African black is a monosyllabic honk, that of the gray forms studied is a disyllabic *kawonk*, with the second syllable higher in pitch. In both species the gular sac is inflated during calling, but it is larger in the eastern and southern populations, and their calls are correspondingly lower in pitch.

The crowned cranes, named for their tuft of golden head feathers, are the most distinctive of all living cranes. Evidence from molecular biology suggests that divergence of the ancestral crowned cranes and the more typical cranes may have occurred as long ago as 10 million years, with the crowned crane lineage seemingly retaining a greater number of "primitive" traits than any of the other living cranes.

Remarkably, fossil cranes about 10 million years old that were recently found in north-central Nebraska, among an assemblage of mammals typical of modern Africa, have been found to be very similar in skeletal respects to modern crowned cranes, even as to their simplified tracheal anatomy. Crowned cranes are also the only surviving crane species with long, prehensile hind toes, which allow them to perch and roost readily in trees (although they rarely nest in trees). The presence of this unique trait might suggest that primitive cranes evolved from perching-adapted ancestors.

Siberian Crane (*Leucogeranus leucogeranus*)

The Siberian crane had until recently been regarded as the second rarest crane in the world, with a total known population of a few hundred birds in the 1970s, making it almost as rare as the whooping crane. In 1980 a major new wintering flock was discovered in eastern China and hopes were raised for the preservation of this beautiful species. It was known to nest in only two areas of Russia, including a very nearly or actually extirpated Western Asian population between the Ob and Pechora Rivers, and a second larger eastern population nesting from the lower Kolyma River basin west to the Indirika and lower Yana Rivers. One part of the western population (the Western Asian flock), now probably extirpated, traditionally wintered along the southern Caspian Sea area of coastal Iran. A second tiny group (the Central Asian flock) formerly wintered in Rajasthan, India, at the Keoladeo Ghana Sanctuary, but only nine individuals were found there in the early 2000s. The East Asian flock breeds near the lower parts of the Ob River and winters in the swampy portions of northern Jiangxi Province at and near Poyang and Dongting Lakes, along the lower Yangtze (Changjiang) River in eastern China. The Eastern Asian population breeds in Yakutia and winters about 6,000

kilometers (3,000 miles) away, with nearly all concentrated at Poyang Lake in southern China.

Siberian cranes are distinctly different from all the other cranes of the world and probably are not close relatives of any of these. Their unison-call behavior and their foraging adaptations suggest affinities with the African wattled crane. Like that species, they have a rather high-pitched and somewhat gooselike voice, and their unison-call ceremony is characterized by its strong wing lowering and extreme neck stretching, especially by the male. Both species also have tracheal windpipes that only slightly penetrate the front of the sternal breastbone.

The unison display of the Siberian crane is also highly distinctive. It is of indeterminate length and is begun by the male rather than the

Fig. 27. Siberian crane, adult.

female. The male first draws his head and neck back behind the vertical until the neck assumes an S-shape. From this posture he quickly rotates the neck downward, ending with the neck held straight downward and the bill turned up toward the breast. At this point he utters a high-pitched call. Then he raises his humeri and lowers his wrists, so the primary feathers are exposed. He then more slowly returns his head until it is extended almost vertically but moving back and forth over a 30-degree arc, while uttering a series of flutelike calls that continue in regular sequence until the end of the display. The neck gradually assumes a vertical position, with the head lowered between calls and raised while making them. The wings remain drooped during this time.

The female typically joins in after the male has begun calling, holding her neck about 70 degrees above the horizontal and moving the head up and down with each call but to a smaller extent than is typical of the male. Her wings are variably drooped during calling. The sexes call alternately, with the female's higher-pitched notes producing the *loo* portion of a *doodle-loo* cadence (Archibald, 1976).

The Siberian crane is considered a critically endangered species by the IUCN, and at about 3,600 to 4,000 birds is the world's third-rarest crane. Recent research using DNA hybridization techniques has shown this to be probably a very isolated species in a genetic sense, second only to the crowned cranes in terms of its isolation from other living species of cranes.

Blue Crane (*Anthropoides paradiseus*)

This beautiful species, sometimes called the Stanley's crane or paradise crane, is one of only two cranes to have been designated as a country's "national bird" (by the Republic of South Africa). It also has one of the most restricted distributions of any crane, being essentially limited to South Africa, including Swaziland and Lesotho, plus a very small and isolated population near the Etosha Pan of Namibia. The blue crane is a close relative of the demoiselle crane and like it is particularly adapted

to arid grasslands. It is especially characteristic of grass-covered hills and valleys with only scattered trees, where grassy cover is thick and short. In Natal, the birds breed in highland "bergveld" areas at 3,300 to 6,500 feet in elevation. There the climate is temperate and most of the precipitation occurs during the summer months, often in the form of hailstorms. During the cold and dry winter season, the birds move to lower elevations.

Blue cranes have short and moderately pointed bills and do most of their foraging from the ground surface or from low vegetation. They have not been found to dig for foods with their bills, or to forage in water, although nighttime roosting in water sometimes occurs among wintering

Fig. 28. Blue crane, adult.

flocks. At that time of year, they are quite gregarious and may form flocks of up to 300 birds. They then may also forage among herds of ungulates, such as springbok antelopes, with which they form an integrated society, the ever-alert cranes sometimes warning the antelopes of possible danger.

According to van Ee (1966), the primary aspect of the blue crane's courtship is the "dance." This activity might last for as much as one to four hours. It begins with the birds running around in circles, as if the male is chasing the female. However, they remain separated by a distance of about ten feet. Suddenly the two birds stop and call in unison. The next phase is characterized by both birds simultaneously picking up bunches of grass, which are thrown into the air. The birds also jump high in the air, stopping very near one another and resuming calling. They then run straight across the field, remaining close to one another. The final phase is once again the throwing up of bunches of grass. This phase never lasts more than ten minutes and is performed with the birds facing one another. At times one bird will snap up the grass that had been thrown up by its partner and toss it up again.

In spite of its small total range, this species is still fairly common locally, no doubt in part because of its special protected status as the national bird of South Africa. In South Africa, populations in the south and southwestern Western Cape and Kwazulu-Natal have increased as the species has recently expanded into agricultural areas, but the national population has fallen greatly since the 1970s. Poisoning associated with farming activities is believed to be the major cause of an apparent marked population decline in recent years. The population in the central Karoo region is presently stable. Tiny relict populations might still exist in Namibia and perhaps Swaziland. The South African population has recently (1996–2005 surveys) been estimated at about 25,000 individuals (IUCN, 2013), but the Namibian flock might be near extinction and is considered critically endangered, with only 23 found in 2013.

Wattled Crane (*Bugeranus carunculatus*)

The distinctive wattled crane of Africa is one of the largest cranes of the world and, with the Australian and the two crowned cranes, is one of the few that are distinctly wattled. Unlike these species, however, in the wattled crane feathers mostly cover the wattle, leaving only the anterior portion bare and reddish. The front of the face, extending back to the eyes, has wartlike papillae in both sexes, and the innermost secondary wing feathers (the so-called "tertials") are greatly elongated, hiding the tail in resting birds. The wattled crane's voice is a high-pitched scream, with the male's slightly lower in pitch than the female's. In both sexes the tracheal windpipe is not deeply convoluted within the sternum.

According to Archibald (1975, 1976), the wattled crane's unison call differs from all other species

Fig. 29. Wattled crane, adult.

except for the Siberian crane. The female begins the display by quickly lowering her head to the shoulders, then instantly extends her coiled neck to the vertical while holding her head about 30 degrees in front of the vertical. This posture is maintained through the rest of the display, which lasts from three to seven seconds. The male joins in the display very soon after the female begins her preliminary movements, and his head movements and initial vocalization closely resemble those of the female, but only initially. While the female utters a series of short evenly spaced calls, the male produces a long call, followed by a series of short calls, and ends with another long call.

This crane is associated with large areas of shallow wetlands. Foraging is done by probing in wet or moist soil for the underground portions of sedges, and by consuming aquatic plants such as water lilies. It may at times also eat such prey as frogs and snakes. Thus, the wattled crane forages in much the same manner as the Siberian crane, a species that is often considered to be the wattled crane's nearest relative.

Wattled cranes are one of the most severely threatened of the African cranes. They are now mostly limited in their distribution to the area of the upper Zambezi drainage, although in earlier times they occurred south to Cape Province and west nearly to the mouth of the Congo. The South African population was estimated at 311 birds in 2014. In south-central Africa there may be about 7,100 birds using five large floodplains, such as the Okavango Delta and Kafue Flats in northern Namibia (100–150 birds). There are also a few in the Democratic Republic of Congo and Zimbabwe. There is an isolated population of perhaps 250 to 300 birds locally in the highlands of Ethiopia. The current status of this last population is precarious, and it is perhaps limited to Bale Mountain National Park, southeastern Ethiopia.

The total population of wattled cranes was probably somewhat over 9,000 birds and was probably declining in the early 2000s, placing them high on the list of cranes that deserve special conservation attention. The available data

suggest marked declines in Mozambique, Zambia, and possibly Botswana. The Okavango Delta in Botswana may now hold the largest single population of about 1,300 birds.

Sarus Crane (*Grus antigone*)

The sarus crane is the tallest of the world's cranes and is also one of the heaviest, with adult males standing nearly six feet in height and averaging more than 18 pounds. The birds range widely over the Indian peninsula, and at least originally also ranged over much of what was then Indochina, even reaching the Philippines. They have been

Fig. 30. Sarus crane, adult.

extirpated from Luzon and a substantial portion of southeast Asia. They remain common in northern India, where the Hindus consider them sacred, and where perhaps they served as the original basis for the mythical garuda bird. In the last few decades, they have managed to reach and colonize a rather large area in northern Australia. As with the Australian brolga, most of the head and upper neck are bare of feathers in the adult sarus crane, and, except for the grayish crown, the entire head region is a startling flesh red. The vernacular name sarus is of Hindi origin. Perhaps because of the bird's bare red head, the Latin name *antigone* was chosen, for the daughter of Oedipus, who hanged herself.

In northern India these birds are associated with a wide variety of wetland habitats, most of which are seasonal wetlands that are flooded during the monsoon period. The arrival of the monsoon rains sets off breeding, but during years when there is no lowland flooding, there may be no nesting. During nonbreeding periods the birds flock to a limited degree, although flock sizes of more than 100 birds are rare. The cranes are omnivorous, consuming not only a wide array of plant materials but also animal foods that range in size from grasshoppers to moderately large water snakes.

Archibald (1975, 1976) states that this species resembles the Australian and white-naped cranes behaviorally. In all, the female begins the call, and during the introductory phase there is a short continuous call that is followed by a pause and then an extended series of sexually distinct calls. In the Indian race of the sarus crane, the introductory note of the female is followed by a rapid series of short notes that transpose gradually into her regular series of calls, which average about two to three notes per note of the male. In the eastern race, the female's calls are more highly pitched, and her notes are not given in synchrony with the regularly spaced notes of the male. In the males of both races, the introductory note is followed by an extended series of pulsed notes that average about a half-second in length, with the total duration of the display dependent upon the intensity of stimulation. Walkinshaw (1973) describes the female's unison call as a series of *tuk* notes, whereas that of the male is a loud, trumpeting *krrr* or *garrrooa*.

The population of the western race of the sarus crane in the early 2000s might have consisted of 13,000 individuals in India, and more than 800 in Nepal. There may also then have been 800 to 1,000 in Cambodia, Laos, and Vietnam, and 300 to 400 in Myanmar. The Australian population was (unreliably) estimated at 5,000 to 10,000 breeding adults in 2000. The world population thus then might have totaled about 19,000 to 22,000 individuals (IUCN, 2013). Because of some ecological advantages over the smaller Australian crane, the sarus may eventually become the dominant crane species over the northern parts of Australia.

Brolga (*Grus rubicunda*)

This Australian crane, called the brolga (a corruption of an aboriginal name) or the native companion, is a close relative to the sarus crane. Both are tall, long-billed, predominantly grayish birds, with a head that is mostly bare in adults. However, the brolga is feathered somewhat farther up the neck, and it has a more distinct wattle or dewlap on the throat as well as blackish rather than reddish legs. Both species utter strong, resonating calls; during the unison call, displaying males of both species strongly arch their wings and throw back their head and neck to a fully vertical position. In the Australian crane the unison calls are somewhat stronger and lower in pitch than are those of the sarus.

The brolga is widespread over the northern portions of Australia and occurs locally as far south as southern Victoria. The largest numbers and densest concentrations are found in Queensland. There the birds seek out freshwater swamps that are dominated by *Eleocharis* sedges, on the tubers of which the cranes forage. For most of the year these tubers, locally called "bulkuru," compose the species' primary food, but in some areas other sedges are also consumed. When natural foods are lacking, such as during Australia's regularly occurring

Fig. 31. Brolga, adult.

drought cycles, the birds will resort to feeding in agricultural fields, bringing them increasingly into conflict with farmers.

According to Walkinshaw (1973) the call of the male during the unison display is one in which the second note is much the loudest, and thereafter the call gradually tapers off: *kawee-kreee-kurr-kurr-kurr-kurr*. The female similarly utters an extended series of *kuk* notes immediately following each syllable of the male's call. According also to Walkinshaw, dancing in this species occurs most commonly during the onset of the wet season and is similar to that of the sarus crane in

that both birds in a dancing pair sometimes bring their throats close together. He also observed tossing behavior during dancing and commented that dancing occurred in a variety of situations as, for example, when he approached a flock or a nest.

Nesting in this species is timed to coincide with the wet season, which in northern Australia usually begins in December, and in southern regions extends from about July to November. The length and severity of the dry season varies considerably from year to year, and so there are considerable variations in the seasonal movements of the cranes. With the onset of the rainy period, there is lowland flooding and filling of seasonal swamps and lagoons. When this occurs, nesting begins immediately, and normally the chicks have already hatched by the time the lagoons begin to dry up once again. At this time there is a gradual movement of adults and young back to the permanent coastal marshes, where some nesting also occurs.

Mixed pairing of brolgas and the invading sarus cranes sometimes occurs, and natural hybridization has been reported in the northern portions of Australia. The brolga had long been abundant there, where the sarus crane was first reported in the 1950s. It has gradually colonized the Cape York region, competing with and perhaps partly displacing the brolga. No recent overall population estimates are available, but earlier ones are in the range of 50,000 to 100,000, and the population has been reported as decreasing (IUCN, 2013). Currently the total brolga population estimate is thought to be about 50,000 birds, but not enough data exists to confirm this.

Demoiselle Crane (*Anthropoides virgo*)

This smallest "damsel-like" and most elegant of all the cranes of the world is a fairly close relative of the blue crane. Like that species, it has a fully feathered crown, highly elongated inner wing feathers, and a somewhat shaggy breast. It is adapted to a dry upland and grass-dominated environment; the demoiselle crane is perhaps the

Fig. 32. Demoiselle crane, adult.

most arid-adapted of all the cranes. The species' main breeding region extends from Turkey and the Black Sea region through the southern Ukraine and Crimea through Kazakhstan, Mongolia, and northeastern China. Its breeding densities across this broad range are generally low, but the birds are notably abundant throughout the vast grasslands of Mongolia, where 40,000 to 70,000 birds might be present. In Kazakhstan the demoiselle may still have a fairly stable population of 50,000 to 60,000 birds, and 30,000 to 40,000 are thought to be present in the Caspian Sea region. However, it has declined over much of its original and now rapidly disappearing steppe range, and in the early 2000s the species' global population was estimated to number about 200,000 to 240,000 individuals.

The demoiselle crane has a wide winter distribution that once included much of northwestern Africa, but it now winters in small numbers in north-central and northeastern Africa. It is especially widespread in the Indian subcontinent, where the largest numbers of birds that breed in central to eastern Asia overwinter. Throughout its breeding range the demoiselle crane occurs in steppelike to semidesert habitats and moves into marshes and swamps only for foraging or roosting. The birds nevertheless prefer to nest no more than about a mile from water, and nests often are located within a few hundred yards of it. During the winter period flocks gather in rice paddies, along the margins of shallow monsoon-dependent wetlands and reservoirs, and in other open and variably moist habitats. Roosts are often located along the sandbars of large rivers or the margins of shallow ponds, as in sandhill cranes.

During the unison-call sequence, both sexes bring their heads back to about 45 degrees behind the vertical. The female may remain in her extreme back-tilted neck position, or may gradually return the head and neck to the vertical. The wings are not lowered and the tertials are not noticeably raised in either sex. The display lasts about three or four seconds (Walkinshaw, 1973).

While performing unison-calling and other mutual displays, dancing often occurs, when the birds bow with spread wings, and they also may throw small objects up into the air (Kozlova, 1975). As these cranes are relatively small, their movements are done with considerable grace and animation. Their dancing is done with the inner wing feathers depressed rather than raised and is more balletlike than in *Grus*, with the birds not jumping so high or so frequently as occurs with other cranes. Occasionally the birds head-bob toward one another, either synchronously or alternately, and move in semicircles around each other, with the tail raised and the wings slightly opened. As in other cranes, there seems to be no differentiation of the sexes during such displays, which most often occur at dawn and especially at dusk. During group display, the birds often form a loose ring around dancing individuals; the participants raise their ear tufts and black neck plumes, and fan their tails while uttering loud calls.

White-Naped Crane (*Grus vipio*)

The white-naped crane is well named; it is the only white-headed crane that has a red facial skin patch extending far enough back to encompass the ear opening, and the only one that has a dark grayish stripe extending up the side of the neck to terminate at a point slightly behind the bare facial region.

During the winter, this crane is found in eastern China (Yangtze River valley), Korea (mainly near the Demilitarized Zone), and southern Japan, where it occupies a restricted area in the Izumi and Akune districts of southwestern Kyushu. It is in the last-named area that the best opportunities for censusing exist, and in recent years about 2,000 wintering birds have been present on Kyushu.

Their wintering habitats are primarily brackish marshlands and rice paddies, with nearby roosting sites on salt marshes, mud flats, or the edges and sandbars of shallow lakes. Currently the Demilitarized Zone of Korea provides a fortuitous refuge for a few hundred migrating and overwintering cranes, but this is a politically based situation that might change without advance warning. The establishment by the Chinese Ministry of Forestry of a nature preserve at Poyang Lake, Jiangxi Province, has been of great value to the white-naped crane; from 2005 to 2012 an average of 1,167 birds were present there during the winter period. In the eastern parts of its range its numbers have increased, with estimates of 6,200 to 6,500 birds between 2012 and 2015.

According to Archibald (1975, 1976), the white-naped crane is part of a species group that also includes the sarus and brolga. In all of these, the female begins the unison call, and the vocal patterns during the introductory phase of the unison display are similar in both sexes, with a short continuous call that is followed by a pause and then by a series of sexually distinct calls. During the introductory portion of her call, the female white-naped crane extends her head and neck farther back behind the vertical than do female sarus or brolga cranes. She then utters a rapid series

Fig. 33. White-naped crane, adult.

of short calls that grade into her more pulsed and broken calls, which are uttered with the neck vertically outstretched, the bill pointed upward, and the wings held against the body. Following his introductory call, the male likewise begins a series of pulsed calls, which are longer and lower in pitch than the female calls, and with each call the male raises his humeri and drops his wrists, while between calls the humeri are lowered and the wrists folded. The neck is thrown back well behind the vertical, and this movement is accentuated by the contrasting neck and nape patterning.

This species has been classified as vulnerable by the IUCN. The total world population was recently estimated at 7,000 to 7,800 individuals, based on estimates of 1,000 to 1,500 individuals wintering in China, and a 2009 count of 1,920 in Korea, and a maximum count of 3,142 in 2009 at Izumi, Japan (IUCN, 2013). Russia has included this crane in its Red Book of threatened and endangered species, and has been making strong efforts to protect it and its breeding habitat, although most of its breeding grounds are in northeastern China and Mongolia.

Eurasian Crane (*Grus grus*)

The Eurasian crane is the familiar "common" crane of Europe and the species with the broadest breeding distribution of any of the Old World cranes. Currently it breeds from Scandinavia and Great Britain on the west to at least Russia's Kolyma River and almost to the Okhotsk Sea on the east. It locally nests south to Germany, Poland, the steppes of eastern Europe and central Asia, and northeastern China. Wintering areas are similarly vast and extend from France to southern China.

Like the fairly closely related sandhill crane, this species is mostly gray, but unlike the sandhill crane it has a white stripe extending from the cheeks back toward the hindneck and a mostly black face, foreneck, and nape. It is only moderately large, with adults weighing about 10 to 13 pounds, or about the size of a greater sandhill crane. Its voice is similarly loud and resonant but not so penetrating as those of the whooping or red-crowned cranes. During the unison call both sexes raise their curved tertial feathers, lower their primaries, and stretch their necks to the vertical.

Dancing behavior can be observed in sexually immature birds during summer and fall and can be seen frequently in winter quarters before the northward migration (Moll, 1963; Glutz von Blotzheim, 1973). Dancing in this species has been described and illustrated by many authors. As in the other *Grus* species, this behavior includes a variety of bobs, bows, pirouettes, and stops interspersed with leaps into the air and the tossing of vegetation above the head. An aggressive "parade march" posturing is also an important part of the

Fig. 34. Eurasian crane, adult.

display repertoire and often immediately precedes attack. A more common form of threat is dorsal-preening, with the wings held slightly away from the body and the inner wing feathers strongly ruffled (Fig. 10). The bare red crown may also be directed toward the opponent, or may be less specifically expanded and exhibited during agonistic display, as for example during the parade-marching behavior. Copulatory behavior in this species is much like that of other cranes, and a precopulatory sequence is illustrated in Figure 9.

Although the Eurasian crane may have lost some breeding areas in the westernmost parts of its range, it is still moderately common in Scandinavia. Its range is also expanding in central Europe. In 2006 it was estimated that Germany supported more than 5,400 pairs. It is also now breeding in small numbers in the Czech Republic and Hungary, and a few now are year-round residents of Great Britain. No recent efforts have been made to estimate the entire European population of Eurasian cranes, but in Europe up to 70,000 winter on the Iberian Peninsula, which together with the wintering cranes of northwestern Africa, the Nile River valley, Sudan, and Ethiopia probably include nearly all of the thriving central European and Scandinavian breeding populations. Wintering also occurs in Israel and the Arabian Peninsula, which probably attracts birds from both eastern Europe and western Russia.

By 2015, the world population was estimated to number about 700,000 individuals, second only to the sandhill crane, with the Western Eurasian population at 590,000 and the Eastern Eurasian population at 110,000 to 112,000 birds. Much of the Siberian and north Chinese population apparently funnels into the Indian subcontinent, whereas those from the easternmost regions of Siberia migrate south to southeastern China. Almost nothing is known of the population sizes of these groups, which have been tentatively estimated at 12,000 birds.

Hooded Crane (*Grus monacha*)

This rather small species of crane is sometimes known by its Latin-based name of "monk crane," in reference to the white "hood" that contrasts with an otherwise dark gray to blackish body. This little-studied crane breeds in sub-Arctic forests of south-central and southeastern Siberia. Breeding also occurs very locally in northeastern China and is suspected to occur in Mongolia. It is a species that has been classified as threatened by the International Council for Bird Preservation (ICBP) and vulnerable by the IUCN. The best estimates are that 11,000 to 12,000 birds were alive in the early 2000s, based mostly on counts of wintering birds

Fig. 35. Hooded crane, adult.

in Honshu and Kyushu, Japan, and in China. The world population was estimated at about 14,500 to 16,000 birds in 2017.

The majority of the world population winters in Japan, with smaller numbers in China and South Korea. More than 80 percent winter at Izumi, southern Japan, where nearly 14,000 were recorded in 2017–18. Another wintering population at Yashiro in western Honshu has declined considerably in the past half-century and has recently supported only a few birds.

It was not until 1974 that the first documented nesting of the hooded crane was obtained, in the Bikin River area of the Ussuri River basin, well to the east of the region previously suspected of hosting breeding birds. Other studies in the Vilyuy River basin of Siberia during the early 1970s indicated that regular nesting occurs in that large but little-studied region. In both regions the birds have been found to prefer mossy hammocks or damp moors in boggy larch forests, at altitudes of about 600 to 2,500 feet. Other regions where the birds have been seen during summer, such as the open steppes and forest-steppes of Transbaikalia, are apparently used only by nonbreeding birds. So far as is known, nearly all breeding is limited to Russia. However, a small amount of nesting habitat occurs in northeastern China, south of the Amur River, where nesting was first discovered in the 1990s, and perhaps some also nest in Mongolia.

The best descriptions of social behavior in the hooded crane come from G. Archibald (1975, 1976), who described the unison-call behavior. He placed the species in the group also containing the Eurasian, whooping, and Japanese cranes but observed that, unlike these other three species, the hooded crane does not usually lower its wrists during high-intensity threat posturing. The female usually utters a long call and a short call for every male call. Male calls tend to be disyllabic. During the unison call the tertial feathers are raised to form a conspicuous bustlelike plume in both sexes, and the head and neck are variably extended upward and backward. In its posturing and calls the hooded crane closely resembles the Eurasian crane, and mixed pairing has been observed under wild conditions. Likewise, the two species often associate on migration. Although dancing behavior and behavior associated with copulation have not been described in detail, at least the dancing behavior does not seem to differ significantly from that of other *Grus* species.

This is one of the species of cranes that can be preserved from extinction only by the cooperation of several nations, particularly Russia, China, Korea, and Japan. Already some important wintering areas in Korea and eastern China have apparently been abandoned, and the wintering grounds in Japan are extremely localized, although they hold about 80 percent of the world population, or 11,500 to 13,000 birds. Perhaps 1,000 to 1,500 also winter in China, and about 1,700 winter in Suncheon Bay, Republic of South Korea.

Black-Necked Crane (*Grus nigricollis*)

The breeding grounds of the black-necked crane are high in the Himalayas, at elevations from about 9,000 to 15,000 feet, an altitude at which few other birds or mammals occur. There, tundralike marshes occur around lake edges and islands. In such locations there are grass- or sedge-dominated areas that have relatively abundant

Fig. 36. Black-necked crane, adult.

aquatic life, and grassy mounds in shallow lakes or ponds exist and serve as nesting sites. It winters in river valleys and along reservoir shorelines in the vicinity of barley and spring wheat fields. Although it prefers breeding around lakes, shallow marshes and meadows are the most important habitat for feeding; its diet consists of roots, tubers, insects, snails, shrimp, fish, small birds, and rodents (IUCN, 2013).

Although little is known of this species' vocalizations and unison-calling, dancing behavior was observed by Gole (1981), who stated that as he approached a pair they engaged in dancing behavior, with the male moving around the female with outstretched wings, trying to lead her. He also observed an apparent courtship dance once. After the pair had alighted, the male began waving his neck up and down, tiptoed several paces ahead, turned, and while spreading his wings came dancing back toward the female. As the male came nearer, the female responded with a similar movement of her neck. The male uttered a short call as he had begun his display, and he responded to the female's neck-waving by standing beside her, still waving his neck. The female did not respond any further.

The breeding season is fairly short at these high elevations, probably confined to the period between late May and August. Evidently there is a fall migration out of the region in October, with many of the cranes wintering in the Yunnan-Guizhou regions of China or in southern Tibet. Wintering also occurs in west-central Bhutan and at least formerly in Assam and Vietnam. During winter the birds mix to some degree with Eurasian cranes; they apparently have rather similar ecological requirements to that species. However, limited information suggests that they have a greater preference for foraging in marshes and other wetlands, and thus may feed to a larger degree on animal materials.

Besides breeding on the Qinghai-Tibetan plateau, China, there is a small nesting population in adjacent Ladakh, India. Several wintering areas have been identified at lower altitudes on China's Qinghai-Tibet and Yunnan-Guizhou plateaus, including both Yunnan and western Guizhou, as well as in Tibet. Small numbers also winter in Bhutan and in Arunachal Pradesh, India, and wintering birds historically occurred in Vietnam. The global winter population during the early 2000s was estimated at about 10,000 to 10,200 birds, including about 5,500 to 7,000 in Tibet, 3,000 in Yunnan, 550 in Bhutan, and a very few in India. A 2020 world population estimate was 12,000 birds.

Much of the known wintering range of this species is in Tibet, and at least until the Chinese influence became strong in the 1950s they were effectively protected by the Tibetans' sacred treatment of all animals. The Chinese government is currently affording the black-necked crane its highest level of official protection and has established one sanctuary specifically for it.

Red-Crowned Crane (*Grus japonensis*)

This marvelous Asian crane is also known by a variety of English names, including Manchurian crane and Japanese crane, but none of these is particularly suitable for such a magnificent bird. It is quite possibly the most beautiful of all cranes, with a snow-white plumage that is set off by a red crown and jet-black flight feathers, plus similar black feathers on its head and upper neck, but with a contrasting white nape and hindneck. Adults are the heaviest of all crane species, with males weighing as much as 25 pounds. Like the similar whooping crane, the red-crowned crane has an extremely loud voice that may easily carry a mile or two under favorable conditions.

The species' unison call has multiple functions, including formation and maintenance of the pair bond, as well as territorial advertisement and agonistic signaling. As described by Archibald (1975, 1976) and other authors, the display begins with the birds standing 3 to 10 feet apart. Either sex can initiate the call, but usually the female does. Both sexes raise their humeri and expose their primaries during the calling, and the latter are usually moved in a rhythmic manner during the calling. The male's wings are usually raised higher than those of the female during display. Both birds call in an antiphonal manner. For each male call, which is typically monosyllabic, the female utters two (in the mainland population) or three to four (in the Japanese population). Unison-calling often provokes the same display from other nearby pairs, sometimes resulting in a synchronous chorus of calling.

Like unison-calling, dancing is a complex behavior having several probable functions. The movements associated with dancing were described by Masatomi and Kitagawa (1974/1975), who recognized eight distinct postures and four types of movements. These movement categories are pumping (of the head and neck), bouncing, pursuing movements (chasing and fleeing behavior), and throwing movements. Dancing often occurs in winter flocks at feeding places, but solitary dancing also sometimes occurs, as when a bird has left the nest after being relieved of incubation.

The red-crowned crane has long been recognized as endangered, and its population in the 1970s was believed to number less than 500 birds. The majority of these were then restricted to Hokkaido, Japan, where the species' largest population still survives and is essentially nonmigratory. The Hokkaido population was for a time believed to be extinct, but a small group of birds was found to be nesting near Kushiro in 1924. This population increased only slowly until the 1950s, when supplemental feeding during winter was begun. By 2017 its population had exceeded 3,400 birds.

On the Asian mainland the species' primary breeding area is in the vicinity of Russia's Lake Khanka and along the Amur and Ussuri Rivers. However, its habitat there has become greatly restricted in recent years, and perhaps now it is more common farther west, in the drainage of the Sungari and Nun Rivers of China. The mainland birds also breed in Inner Mongolia and in adjoining northeastern China (Heilongjiang, Julin, and Liaoning provinces). The more western breeders winter along coastal China, whereas the eastern birds winter in the vicinity of the Demilitarized Zone of Korea.

The red-crowned crane's migratory population was recently estimated at about 2,800 to 3,430 birds. It is probably declining on mainland Asia, with an estimate of 1,400 birds; the wintering population in China totaled about 400 to 500 birds. Another 1,000 to 1,050 birds winter in Korea (IUCN, 2013). Part of the mainland breeding flock winters in China along the coast of China's Jiangsu Province (about 580 birds), and about 1,250 winter in Korea, mainly around the Demilitarized Zone.

Fig. 37. Red-crowned crane, adult.

Following pages: Whooping cranes, Saskatchewan, Canada

IV Cranes in Lore, Legend, and Myth

Adapted in part from *Cranes of the World*
(Johnsgard, 1983a)

American Crane Lore and Legends

Crane clans occur in many Native American tribes, from the northern Ojibwas of eastern Canada and the Great Lakes region to the southwestern desert pueblo tribes, such as the Hopis, who have both crane and sandhill crane clans. The northern Ojibwas and the Muskogees of the southeastern states perform ritualized crane dances, and the Chumash tribe of coastal California dances in reverence to cranes, whose presence indicates an abundance of fish in nearby waters.

In many Native American tribes, cranes are associated with good luck or peacemaking, and to the woodland-dwelling Ojibwas they represent leadership. Cranes ("Echomakers") are also the most important and most vocal of their several bird and mammal totems. In some tribes' folklore the crane serves as an experienced animal guide, usually leading a younger individual into exciting adventures or out of danger. According to one tale, by using his long legs as a bridge Grandfather Crane helped other animals cross a river to escape their enemies. He then also offered to carry their pursuers across, but halfway across he dumped them in the water!

Like many world cultures that believe cranes will carry small birds on their backs to help them on their long migrations, the Crow tribe of Montana believed that the sandhill crane carries small birds on its long migratory flights. This small bird supposedly accompanies the cranes and flutters up to settle among a bird's back feathers when it takes off. At such times, the bird utters a chattering whistle to encourage it and help direct it on its route, which is why Crow and Cheyenne warriors blew a whistle made from the wing bone of a sandhill crane to give them courage as they left their camp to do battle.

Not only do cranes often transport small birds on their backs but at times they even steal humans, according to the folklore of Eskimos living along Alaska's western coast. One autumn day, very long ago, the cranes were preparing to go southward. As they were gathered in the great flock they saw a beautiful young woman standing alone near the village. Admiring her greatly, the cranes gathered about, and lifting her on their widespread wings, bore her far up in the air and away. While the cranes were taking her skyward, they circled below her so closely that she could not

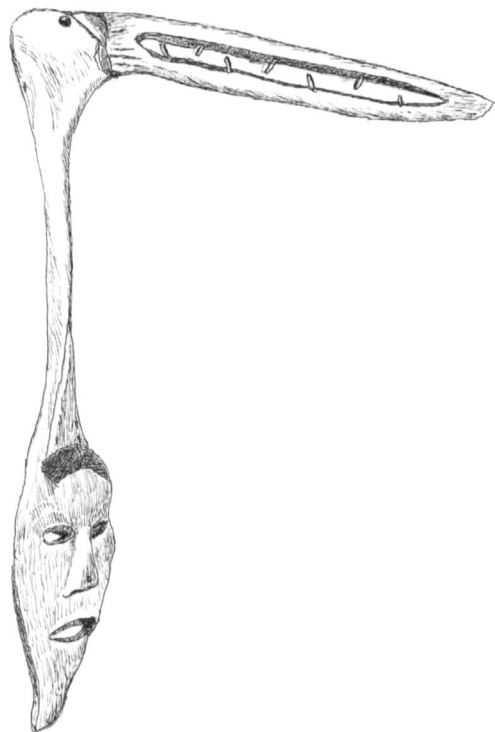

Fig. 38. Eskimo sandhill crane facial mask. After Nelson, 1899.

fall, and their loud, hoarse cries drowned out her calls for help, as she was carried away and never seen again. Ever since then the cranes always circle about as they begin to depart in autumn, uttering their loud cries at the start of their long journey southward, just as they did at that time.

There is an area in eastern Nebraska where the Platte River, after flowing northeastwardly from the vicinity of Grand Island for nearly 100 miles, enters the glacial drift bordering the Missouri River valley and turns directly east. Along its eastward course, the river forms a shallow and wide sandy channel that is bounded to the south by variably tall, forested bluffs and to the north by a wide wooded floodplain. The resident historic Pawnee tribe, who lived throughout the Platte valley, knew one of these tall bluffs as Pahaku. This Pawnee word may be roughly translated as "mound on or over water," or "headland." Pahaku is one of four natural sites along the Platte River that were considered sacred to the Pawnees and is the only remaining sacred location that is still biologically intact.

According to Pawnee legend, a young boy once lay at the edge of the bluff, hoping to shoot a bird with his bow and arrows. Growing at the base of the bluff was a tall cedar tree, marking the entrance to a huge cave that was the lodge of many animals. Several eagles and a hawk sat on the cedar tree, perhaps serving as guardians. A second entrance to the cave also existed, which could be reached only by following a kingfisher as a guide. The chief of the animals living in the lodge was a giant beaver, but the lodge also was the home of other spiritually significant and wise animals, including cranes.

Cranes and other larger birds and mammals were considered sacred animals by the Pawnee, and in this cave the animals periodically held council. There they also endowed the young Pawnee boy with special healing powers, which he later passed on to others of his village. At times he and other medicine men visited Pahaku to renew their healing abilities and to give thanks.

Of all the Pawnee animals having spiritual powers, birds were especially important. They served as direct messengers to the gods and played significant roles in major Pawnee ceremonies. Eagles were the most preeminent and powerful of these totemic birds, and hawks were also notable, as were their feathers. Owls were particularly significant in Pawnee healing ceremonies, while other species such as jays, magpies, and woodpeckers were each appreciated for their own valuable attributes. For example, the intelligent magpie helped the Pawnee child find the hidden entrance to the Pahaku cave. There possibly once was an actual cave at this site, as several of the Pawnees' sacred sites along rivers consisted of bluffs with caves, but erosion no doubt long ago destroyed any cave that might have been present.

Not far from the riverside bluff is the oldest bur oak in the area, which no doubt was already an impressive tree in the early 1800s while the Pawnees were still living peacefully along the Platte. This gigantic oak is still producing a few acorns but is slowly dying; by 2010 one of its largest lower branches had broken off and lay desolate on the ground. The tree's twisted shape is reminiscent of an ancient Pawnee holy man, his body misshapen and bent with age but lifting his arms in anguish toward the sky and lamenting the fate of his dispersed people, who now live in an arid Oklahoma reservation more than 500 miles away from their homeland.

Pahaku is nearly 100 miles east of the sandhill crane's main migration pathway, and the downstream shorelines and islands of this now greatly altered river are too overgrown and developed to attract any large water birds, except for a few great blue herons. However, migrating cranes sometimes fly over the Platte at this point and perhaps look down on it from thousands of feet above. Maybe their archaic memories are somehow stirred by the holiness of the place, and they might briefly slow down in their flight long enough to remember a time when men and women alike honored and revered cranes, rather than perhaps having no more interest in them than as tempting creatures to kill for idle sport.

European Crane Lore and Legends

Among the best sources of information about crane lore and legends for England and southern Europe are the writings of Edward Topsell (1572–1625), whose compositions on birds have been updated and reprinted (Topsell, 1972). Topsell reported that "when fables ruled the world" it was believed that a proud queen of pygmies named Oenoe or Gerania was turned into a crane by Juno and Diana because she taught her people to neglect other gods and worship her. Gerania thereafter began an irreconcilable war between cranes and pygmies that has persisted ever since. Aristotle, Homer, and many other early authors also believed that cranes regularly engaged in warfare with evil pygmies. These pygmies were thought to live in caves and were called Troglodytes (which is the Latin name for wrens, tiny birds that nest in cavities).

From this legend, perhaps, came the Greek name *geranos* or *gereunos* for cranes. Cranes occur in many of Greece's historical and allegorical stories, one involving a city in Thrace and a mountain near Corinth that were both called Gerania. *Geranos* is the Greek word for crane. The mountain, now named Yerania, was so named because the people followed the calls of fleeing cranes at the time of a flood, thereby reaching higher ground and saving themselves from drowning. Similarly, *Geranium* is the Latinized botanical name for the geranium plant. The geranium is also known as the crane-bill because of its diagnostic flower, which has a distinctive beak-shaped ovary. In Europe, wild cranes have historically been captured or killed by the use of falcons or small eagles. In Germany, such large falcons were called "girfalcons" (now gyrfalcons).

Cranes were also evidently raised as pets or fattened for the pot in ancient Greece. Plutarch referred to the practice of fattening them by sewing shut their eyelids, which quiets the birds (from which the English term "hoodwinking" derives), and a design on an ancient Greek vase in the Hermitage Museum of Leningrad shows a seated woman offering a morsel of food to a crane. Cranes were believed by the Greeks to give equal honor to all, for their leaders regularly give up their foremost position in flight to go to the rear of the flock, and thus the last becomes first, and the birds can live in freedom without king or tyrant. The modern democratic form of government was first established more than 2,000 years ago in Athens and was associated with the congruent behavior of cranes in which all the populace participates in important decisions.

In contrast, the Romans called cranes *grues*, evidently because of their grunting voices. The Eurasian crane was familiar to the early Romans through its regular migrations, and the Romans were greatly impressed by its longevity in captivity. According to Topsell, even the African crowned cranes were well known to Pliny and other early Roman writers, no doubt because of the many early contacts between Rome and Egypt. Soon after the Norman Conquest of England, a general interest developed in genealogy, and the branching form of a family tree was referred to as a "crane's foot," or *pied de grue*, from which is derived the present word "pedigree." The calling of cranes, or *iangling*, also gave rise to the modern English word "jangling." The Latin *congruere*, meaning an agreement or consent, is the origin of the English word "congruence."

The migrations of cranes, marked by large flocks and clamoring calls, were well known to both the Greeks and Romans, and were used to mark the changing of the seasons. Topsell observed that the birds have keen senses of sight, hearing, and smell. Further, like the kings of Persia, the cranes have both summer and winter dwellings, and they follow certain determinate schedules during which they change their habitations.

Topsell noted that during flight, the birds attain unusual heights and fly in triangular formation, and he believed that unlike other birds they fly both night and day. Their high flight was attributed to the birds' desire to see great distances ahead, and perhaps foresee the onset of rains or storms in order that they might avoid them. Furthermore, when flying at such heights the stragglers can better be observed and helped. The usual triangular formation, like the Greek letter lambda, allows the birds to cut the air more readily, whereas during high winds they tend to fly in the form of a half-moon. Topsell judged that the three most likely Greek letters to have been extracted from the flight of cranes were alpha, lambda, and upsilon.

Topsell also noted that cranes sometimes change places in flight formation, and by this regular changing of formation various letters of the alphabet are imitated. Topsell believed that, while in flight, cranes always treat the foremost of them as captain and arrange themselves so as not to obscure the view of the lead bird. The older birds take turns being leader, and should any of the flock become weary before reaching their destination two other birds will take the tired individual on their backs or wings, or support it with their outstretched legs. Topsell observed that cranes rarely fly against the wind, except when being chased, and they also avoid strong backwinds that might ruffle their feathers and weaken them; of the two they prefer to fly against the wind.

More remarkably, Cicero believed that each crane rested its head on the back of the bird flying immediately ahead of it. The lead crane, having no bird to rest its head upon, eventually retired to the end of the line, to place its head on the back of the trailing bird, which had previously supported none. Many early writers believed that when cranes flew long distances they would swallow a heavy stone that served as ballast, to strengthen themselves against sudden gusts of wind. Others believed that the birds carried the stone so that when nearing the end of their journey they could drop the stone, and on hearing it land could determine whether or not they had crossed the ocean. Others believed that the birds kept the stones in their mouths to stop their voices and thus escape detection from eagles. Some believed that they held the stone with their toes, and Topsell suggested that perhaps the carrying of stones by the individuals that were swiftest of flight prevented them from flying so fast that they might outstrip and lose contact with the slower ones.

On their migration to Egypt the cranes were believed to choose a captain, since they knew they would meet with enemies there, but on their return flight to Europe they neither chose a captain nor posted watches. In their choice of a guide, they selected one of the strongest and oldest birds best able to find the proper way, and strong enough to withstand the wind. In the middle of the flock the youngest and weakest birds fly, so that they might be encouraged by those both in front and behind; a pattern of formation structure in migrating whooping cranes that is essentially correct (Kuyt, 1984). Other watchmen and officers are placed at the rear of the group to call to the captain and inform him that all are following. The flock's captain must not only fly in the foremost position and guide the flock properly but also help stand guard while the flock rests at night.

Topsell stated that cranes fly remarkably swiftly, although they fly so high that from the earth it would seem that they are actually flying very slowly. Further, by flying at night as well as during the day, they are able to cover great distances in a short time. At night they utter almost continuous calls to keep others informed of their positions, and by flying very high they are able to see well enough and far enough to find their way. When the birds do stop to sleep at night, they raise one leg and place the head upon the wing while standing, by which the heat of the body is transmitted to the brain; thus the bird is able to sleep more easily, all according to Topsell.

Many watchmen are also posted at roosting sites at night, when each of the others in the flock sleeps with one leg lifted and its head under a wing. However, the watchman crane stands on one leg and holds a stone in the claws of the other foot, so that if sleep should overtake it, the bird would drop the stone, awakening itself and the other sleeping birds.

Topsell stated that cranes eat all kinds of wild grain as well as snakes, and that in Thessaly (now part of east-central Greece and the mythic birthplace of Achilles), were it not for storks and cranes, the people would be forced to leave the country. Thus, they were forbidden to kill the birds. According to Topsell, when the cranes have reached three years of age they leave the cold climates for their breeding grounds. Then the birds form couples, and the males fertilize their mates while the latter are standing upright, rather than while lying on the earth. In addition to two eggs, a stone was also believed to be placed in the nest, perhaps to confuse or dissuade predators from trying to steal and eat the eggs.

Topsell commented that cranes also exhibit hostility toward eagles and hawks, and when cranes see such predators they usually flee with haste and utter loud calls. Yet, when there are enough cranes present to resist, he said that they would gather into a circle or ring and, with their heads lifted to the highest, would advance on the eagle or hawk and force it to depart. This exact behavior can often still be seen during spring on the Platte River, when an immature bald eagle lands on a sandbar where a group of sandhill cranes is already present. Standing close together, and with heads held high, they slowly advance on the eagle until it is forced to fly. However, far greater respect is shown to adult-plumaged bald eagles, which are known to occasionally attack sandhill cranes. Besides protecting one another, cranes show a special love for their own young, and at times the pair will fight with one another over the education of their young, according to Topsell.

The great flying ability of cranes was associated with that of a wise man who had studied astronomy or some other "lofty and sublime" study. The seasonal appearance of migrating cranes in the spring has often been associated with a resurgent sun-god in the east (and is the original pagan basis for celebrating Easter), and their dancing behavior has epitomized fertility in some cultures. According to Plutarch, when Theseus (the mythical king and founder of Athens) returned from Crete after slaying the Minotaur, he and his friends danced the geranos, or crane dance, thereby repeating the convoluted route they had used while navigating the tortuous Cretan labyrinth.

The murder of Ibycus, a well-known Greek lyric poet from the sixth century BC, is probably the most famous of all crane stories from ancient Greece. While out walking one day this poet was reputedly set upon by robbers but before expiring looked up to see a flock of migrating cranes flying overhead. With his dying breath he cried out to the cranes high above to somehow avenge his death. Much later, while in the marketplace of Corinth, the robbers saw a group of cranes flying overhead, and one fearfully exclaimed to the others, "Behold, the cranes of Ibycus!" On being thus overheard, the men were detained and questioned by authorities. They then confessed their crime and were put to death for the murder.

Asian Crane Lore and Legends

Crane dancing has had its counterparts in various Asian cultures. For example, the tundra-dwelling people of Siberia dressed in crane skins and performed funereal dances, and similar dances were also associated with Chinese funerals. Crane dancing also occurs in the ceremonies of China and Japan. In Japan, especially among the Ainu people of the northernmost island Hokkaido, women perform a crane dance while imitating their calls, holding their shawls over their heads and spreading them outward so that they resemble the wings of a crane.

These and related dances variously drive away evil spirits, show gratitude for successful harvests and fishing, and offer prayers to the spirits. Although the purposes of dancing by real cranes are still uncertain, they probably include establishing social relationships, maintaining pair-bonds, and perhaps even exercising their growing young and training them to dance too.

In Chinese tradition the crane is a common symbol of longevity, and the soul of the dead is often represented as riding to heaven on a crane's back. Likewise in ancient Chinese tradition, old pine trees sometimes are transformed into cranes, since both are long-lived, and the two are often thus associated in Chinese and Japanese art. As the Chinese culture gradually came to influence Japan, the Japanese adopted the image of a crane as a symbol of longevity, and gradually modified it to additionally be an emblem of joy. Since the ninth century, in Japan cranes have also been regarded as a symbol of happiness, and typically in the marriage ceremony a design incorporating both the crane and the long-lived tortoise is often used to predict both happiness and longevity.

In a famous Japanese crane-maiden legend, a nobleman named Tochiro lost his wealth and moved to the remote woods of Hokkaido to become a woodcutter. One day while chopping wood he saw a hunter who had captured a crane and was about to kill it. Tochiro begged the hunter to spare its life, but the hunter would do so only in exchange for Tochiro's sword, his last possession of any value. The following night a young woman appeared at the door of his hut. She was dressed in white rags that were mud-stained with black at their edges. She said her name was Tsuru and asked him for shelter, explaining that she had been driven from her home by a cruel stepmother. Tochiro admitted her, and soon the two fell in love and were married. Months later, the local feudal lord decided to host a hunting party. As the hunters approached Tochiro's hut, Tsuru confessed to Tochiro that she was actually the crane that he had saved, and that she must flee. Together they quickly left the hut and went to live in the palace of Tsuru's crane parents, where they had long and happy lives.

In a similar but much sadder version, Tsuru remained in the house of Tochiro and his wife, where Tsuru helped with housework. During a very harsh winter, heavy snows made it impossible for Tochiro to go out and chop wood to sell, and the family became ever more desperate. Finally, Tsuru promised to make a beautiful quilt that Tochiro could sell for a high price at the local market. She asked that she not be disturbed for any reason while she was sewing it and closed her bedroom door. Months passed, and there were no sounds to be heard from the room. Finally, fearing the worst, Tochiro opened her door and peeked in. He saw an immaculate white crane with black wingtips silently plucking white feathers from her breast to weave into the most beautiful quilt that could be imagined on earth. Thus discovered,

Tsuru shrieked loudly and flew out through the open door, disappeared into the snow-filled sky, and was never seen again.

A more touching and even sadder crane story that is entirely true concerns a Japanese girl named Sadako Sasaki, who was born in Hiroshima in 1943. During August of 1945, the last year of World War II and when Sadako was two years old, an American B-29 bomber dropped on Hiroshima the first nuclear bomb ever used in warfare. Although more than 100,000 people died almost immediately, Sadako somehow survived and eventually entered grade school, where she became a very good runner. However, she gradually became increasingly dizzy when she ran and was sent to a hospital for observation and treatment. There it was discovered that she had developed leukemia,

Fig. 39. Red-crowned crane dancing.

a then-fatal blood disease closely associated with exposure to nuclear radiation.

While at the hospital Sadako heard from friends the belief that if she folded 1,000 origami cranes, the gods would heal her. In spite of becoming increasingly weaker, Sadako began making paper cranes. She died in 1955, after having completed 644 cranes. Her story has lived on as a testimony to her faith and courage; a bronze statue of her lifting a crane to the sky can be seen in Hiroshima Peace Park. A somewhat similar statue of her holding an origami crane can be found in Seattle's Peace Park.

How to Make an Origami Crane

Note: Various video instructions can be found on the Internet, such as https://www.wikihow.com/Fold-a-Paper-Crane

1. Using a square piece of paper, fold it in half to form a triangle. If using paper that is colored on one side, begin with the colored side facing up. Unfold the paper and repeat to make fold diagonally across the other two ends of the paper, making an X folding pattern (Sketch 1).

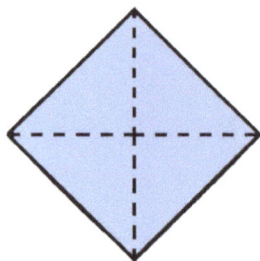

2. Turn the paper over so the colored side is down and fold the paper in half horizontally, with the crease down the middle. Unfold and fold it vertically (Sketch 2). Now fold along all four corners, forming a square with the open end toward you (Sketch 3).

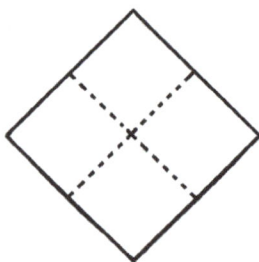

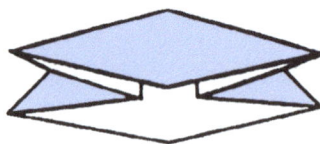

3. Make two folds at points a and b and crease them, forming a kite-like shape (Sketch 4). Repeat on the other side. Then fold the top of the kite down and make a crease above the other two folds (Sketch 5).

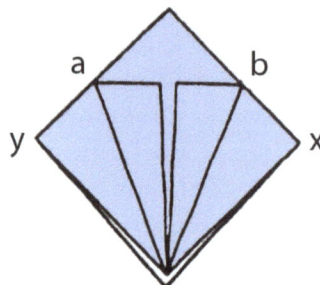

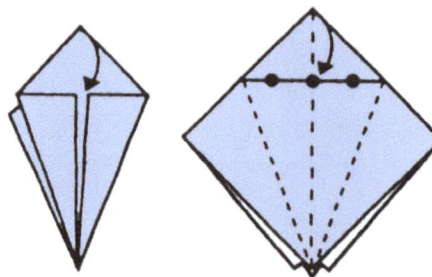

4. Pull the top layer of the bottom corner up and above the top corner (Sketch 6). Press flat, and do the same thing with other side to make a broad diamond or kite.

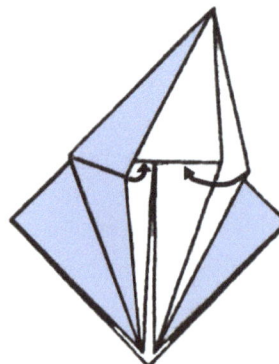

5. Now fold the two sides inward to make a narrow diamond (or kite) shape. Do the same on the other side (Sketch 7). Press flat.

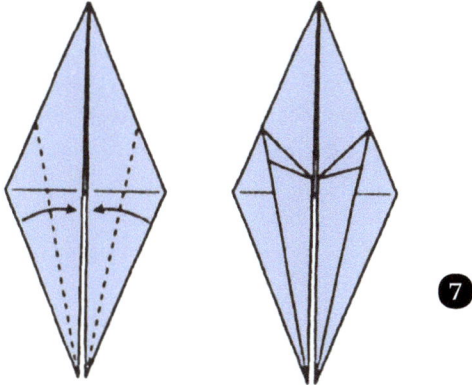

6. Fold the top layer to lay on the tip of the left side, like the pages of a book (Sketch 8).

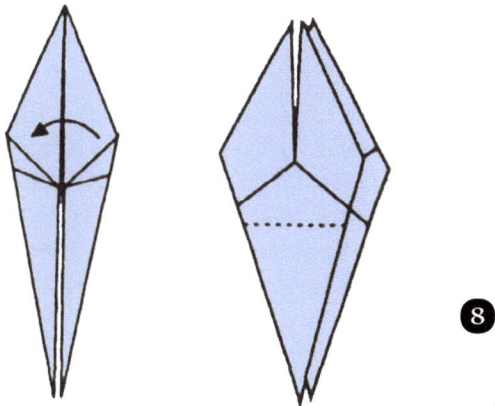

7. Fold up the bottom of the diamond as far as you can, on each side (Sketch 9).

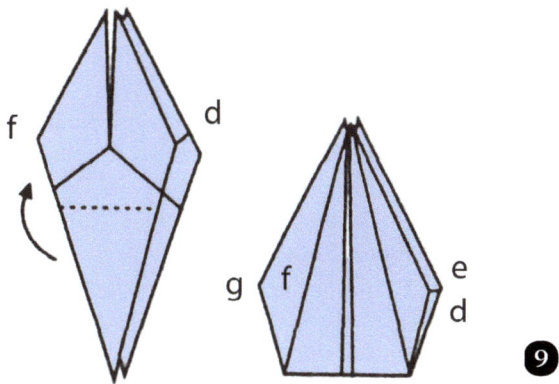

8. Bring points f and d together on the front, and **g** and **e** together behind (Sketch 10). Press flat.

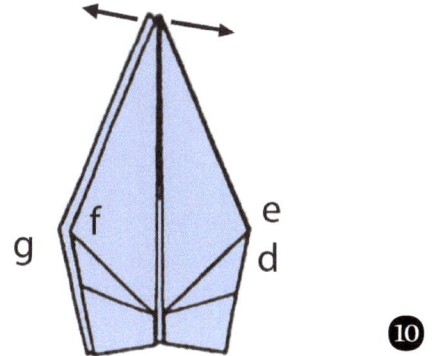

9. Then pinch the base with your right hand while the left pulls out the neck slightly. Next, pinch the base with your left hand and pull out the tail (Sketch 11).

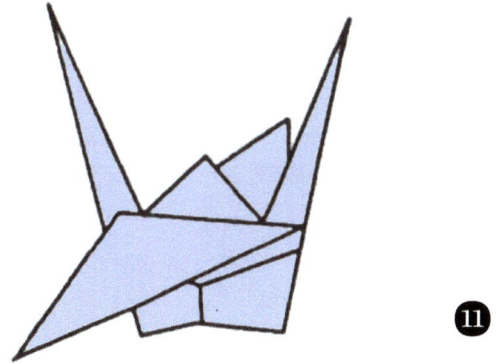

10. Pull the wings out to expand the body. Also pull out and fold down the beak (Sketch 12).

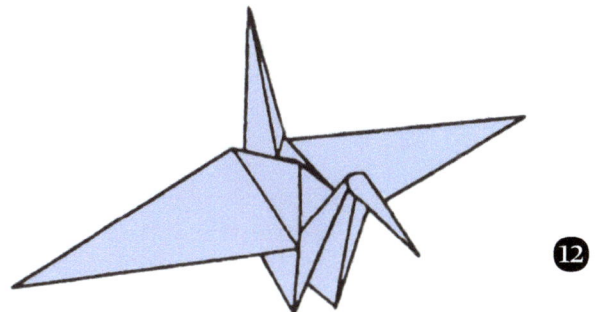

References

Printed Crane Resources

Comprehensive Books and Single-Subject Monographs

Ellis, D. H., G. F. Gee, and C. F. Mirande. 1996. *Cranes: Their Biology, Husbandry, and Conservation*. Washington, DC: US Department of the of Interior, National Biological Service, and Baraboo, WI: International Crane Foundation. See https://pubs.er.usgs.gov/publication/5200136

French, J. B., Jr, S. J. Converse, and J. E. Austin, eds. 2018. *Whooping Cranes: Biology and Conservation*. Biodiversity of the World: Conservation from Genes to Landscapes. San Diego, CA: Academic Press. 344 pp.

Glutz von Blotzheim, U. N., ed. 1973. *Handbuch der Vögel Mitteleuropas* [Handbook of the birds of central Europe]. Band 5. Weisbaden, Germany: Akademische Verlagegellschaft. 699 pp.

Hughes, J. M. 2008. *Cranes: A Natural History of a Bird in Crisis*. Buffalo, NY: Firefly Books. 256 pp.

Johnsgard, P. A. 1983a. *The Cranes of the World*. Bloomington: Indiana University Press. 256 pp. See https://digitalcommons.unl.edu/bioscicranes/24/

———. 1991. *Crane Music: A Natural History of American Cranes*. Washington, DC: Smithsonian Institution Press. 136 pp.

———. 2011. *Sandhill and Whooping Cranes: Ancient Voices over America's Wetlands*. Lincoln: University of Nebraska Press. 155 pp.

———. 2015. *A Chorus of Cranes: The Cranes of North America and the World*. Boulder: University Press of Colorado. 242 pp.

Matthiessen, P. 2001. *The Birds of Heaven: Travels with Cranes*. New York: North Point Press. 349 pp.

Meine, C. D., and G. W. Archibald, eds. 1996. *The Cranes: Status Survey and Conservation Action Plan*. Gland, Switzerland: IUCN. 282 pp.

Mirande, C. M., and J. T. Harris, eds. 2019. *Crane Conservation Strategy*. Baraboo, WI: International Crane Foundation. 455 pp. Available at https://www.savingcranes.org/wp-content/uploads/2019/10/crane_conservation_strategy_web_2019-1.pdf (whooping crane, pp. 223–243; sandhill crane, pp. 425–450).

Prange, H. 2016. *Die Welt der Kraniche: Leben, Umfeld, Schutz, Verbreitung der 15 Arten* [The world of cranes: Life, environment, protection, distribution of the 15 species]. Germany: Christ Media Natur Verlag. 896 pp.

von Treuenfels, C.-A. 2007. *The Magic of Cranes*. New York: H. Abrams. 240 pp.

Walkinshaw, L. H. 1949. *The Sandhill Crane*. Bloomfield Hills, MI: Cranbrook Institute of Science Bulletin 29. 202 pp.

———. 1973. *Cranes of the World*. New York: Winchester Press. 370 pp.

Nontechnical and Illustrated Books

Archibald, G. 2016. *My Life with Cranes: A Collection of Stories by George Archibald*. Baraboo, WI: International Crane Foundation. 160 pp.

Britton, D. G., and T. Hayashida. 1981. *The Japanese Crane: Bird of Happiness*. Tokyo: Kodansha International. 63 pp.

Forsberg, M. 2004. *On Ancient Wings: The Sandhill Cranes of North America*. Lincoln: University of Nebraska Press. 168 pp.

Grooms, G. 1991. *Cry of the Sandhill Crane*. Minaqua, WI: North Wood Press. 160 pp.

Hayashida, T. 2002. *Cranes of Japan*. Japan: Heibonsha. (photographic survey of Japanese cranes)

Johnsgard, P. A. 1981. *Those of the Gray Wind: The Sandhill Cranes*. 1981. New York: St. Martin's Press. 150 pp.

———. 2020. *Audubon's Lillian Annette Rowe Sanctuary: A Refuge, a River, and a Migration*. Lincoln, NE: Infusion Media. 203 pp.

Kaska, K. 2012. *The Man Who Saved the Whooping Crane: The Robert Porter Allen Story*. Gainesville: University Press of Florida. 224 pp.

Matthiessen, P. 2001. *The Birds of Heaven: Travels with Cranes*. New York: North Point Press. 349 pp.

McNulty, F. 1966. *The Whooping Crane: The Bird That Defies Extinction*. New York: E. P. Dutton.

Prange, H., ed. 1989. *Der Graue Kranich*. Die Neue Brehm-Bücherei. Wittenberg, Germany: A. Ziemsen Verlag. 272 pp. (Eurasian crane biology)

Pratt, J. J. 1996. *The Whooping Crane: North America's Symbol of Conservation*. Sierra Vista, CA: Castle Rock Publishing.

Schuff, G. H. 1981. *Reflections: The Story of Cranes*. Baraboo, WI: International Crane Foundation. 40 pp.

Wu, C. 2002. *A Thousand Cranes*. Teipei: Crane Publishing Co. (photographic essay)

———. 2003. *The Propitious Crane*. Taipei. Crane Publishing Co. 184 pp. (text in Chinese and English; photographs of all 15 species of cranes)

Single-Species Studies

Sandhill Crane

August, C. W. 2011. Demography of greater sandhill cranes in northeast Nevada. MS thesis. University of Nevada Reno, Reno. 73 pp.

Austin, J. E., A. R. Henry, and I. J. Ball. 2007. Sandhill crane abundance and nesting ecology at Grays Lake, Idaho. *Journal of Wildlife Management* 71: 1067–1079.

Barcelo, I. 2012. Winter ecology of sandhill cranes (*Grus canadensis*) in northern Mexico. PhD dissertation. University of Nebraska, Lincoln. 246 pp.

Bennett, A. J., and L. A. Bennett. 1990. Survival rates and mortality factors of Florida sandhill cranes in Georgia. *North American Bird Bander* 15: 86–88.

Boise, C. M. 1977. Breeding biology of the lesser sandhill crane *Grus canadensis canadensis* (L.) on the Yukon–Kuskokwim delta, Alaska. MS thesis. University of Alaska, Fairbanks. 79 pp.

Caven, A. J., D. M. Varner, and J. Drahota. 2020. Sandhill crane abundance in Nebraska during spring migration: Making sense of multiple data-points. *Nebraska Academy of Sciences* 40: 6–18.

Collins, D. P., B. A. Grisham, C. M. Conring, J. M. Knetter, W. C. Conway, S. A. Carleton, and M. S. Boggie. 2015. New summer areas and mixing of two greater sandhill crane populations in the Intermountain West. *Journal of Fish and Wildlife Management* 7: 141–152.

Collins, D. P., T. Cooper, J. Dubovsky, and D. Fronczak. 2016. *Priority Information Needs for Sandhill Cranes II*. Association of Fish and Wildlife Agencies' Migratory Shore and Upland Game Bird Support Task Force. 17 pp.

Drewien, R. C. 1973. Ecology of Rocky Mountain greater sandhill cranes. PhD dissertation. University of Idaho, Moscow. 152 pp.

Drewien, R. C., and W. M. Brown. 1996. Distribution and abundance of sandhill cranes in Mexico. *Journal of Wildlife Management* 60: 270–285.

Drewien, R. C., W. M. Brown, and K. R. Clegg. 2010. Longevity records of Rocky Mountain greater sandhill cranes banded during 1969–1987 in Idaho, Montana, Utah, and Wyoming. In *Proceedings of the Eleventh North American Crane Workshop*, edited by B. K. Hartup, 199. Baraboo, WI: North American Crane Working Group.

Drewien, R. C., W. M. Brown, and W. L. Kendall. 1995. Recruitment in Rocky Mountain greater sandhill cranes and comparison with other crane populations. *Journal of Wildlife Management* 59(2): 339–356.

Dubovsky, J. A. 2018. *Status and Harvests of Sandhill Cranes Mid-Continent, Rocky Mountain, Lower Colorado River Valley and Eastern Populations*. Lakewood, CO: Administrative Report, US Fish and Wildlife Service. 15 pp.

Dwyer, J. F., A. K. Pandey, L. E. McHale, and R. E. Harness. 2019. Near-ultraviolet light reduced sandhill crane mortality with a power line by 98%. *Condor* 121: 1–10.

Fronczak, D. L. 2014. Distribution, migration chronology, and survival rates of Eastern Population sandhill cranes. MS thesis. University of Minnesota, Minneapolis. 64 pp.

Galvez-Aguilera, X., and F. Chavez-Ramirez. 2010. Distribution, abundance, and status of Cuban sandhill cranes (*Grus canadensis nesiotes*). *Wilson Journal of Ornithology* 122: 556–562.

Gerber, B. D., J. F. Dwyer, S. A. Nesbitt, R. C. Drewien, C. D. Littlefield, T. C. Tacha, and P. A. Vohs. 2014. Sandhill Crane (*Antigone canadensis*), version 2.0. In *The Birds of North America*, edited by A. F. Poole. Ithaca, NY: Cornell Lab of Ornithology. https://doi.org/10.2173/bna.31

Happ, C. Y., and G. Happ. 2017. *Sandhill Crane Display Dictionary: What Cranes Say with Their Body Language*. 2nd ed. Wildlife and Nature Identification Series. Safety Harbor, FL: Waterford Press. (Fold-out guide)

Hayes, M. A. 2015. Dispersal and population genetic structure in two flyways of sandhill cranes (*Grus canadensis*). PhD dissertation. University of Wisconsin, Madison. 287 pp.

Hayes, M. A., and J. A. Barzen. 2006. Dynamics of breeding and nonbreeding sandhill cranes in south central Wisconsin. *Passenger Pigeon* 68: 345–352.

———. 2016. Dispersal patterns and pairing behaviors of nonterritorial sandhill cranes. *Passenger Pigeon* 78: 411–425.

Hayes, M. A., H. B. Britten, and J. A. Barzen. 2006. Extra-pair fertilizations in sandhill cranes revealed using microsatellite DNA markers. *Condor* 108: 970–976.

Hereford, S. 2018. Mississippi sandhill crane update. *Unison Call* 28(2): 16–17.

Hereford, S. G., and L. E. Bilodeaux. 2010. Mississippi sandhill crane conservation update, 2006–2009. In *Proceedings of the 11th North American Crane Workshop*, edited by B. Hartup, 189–191. Baraboo, WI: International Crane Foundation.

Hunt, H. E., and R. D. Slack. 1989. Wintering diets of whooping and sandhill cranes in south Texas. *Journal of Wildlife Management* 53: 1150–1154.

Iverson, G. C., T. C. Tacha, and P. A. Vohs. 1982. Food contents of sandhill cranes during winter and spring. In *Proceedings of the 1981 Crane Workshop*, edited by J. Lewis, 95–98. Taverneir, FL: National Audubon Society.

Ivey, G. L., B. D. Dugger, C. P. Herziger, M. L. Casazza, and J. P. Fleskes. 2014a. Distribution, abundance, and migration timing of greater and lesser sandhill cranes wintering in the Sacramento–San Joaquin River delta region of California. In *Proceedings of the Twelfth North American Crane Workshop*, edited by D. A. Aborn and R. A. Urbenek, 1–11. Madison, WI: North American Crane Working Group.

Ivey, G. L., B. D. Dugger, M. L. Casazza, J. P. Fleskes, and C. P. Herziger. 2014b. Movements and home range size of greater and lesser sandhill cranes wintering in central California. (Abstract) In *Proceedings of the Twelfth North American Crane Workshop*, edited by D. A. Aborn and R. A. Urbenek, 94. Madison, WI: North American Crane Working Group.

Ivey, G. L., C. P. Herzinger, and T. J. Hoffmann. 2005. Annual movements of Pacific Coast sandhill cranes. In *Proceedings of the Ninth National Crane Workshop*, edited by F. Chavez-Ramirez, 25–35. Sacramento, CA: North American Crane Working Group.

Ivey, G. L., J. D. Engler, M. J. St. Louis, M. A. Stern, and S. Cross. 2010. Winter distribution of greater sandhill cranes marked at breeding areas in California, Washington and Oregon. (Abstract) In *Proceedings of the 11th North American Crane Workshop*, edited by B. Hartup, 206. Baraboo, WI: International Crane Foundation.

Johnsgard, P. A., and K. Gill. 2011. Sandhill cranes: Nebraska's avian ambassadors at large. *Prairie Fire*, March 2011. Pp. 14, 15, 20.

Johnson, D. H. 1979. *Modeling Sandhill Crane Population Dynamics*. US Fish and Wildlife Service, Special Scientific Report (Wildlife), No. 222. 10 pp.

Johnson, D. H., J. E. Austin, and J. A. Shaffer. 2005. A fresh look at the taxonomy of midcontinental sandhill cranes. In *Proceedings of the Ninth National Crane Workshop*, edited by F. Chavez-Ramirez, 37–45. Sacramento, CA: North American Crane Working Group.

Jones, K. L., G. L. Krapu, D. L. Brandt, and M. V. Ashley. 2005. Population genetic structure in migratory sandhill cranes and the role of Pleistocene glaciations. *Molecular Ecology* 14: 2645–2657.

Krapu, G. L., and D. A. Brandt. 2005. Migration routes, staging areas, and wintering grounds of sandhill cranes that breed in Siberia. In *Proceedings of the Ninth North American Crane Workshop*, edited by F. Chavez-Ramirez, 205. Sacramento, CA: North American Crane Working Group.

Krapu, G. L., D. A. Brandt, K. L. Jones, and D. H. Johnson. 2011. *Geographic Distribution of the Mid-Continent Population of Sandhill Cranes and Related Management Implications*. Wildlife Monographs 175. 38 pp.

Krapu, G. L., D. A. Brandt, P. J. Kinzel, and A. T. Pearse. 2014. *Spring Migration Ecology of the Mid-Continent Sandhill Crane Population with Emphasis on Use of the Central Platte River Valley, Nebraska*. Wildlife Monographs 189. 41 pp.

Krapu, G. L., G. I. Ivey, and J. A. Barzen. 2019. Species review: Sandhill crane (*Grus canadensis*). In *Crane Conservation Strategy*, edited by C. M. Mirande and J. T. Harris, 425–450. Baraboo, WI: International Crane Foundation.

Lacy, A. E., J. A. Barzen, D. M. Moore, and K. E. Norris. 2015. Changes in the number and distribution of greater sandhill cranes in the Eastern Population. *Journal of Field Ornithology* 86: 317–325.

Lewis, J. C. 1979. Field identification of juvenile sandhill cranes. *Journal of Wildlife Management* 41: 211–214.

Littlefield, C. D., and R. A. Ryder. 1968. Breeding biology of the greater sandhill crane on Malheur National Wildlife Refuge, Oregon. *Transactions North American Wildlife and Natural Resources Conference* 33: 444–454.

Littlefield, C. D., and S. P. Thompson. 1987. Distribution and status of the Central Valley Population of greater sandhill cranes. In *Proceedings of the 1978 Crane Workshop*, edited by J. C. Lewis, 113–120. Fort Collins: Colorado State University Printing Service.

McKinney, L., J. A. Barzen, J. Riddle, S. Dubay, and T. Ginnett. 2016. Differential detection of territorial and nonterritorial greater sandhill cranes in summer. In *Proceedings of the 13th North American Crane Workshop*, edited by D. A. Aborn, 25–32. Madison, WI: North American Crane Working Group.

McWethy, D. B., and J. E. Austin. 2009. Nesting ecology of greater sandhill cranes (*Grus canadensis tabida*) in riparian and palustrine wetlands of eastern Idaho. *Waterbirds* 32: 106–115.

Melvin, S. M., and S. A. Temple. 1980. Migration Ecology and Wintering Grounds of Sandhill Cranes from the Interlake Area of Manitoba. Unpublished report to the US Fish and Wildlife Service. 60 pp.

Nesbitt, S. A. 1989. The significance of mate loss in Florida sandhill cranes. *Wilson Bulletin* 101: 648–651.

———. 1996. Florida sandhill crane. In *Rare and Endangered Biota of Florida, Vol. 5: Birds*, edited by J. A. Rodgers, Jr., H. W. Kale II, and H. T. Smith, 219–229. Gainesville: University Press of Florida.

———. 1997. Florida sandhill crane (*Grus canadensis pratensis*), Family Gruidae, Order Gruiformes. In *Rare and Endangered Biota of Florida. Vol. 5: Birds*, rev. ed., edited by J. A. Rogers, Jr., H. W. Kale II, and H. T. Smith, 219–229. Gainesville: University Press of Florida.

Nesbitt, S. A., and A. S. Wenner. 1987. Pair formation and mate fidelity in sandhill cranes. In *Proceedings of the 1985 Crane Workshop*, edited by J. Lewis, 117–122. Grand Island, NE: Platte River Whooping Crane Habitat Maintenance Trust and US Fish and Wildlife Service.

Nesbitt, S. A., and G. Archibald. 1981. The agonistic repertoire of sandhill cranes. *Wilson Bulletin* 93: 99–103.

Nesbitt, S. A., and J. L. Hatchitt. 2008. Trends in habitat and population of Florida sandhill cranes. In *Proceedings of the 10th North American Crane Workshop*, edited by M. J. Folk and S. A. Nesbitt, 40–42. Leesburg, FL: North American Crane Working Group. https://digital-commons.unl.edu/nacwgproc/189/

Nesbitt, S. A., and J. W. Carpenter. 1993. Survival and movements of greater sandhill cranes experimentally released in Florida. *Journal of Wildlife Management* 57(4): 673–679.

Nesbitt, S. A., and R. A. Bradley. 1997. Vocalizations of sandhill cranes In *Proceedings of the Seventh North American Crane Workshop*, edited by R. P. Urbanek and D. W. Stahlecker, 25–35. Biloxi, MS: North American Crane Working Group.

Nesbitt, S. A., and T. C. Tacha. 1997. Monogamy and productivity in sandhill cranes. In *Proceedings of the Seventh North American Crane Workshop*, edited by R. P. Urbanek and D. W. Stahlecker, 10–13. Biloxi, MS: North American Crane Working Group. https://digitalcom-mons.unl.edu/nacwgproc/228

Niemeier, M. M. 1979. Structural and functional aspects of vocal ontogeny in *Grus canadensis* (Gruidae: Aves). PhD dissertation. University of Nebraska, Lincoln.

Petersen, J. L., L. R. Bischof, G. L. Krapu, and A. L. Szalanski. 2003. Genetic variation in the Mid-continental Population of sandhill cranes *Grus canadensis*. *Biochemical Genetics* 41: 1–12.

Petrula, M. J., and T. C. Rothe. 2005. Migration chronology, routes, and distribution of Pacific Flyway Population of lesser sandhill cranes. In *Proceedings of the 9th North American Crane Workshop*, edited by F. Chavez-Ramirez, 53–67. Chihuahua City, Mexico: North American Crane Working Group.

Pogson, T. H., and S. M. Lindstedt. 1991. Distribution and abundance of large sandhill cranes, *Grus canadensis*, wintering in California's Central Valley. *Condor* 93: 266–278.

Poulin, R. G., G. L. Krapu, D. A. Brandt, and P. J. Kinzel. 2010. Changes in agriculture and abundance of snow geese affect carrying capacity of sandhill cranes in Nebraska. *Journal of Wildlife Management* 74: 479–488.

Rhymer, J. M., M. G. Fain, J. E. Austin, D. H. Johnson, and C. Krajewski. 2001. Mitochondrial phylogeography, subspecific taxonomy, and conservation genetics of sandhill cranes *Grus canadensis* (Aves: Gruidae). *Conservation Genetics* 2: 203–218.

Subcommittee on Rocky Mountain Greater Sandhill Cranes. 2007. *Management Plan of the Pacific and Central Flyways for the Rocky Mountain Population of Greater Sandhill Cranes*. Portland, OR: US Fish and Wildlife Service, MBMO (Rocky Mountain Population of Greater Sandhill Cranes Committee, Pacific Flyway Study Committee, and Central Flyway Webless Migratory Game Bird Technical Committee). 97 pp.

Tacha, T. C. 1988. *Social Organization of Sandhill Cranes from Mid-continental North America*. Wildlife Monographs 99. 37 pp.

Tacha, T. C., S. A. Nesbitt, and P. A. Vohs. 1994. Sandhill crane. In *Migratory Shore and Upland Game Bird Management in North Americas*, edited by T. C. Tacha and C. E. Braun, 76–94. Washington, DC: International Association of Fish and Wildlife Agencies.

Toepler, J. E., and R. A. Crete. 1979. Migration of radio-tagged greater sandhill cranes from Minnesota and Wisconsin. In *Proceedings 1978 Crane Workshop*, edited by J. Lewis, 159–174. Fort Collins: Colorado State University.

Valentine, J. M., Jr., and R. E. Noble. 1970. A colony of sandhill cranes in Mississippi. *Journal of Wildlife Management* 34(4): 761–768.

Van Horn, K., T. White, W. Atkins, T. Cooper, R. Urbanek, D. Holm, D. Sherman, D. A. Aborn, J. Suckow, K. Cleveland, and R. Brook. 2010. *Management Plan for the Eastern Population of Sandhill Cranes*. US Fish and Wildlife Service, Ad hoc Eastern Population Sandhill Crane Committee. 34 pp.

Voss, K. S. 1976. Behavior of the greater sandhill crane. MS thesis. University of Wisconsin, Madison.

Walkinshaw, L. H. 1965a. One hundred thirty-three Michigan sandhill crane nests. *Jack-Pine Warbler* 43: 137–142.

———. 1965b. Territories of cranes. *Papers of the Michigan Academy of Science, Arts and Letters* 50: 75–88.

———. 1965c. Sandhill crane studies on Banks Island, N.W.T. *Blue Jay* 23: 66–72.

———. 1976. Sandhill crane on and near the Kissimmee Prairie, Florida. In *Proceedings of the 1975 International Crane Workshop*, edited by J. C. Lewis, 1–18. Stillwater, OK: University Publishing and Printing Department.

———. 1978. Sandhill crane studies in Michigan's Upper Peninsula. *Jack-Pine Warbler* 56: 107–121.

———. 1982. Nesting of the Florida sandhill crane in central Florida. In *Proceedings 1981 Crane Workshop*, edited by J. Lewis, 53–62. New York: National Audubon Society.

Weekly, F. 1965. Individual and regional variation in calls of the greater sandhill cranes. MS thesis. University of Wisconsin, Stevens Point.

Wheeler, M. E, J. A. Barzen, S. Crimmins, and T. R. Van Deelen. 2019. Effects of territorial status and life history on sandhill crane population dynamics in south central Wisconsin. *Canadian Journal of Zoology* 97: 112–120.

Windingstad, R. M. 1988. Nonhunting mortality in sandhill cranes. *Journal of Wildlife Management* 52: 260–263.

Wolfson, D., J. Fieberg, J. Lawrence, T. Cooper, and D. E. Anderson. 2017. Range overlap between Mid-Continent and Eastern sandhill cranes revealed by GPS-tracking. *Wildlife Society Bulletin* 41: 489–498.

Wright, G. D., T. J. Smith, R. K. Murphy, J. T. Runge, and R. R. Harms. 2010. Mortality of cranes (Gruidae) associated with power lines over a major roost on the Platte River, Nebraska. *Prairie Naturalist* 41: 116–120.

Whooping Crane

Allen, R. P. 1952. *The Whooping Crane. Research Report No. 2.* New York: National Audubon Society.

———. 1956. *A Report on the Whooping Crane's Northern Breeding Grounds. Supplement to Research Report No. 2,* 1–60. New York: National Audubon Society.

Austin, J. E., and A. L. Richert. 2001. *A Comprehensive Review of Observational and Site Evaluation Data of Migrant Whooping Cranes in the United States, 1943–99.* Jamestown, ND: US Geological Survey Report, Northern Prairie Wildlife Research Center. 157 pp.

Austin. J. E., M. A. Hayes, and J. A. Barzen. 2018. Revisiting the historic distribution and habitats of the whooping crane. In *Whooping Cranes: Biology and Conservation,* edited by J. B. French et al., 25–88. San Diego, CA: Academic Press.

Belaire, J. A., B. A, Kreakie, T. T. Keitt, and E. Minor. 2014. Predicting and mapping potential whooping crane stopover habitat to guide site selection for wind energy projects. *Conservation Biology* 28: 541–550.

Bergeson, D. G., B. W. Johns, and G. Holroyd. 2001. Mortality of whooping crane colts at Wood Buffalo National Park, Canada. In *Proceedings of the 8th North American Crane Workshop,* edited by D. H. Ellis, 6–10. Seattle, WA: North American Crane Working Group.

Blankinship, D. R. 1976. Studies of whooping cranes on the wintering grounds. In *Proceedings of the International Crane Workshop,* edited by J. Lewis, 197–206. Stillwater, OK: State University Publishing and Printing Department.

Butler, M. J., and W. Harrell. 2018. *Whooping Crane Survey Results: Winter 2017–2018.* US Fish and Wildlife Service Report. Washington, DC: US Fish and Wildlife Service. 3 pp.

Butler, M. J., G. M. Harris, and B. N. Strobel. 2013. Influence of whooping crane population dynamics on its recovery and management. *Biological Conservation* 162: 89–99.

Butler, M. J., K. L. Metzger, and G. M. Harris. 2017. Are whooping cranes destined for extinction? Climate change imperils recruitment and population growth. *Ecology and Evolution* 2017: 1–14.

Canadian Wildlife Service and US Fish and Wildlife Service. 2005. *International Recovery Plan for the Whooping Crane.* Ottawa, ON, and Albuquerque, NM: Recovery of Endangered Wildlife (RENEW) and US Fish and Wildlife Service. 162 pp.

Carlson, G. 1991. The feasibility of individual identification and sex determination of whooping cranes (*Grus americana*) by vocalizations. MS thesis. Idaho State University, Pocatello.

Carlson, G., and C. H. Trost. 1992. Sex determination of the whooping crane by analysis of vocalizations. *Condor* 94: 532–536.

Caven, A. J., J. D. Wiese, W. R. Wallauer, and K. J. Mosher. 2018. First description of a bald eagle (*Haliaeetus leucocephalus*) actively depredating an adult sandhill crane (*Antigone canadensis*). *Western North American Naturalist* 11(1): 3.

Caven, A. J., J. Malzahn, K. D. Koupal, E. M. Brinley Buckley, J. D. Weise, R. Rasmussen, and C. Steenson. 2019. Adult whooping crane consumption of juvenile channel catfish (*Ictalurus punctatus*) during the avian spring migration in the central Platte River valley. *Western North American Naturalist* 11(1): 2.

Caven, A. J., M. Rabbe, J. Malzahn, and A. E. Lacy. 2020. Trends in the occurrence of large whooping crane groups during migration in the Great Plains, USA. *Heliyon* 6: e03549.

Chavez-Ramirez, F. 1996. Food availability, foraging ecology, and energetics of whooping cranes wintering in Texas. PhD dissertation. Texas A&M University, College Station. 104 pp.

Converse, S. J., B. N. Strobel, and J. A. Barzen. 2018. In *Whooping Cranes: Biology and Conservation,* edited by J. B. French et al., 161–178. San Diego, CA: Academic Press.

Conway, W. G. 1957. Three days with a family of whooping cranes. *Animal Kingdom* 40(4): 98–106.

Dellinger, T. A. 2018. Florida's non-migratory whooping cranes. In *Whooping Cranes: Biology and Conservation,* edited by J. B. French et al., 179–194. San Diego, CA: Academic Press.

Derrickson, S. R. 1980. *Whooping Crane Recovery Plan. Report Prepared by the Whooping Crane Recovery Team.* Washington, DC: US Fish and Wildlife Service. 206 pp.

Environment Canada. 2007. *Recovery Strategy for the Whooping Crane (Grus americana) in Canada.* Species at Risk Recovery Strategy Series. Ottawa, ON: Environment Canada. 27 pp.

French J. B., Jr, S. J. Converse, and J. E. Austin, eds. 2018a. *Whooping Cranes: Biology and Conservation.* San Diego, CA: Academic Press. 455 pp.

———. 2018b. Whooping cranes past and present. In *Whooping Cranes: Biology and Conservation*, edited by J. B. French et al., 3–16. San Diego, CA: Academic Press.

Gil-Weir, K. C., W. E. Grant, R. D. Slack, H. Wang, and M. Fujiware. 2012. Demography and population trends of whooping cranes. *Journal of Field Ornithology* 83: 1–10.

Gomez, G. 1992. Whooping cranes in southwest Louisiana: History and human attitudes. In *Proceedings of the 6th North American Crane Workshop*, edited by D. W. Stahlecker and R. P. Urbanek, 19–23. Albuquerque, NM: North American Crane Working Group and Guynes Printing Company.

Gossens, A. P. 2018. Habitat use of the reintroduced Eastern Migratory Population of whooping cranes. In *Whooping Cranes: Biology and Conservation*, edited by J. B. French et al., 307–325. San Diego, CA: Academic Press.

Howe, M. A. 1989. *Migration of Radio-marked Whooping Cranes from the Aransas–Wood Buffalo Population: Patterns of Use, Behavior, and Survival*. US Fish and Wildlife Service Technical Report 21. Washington, DC: US Department of the Interior. 33 pp.

Hunt, H. E., and R. D. Slack. 1989. Wintering diets of whooping and sandhill cranes in south Texas. *Journal of Wildlife Management* 53: 1150–1154.

Johnsgard, P. A. 2014. Aransas National Wildlife Refuge: The whooping crane's vulnerable winter retreat. *Prairie Fire*, May 2014, pp. 12–13.

King, S. L., W. Selman, P. Vasseur, and S. Zimorski. 2018. Louisiana non-migratory whooping crane reintroduction. In *Whooping Cranes: Biology and Conservation*, edited by J. B. French et al., 469–484. San Diego, CA: Academic Press.

Kuyt, E. 1976. Recent clutch size data for whooping cranes, including a three-egg clutch. *Blue Jay* 34: 82–83.

———. 1979. Banding of juvenile whooping cranes and discovery of the summer habitat used by nonbreeders. In *Proceedings of the 1978 Crane Workshop*, edited by J. C. Lewis, 109–112. Fort Collins: Colorado State University Printing Service.

———. 1981a. Clutch size, hatching success and survival of whooping crane chicks, Wood Buffalo National Park, Canada. In *Crane Research around the World, Proceedings of the International Crane Symposium*, edited by J. C. Lewis and H. Masatomi, 126–129. Baraboo, WI: International Crane Foundation.

———. 1981b. Population status, nest site fidelity, and breeding habitat of whooping cranes. In *Crane Research around the World, Proceedings of the International Crane Symposium*, edited by J. C. Lewis and H. Masatomi, 119–125. Baraboo, WI: International Crane Foundation.

———. 1984. Radio-tracking of whooping cranes during fall migration from Wood Buffalo National Park to Aransas National Wildlife Refuge, August–November, 1982. Canadian Wildlife Service Report. 92 pp.

———. 1992. *Aerial Radio-tracking of Whooping Cranes Migrating between Wood Buffalo National Park and Aransas National Wildlife Refuge*. Occasional Paper No. 74. Ottawa, ON: Canadian Wildlife Service. 53 pp.

Lewis, J. C., E. Kuyt, K. E. Schwindt, and T. V. Stehn. 1992. Mortality in fledged cranes of the Aransas–Wood Buffalo population. In *Proceedings of 1988 North American Crane Workshop*, edited by D. A. Wood, 145–148. Tallahassee: Florida Game and Fish Commission.

Maroldo, G. 1980. Crip, the constant dancer. *Blue Jay* 38: 147–161.

Miller, P. S., M. Butler, S. Converse, K. Gil-Weir, W. Selman, J. Straka, K. Traylor-Holzern, and S. Wilson, eds. 2016. *Recovery Planning for the Whooping Crane Workshop 1: Population Viability Analysis*. Apple Valley, MN: IUCN/SSC Conservation Breeding Specialist Group. 34 pp.

Mueller, T., C. S. Teitelbaum, and W. F. Fagan. 2018. Movement ecology of reintroduced migratory whooping cranes. In *Whooping Cranes: Biology and Conservation*, edited by J. B. French et al., 217–238. San Diego, CA: Academic Press.

Mueller, T., R. B. O'Hara, S. J. Converse, R. P. Urbanek, and W. F. Fagan. 2013. Social learning of migratory performance. *Science* 341: 999–1002.

Niemuth, N. D., A. J. Ryba, A. T. Pearse, S. M. Kvas, D. A. Brandt, B. Wangler, and J. E. Austin. 2018. Opportunistically collected data reveal habitat selection by migrating whooping cranes in the US Northern Plains. *Condor* 120: 343–356.

Novakowski, N. S. 1966. *Whooping Crane Population Dynamics on the Nesting Grounds, Wood Buffalo National Park, Northwest Territories, Canada*. Canadian Wildlife Service Research Reports, Series 1. Ottawa, ON: Canadian Wildlife Service. 20 pp.

Pearse, A. T., D. A. Brandt, B. K. Hartup, and M. Bidwell. 2019. Mortality in Aransas–Wood Buffalo whooping cranes: Timing, location, and causes. In *Whooping Cranes: Biology and Conservation*, edited by J. B. French et al., 135–138. San Diego, CA: Academic Press.

Pearse, A. T., K. L. Metzger, D. A. Brandt, M. T. Bidwell, M. J. Harner, D. M. Baasch, and W. Harrell. 2020. Heterogeneity in migration strategies of whooping cranes. *Condor* 122: 1–15.

Pearse, A. T., M. Rabbe, L. M. Juliusson, M. T. Bidwell, L. Craig-Moore, D. A. Brandt, and W. Harrell. 2018. Delineating and identifying long-term changes in the whooping crane (*Grus americana*) migration corridor. *PloS ONE* 13(2): e0192737. https://doi.org/10.1371/journal.pone.0192737

Smith, E., ed. 2019. Species Review: Whooping crane (*Grus americana*). In *Crane Conservation Strategy*, edited by C. M. Mirande and J. T. Harris, 223–243. Baraboo, WI: International Crane Foundation.

Smith, E. H., F. Chavez-Ramirez, and L. Lumb. 2018. Winter habitat ecology, use, and availability for the Aransas Wood Buffalo population of whooping cranes. In *Whooping Cranes: Biology and Conservation*, edited by J. B. French et al., 269–306. San Diego, CA: Academic Press.

Spalding, M. G., M. J. Folk, S. A. Nesbitt, M. L. Folk, and R. Kiltie. 2009. Environmental correlates of reproductive success for introduced resident whooping cranes in Florida. *Waterbirds* 32: 538–547.

Stehn, T. V., and C. L. Haralson-Strobel. 2014. An update on mortality of fledged whooping cranes in the Aransas/Wood Buffalo population. In *Proceedings of the 12th North American Crane Workshop*, edited by D. A. Aborn, 43–50. Madison, WI: North American Crane Working Group.

Stehn, T. V., and F. Prieto. 2010. Changes in winter whooping crane territories and range, 1950–2006. In *Proceedings of the 11th North American Crane Workshop*, edited by B. K. Hartup, 40–56. Laurel, MD: North American Crane Working Group.

Stephenson, J. D. 1971. Plumage development and growth of young whooping cranes. MS thesis. Oregon State University, Corvallis.

Teitelbaum, C. S., S. J. Converse, W. F. Fagan, K. Böhning-Gaese, R. B. O'Hara, A. E. Lacy, and T. Mueller. 2016. Experience drives innovation of new migration patterns of whooping cranes in response to global change. *Nature Communications* 7: 12793.

Timoney, K. 1999. The habitat of nesting whooping cranes. *Biological Conservation* 89: 189–197.

Urbanek, R. P., and J. C. Lewis. 2015. Whooping crane (*Grus americana*), version 2.0. In *The Birds of North America*, edited by A. F. Poole. Ithaca, NY: Cornell Lab of Ornithology. https://doi.org/10.2173/bna.153

Urbanek, R. P., E. K. Szyszkoski, and S. E. Zimorski. 2014. Winter distribution dynamics and implications to a reintroduced population of migratory whooping cranes. *Journal of Fish and Wildlife Management* 5: 340–362.

Urbanek R. P., L. E. A. Fondow, and S. E. Zimorski. 2010. Survival, reproduction, and movements of migratory whooping cranes during the first seven years of reintroduction. In *Proceedings of the 11th North American Crane Workshop*, edited by B. K. Hartup, 124–132. Laurel, MD: North American Crane Working Group.

Weir, K. G., and P. A. Johnsgard. 2010. The whooping cranes: Survivors against all odds. *Prairie Fire*, September 2010, pp. 12–22.

Wilson, S., K. C. Gil-Weir, R. G. Clark, G. J. Robertson, and M. T. Bidwell. 2016. Integrated population modeling to assess demographic variation and contributions to population growth for endangered whooping cranes. *Biological Conservation* 197: 1–7.

Multispecies and General Studies

Archibald, G. W. 1975. The unison call of cranes as a useful taxonomic tool. PhD dissertation. Cornell University, Ithaca, NY.

———. 1976. Crane taxonomy as revealed by the unison call. In *Proceeding of the International Crane Workshop, 3–6 September 1973, International Crane Foundation, Baraboo, Wisconsin*, edited by J. C. Lewis, 225–251. Stillwater: Oklahoma State University Publishing and Printing Department.

Brown, M. B., and P. A. Johnsgard. 2013. *Birds of the Central Platte River Valley and Adjacent Counties*. Lincoln: University of Nebraska–Lincoln Digital Commons and Zea Books. 182 pp. http://digitalcommons.unl.edu/zeabook/15/

Currier, P. J., G. R. Lingle, and J. G. VanDerwalker. 1985. *Migratory Bird Habitat on the Platte and North Platte Rivers in Nebraska*. Grand Island, NE: Whooping Crane Habitat Maintenance Trust. 177 pp.

Dinets, V. 2013. Crane dances as play behavior. *Ibis* 155: 424–425.

Ellis, D. H., S. R. Swengel, G. Archibald, and C. B. Kepler. 1998. A sociogram for the cranes of the world. *Behavioral Processes* 43: 25–51.

Emanuel, V. L. 1982. South Texas region. In The autumn migration August 1–November 30, 1981. *American Birds* 36(2): 196.

Faanes, C. E., and G. R. Lingle. 1995. *Breeding Birds of the Platte Valley of Nebraska*. Jamestown, ND: US Geological Survey, Northern Prairie Wildlife Research Center.

Graf, W. L., J. A. Barzen, F. Cuthbert, H. Doremus, L. M. Butler-Harrington, E. E. Herricks, K. L. Jacobs, W. C. Johnson, F. Lupi, D. D. Murphy, R. N. Palmer, E. J. Peters, H. W. Shen, and J. A. Thompson. 2005. *Endangered and Threatened Species of the Platte River*. Washington, DC: Natural Resources Council of the National Academies, National Academy of Science. 299 pp.

Johnsgard, P. A. 1983b. The Platte: A river of birds. *Nature Conservancy News* 33: 6–10.

———. 2001. *The Nature of Nebraska: Ecology and Biodiversity*. Lincoln: University of Nebraska Press. 402 pp.

———. 2003. Great gathering on the Great Plains. *National Wildlife* 41(3): 20–29. https://digitalcommons.unl.edu/johnsgard/38/

———. 2007. *A Guide to the Natural History of the Central Platte Valley of Nebraska*. Lincoln: University of Nebraska–Lincoln Digital Commons and Zea Books. 156 pp. https://digitalcommons.unl.edu/biosciornithology/40/

———. 2008a. *The Platte: Channels in Time*. Lincoln: University of Nebraska Press. 176 pp.

———. 2008b. The Platte: River of dreams or river of dust? *Prairie Fire*, May 2008, pp. 12–19.

———. 2009a. The wings of March. *Prairie Fire*, March 2009, pp. 1, 17, 18, 19.

———. 2009b. *Four Decades of Christmas Bird Counts in the Great Plains: Ornithological Evidence of a Changing Climate*. Lincoln: University of Nebraska–Lincoln Libraries. 334 pp. http://digitalcommons.unl.edu/biosciornithology/46/

———. 2010. Snow geese of the Great Plains. *Prairie Fire*, February 2010, pp. 12–15.

———. 2012a. *Nebraska's Wetlands: Their Wildlife and Ecology*. Lincoln: University of Nebraska School of Natural Resources, Conservation and Survey Division, Water Survey Paper No. 78.

———. 2012b. *Wings over the Great Plains: Bird Migrations in the Central Flyway*. Lincoln: University of Nebraska–Lincoln Digital Commons and Zea Books. 249 pp. http://digitalcommons.unl.edu/zeabook/13/

———. 2014a. The allure of cranes. *Prairie Fire*, March 2014, pp. 1, 3, 4.

———. 2014b. Secrets of the very long dead: Ashfall Fossil Beds State Historical Park. *Prairie Fire*, October 2014, pp. 1, 3, 4. (Describes a fossil crane closely related to modern crowned cranes)

———. 2013. *The Birds of Nebraska*. Rev. ed. Lincoln: University of Nebraska–Lincoln Digital Commons and Zea Books. 307 pp. https://digitalcommons.unl.edu/zeabook/17/

———. 2020. *Nebraska Wildlife: A Natural History*. Lincoln: University of Nebraska Press.

Jorgensen, J. 2012. *Birds of the Rainwater Basin, Nebraska*. Lincoln: Nebraska Game and Parks Commission.

Krajewski, C. 2018. Phylogenetic taxonomy of cranes and the evolutionary origin of the whooping crane. In *Whooping Cranes: Biology and Conservation*, edited by French et al., 17–24. San Diego, CA: Academic Press.

Krajewski, C., and J. W. Fetzner. 1994. Phylogeny of cranes (Gruiformes: Gruidae) based on cytochrome-B DNA sequences. *Auk* 111: 351–365.

Krajewski, C., J. T. Sipiorski, and F. E. Anderson. 2010. Complete mitochondrial genome sequences and the phylogeny of cranes (Gruiformes: Gruidae). *Auk* 127(2): 440–452. (The sarus crane, brolga, white-naped crane, and sandhill crane, which had been placed in *Antigone* on the basis of molecular data, are returned to *Grus*.)

Krapu, G. L., ed. 1981. *The Platte River Ecology Study: Special Research Report*. Jamestown, ND: US Geological Survey, Northern Prairie Wildlife Research Station. 186 pp.

Martin, G. R., and J. M. Shaw. 2010. Bird collisions with power lines: Failing to see the way ahead? *Biological Conservation* 143(11): 2695–2702.

Møller, A. P., W. Fiedler, and P. Berthold, eds. 2004. *The Effect of Climatic Change on Birds, Advances in Ecological Research*. New York: Academic Press.

Naves, L. C., and J. M. Keating. 2017. *Alaska Subsistence Harvest of Birds and Eggs*. Technical Paper No. 443. Anchorage: Alaska Department of Fish and Game and Alaska Migratory Bird Co-Management Council. 70 pp.

Roberts, T. S. 1880. The convolution of the trachea in the sandhill and whooping cranes. *American Naturalist* 14: 108–114.

Old World Crane Research

Note: For a more comprehensive bibliography of the Old World cranes, see Mirande and Harris, 2019 (listed in the section Comprehensive Books and Single-Subject Monographs). Many of the following foreign references can be found in the International Crane Foundation's Ron Sauey Memorial Library for Bird Conservation.

Single-Species Research

Allan, D. G. 1993. Aspects of the biology and conservation status of the blue crane *Anthropoides paradiseus*, and the Ludwig's *Neotis ludwigii* and Stanley's *N. denhami stanleyi* bustards in Southern Africa. MS thesis. University of Cape Town, Cape Town, South Africa.

Archibald, G. W. 1994. Siberian cranes. *National Geographic* 185(5): 124–136.

Beilfuss, R., W. Tarboton, and N. Gichuki, eds. 1994. Proceedings of the 1993 African Crane and Wetland Training Workshop, 1993. Maun: Botswana. (Includes papers from the *1992 International Conference on the Black Crowned Crane and Its Habitats in West and Central Africa*.) Baraboo, WI: International Crane Foundation.

Bento, C. M. 2002. The status and prospects of wattled cranes *Grus carunculatus* in the Marromeu complex of the Zambezi Delta. MS thesis. University of Cape Town, Cape Town, South Africa.

Bragina, E., and I. Beme. 2013. Sexual and individual features in the long-range and short-range calls of the white-naped crane. *Condor* 115: 501–507.

Bysykatova, G., L. Krapu, N. I. Germogenov, and D. A. Buhl. 2014. Distribution, densities and ecologies of Siberian cranes in the Khroma River region of northern Yakutia in northeastern Russia. In *Proceedings of the Twelfth North American Crane Workshop*, edited by D. A. Aborn and R. A. Urbenek, 51–64. Madison, WI: North American Crane Working Group.

Chandan, P., et al. 2014. Status and distribution of black-necked crane (*Grus nigricollis*) in India. *Zoological Research* 35(S1): 39–50.

Frame, G. W. 1982. East African crowned crane (*Balearica regulorum gibbericeps*): Ecology and behavior in Tanzania. *Scopus* 6: 60–69.

Gichuki, C. M. 2004. *Study of Black Crowned Cranes in Northern Kenya: A Search for the Lost Queen of the Jade Sea*. Nairobi, Kenya: Kenya Museum Society. 29 pp.

Gole, P. 1981. Black-necked crane in Ladakh. In *Crane Research around the World: Proceedings of the International Crane Symposium at Sapporo Japan in 1980 and Papers from the World Working Group on Cranes, International Council for Bird Preservation*, edited by J. C. Lewis and H. Masatomi, 197–203. Baraboo, WI: International Crane Foundation.

Hachfeld, B. 1989. *Der Kranich: Ein Lebenbild*. Hannover: Schlütersche Verlagsanstalt. 160 pp. (Eurasian crane life history)

Hansbauer, M., Z. Vegvri, and J. T. Harris. No date. *Eurasian Cranes and Climate Change*. Baraboo, WI: International Crane Foundation. 21 pp.

Harris, J. 2009. *Safe Flyways for the Siberian Crane: A Flyway Approach Conserves Some of Asia's Most Beautiful Wetlands and Waterbirds*. Baraboo, WI: International Crane Foundation. 99 pp.

Hayashida, T. 1983. The Japanese crane, bird of happiness. *National Geographic* 164(4): 542–556.

Hermansson, C., and A. Karlsson. 2013. *Tranorna vid Hornborgasjön* [Cranes at Hornborgasjön]. Hornborgasjöns Fältstation, Broddetorp. 96 pp. (Eurasian cranes at Lake Hornborga, in Swedish)

Higuchi, H., and J. Minton. 2017. Migratory routes across the Himalayas used by demoiselle cranes. In *Bird Migration Across the Himalayas: Wetland Functioning Amidst Mountain and Glaciers*, edited by H. H. T. Prins and T. Namgail, 45–57. Cambridge, UK: Cambridge University Press.

Iqubal, P. 1992. Breeding behaviour in the sarus crane (*Grus antigone antigone*). MS thesis. Aligarh Muslim University, Aligarh, India.

Johnson, D. N., and P. R. Barnes. 1991. The breeding biology of the wattled crane in Natal. In *Proceedings 1987 International Crane Workshop, 1–10 May 1987, Qiquihar, Heilongjiang Province, People's Republic of China*, edited by J. Harris, 377–386. Baraboo, WI: International Crane Foundation.

Kanai, Y., M. Ueta, N. Germogenov, M. Nagendran, N. Mitta, and H. Higuchi. 2002. Migration routes and important resting areas of Siberian cranes (*Grus leucogeranus*) between northeastern Siberia and China as revealed by satellite tracking. *Biological Conservation International* 106: 339–346.

Klenova, A. V., I, A. Volodin, and E. V. Volodina. 2007. The vocal development of the red-crowned crane *Grus japonensis*. *Ornithological Science* 6(2): 107–119.

———. 2008. Duet structure provides information about pair identity in the red-crowned crane (*Grus japonensis*). *Journal of Ethology* 26(3): 317–325.

Klenova, A., I. A. Volodin, E. V. Volodina, and K. A. Postelnyk. 2010. Voice breaking in adolescent red-crowned cranes (*Grus japonensis*). *Behaviour* 147(4): 505–524.

Kozlova, E. V. 1975. (Birds of the zonal steppes and wastelands of Central Asia.) *Trudy Zoologischeskogo Instituta* 59: 8–239. (In Russian)

Li, F. 2014. IUCN Black-necked crane (*Grus nigricollis*) conservation plan. *Zoological Research* 35(S1): 3–9.

Liu, Q., F. Li, P. Buzzard, F. Qian, F. Zhang, J. Zhao, J. Yang, and X. Yang. 2012. Migration routes and new breeding areas of black-necked cranes. *Wilson Journal of Ornithology* 124: 702–710.

Masatomi, H. 1991. Population dynamics of red-crowned cranes in Hokkaido since the 1950s. In *Proceedings 1987 International Crane Workshop, 1–10 May 1987, Qiquihar, Heilongjiang Province, People's Republic of China*, edited by J. Harris, 297–299. Baraboo, WI: International Crane Foundation.

———. 2004. Individual (non-social) behavioral acts of hooded cranes *Grus monachus* wintering in Izumi, Japan. *Journal of Ethology* 22: 69–83.

Masatomi, H., and T. Kitagawa. 1974/1975. Bionomics and sociology of tancho or the Japanese crane, *Grus japonensis*. I. Distribution, habitat and outline of annual cycle. II. Ethogram. *Journal of the Faculty of Science* (Hokkaido University, Sapporo, Japan) 19(2): 777–802; 19(4): 834–878.

Matthiessen, P. 1994. At the end of Tibet. *Audubon Magazine*, March–April 1994. (Black-necked crane)

———. 1995. The cranes of Hokkaido. *Audubon Magazine*, July–August 1995. (Red-crowned crane)

Munier, V., and Z. Bisnau. 2004. *Tanchu*. Buxieres-les-Villiers. (Red-crowned crane)

Neufeldt, I. A., and J. Kespaik, eds. 1989. *Common Crane Research in the USSR: Papers Prepared by the USSR Working Group on Cranes*. Tartu, USSR (Estonia): Communications of the Baltic Commission for the Study of Bird Migration No. 21. 185 pp. (In Russian, with English summaries)

Nevard, T. D., M. Haase, G. Archibald, and I. Leiper. 2019. The sarolga: Conservation implications of genetic and visual evidence for hybridization between the brolga *Antigone rubicunda* and the Australian sarus crane *Antigone antigone gillae*. *Oryx* 54: 40–51.

Pae, S. H., and P. Won. 1994. Wintering ecology of red-crowned cranes and white-naped cranes *Grus japonensis* and *G. vipio* in the Cheolwon Basin, Korea. In *The Future of Cranes and Wetlands: Proceedings of the International Symposium*, 97–196. Tokyo: Wild Bird Society of Japan.

Pfister, O. 1998. The breeding ecology and conservation of the black-necked crane (*Grus nigricollis*) in Ladakh/India. Thesis. University of Hull, Kingston upon Hull, UK. 124 pp.

Pomeroy, D. E. 1980. Aspects of the ecology of crowned cranes *Balearica regulorum* in Uganda. *Scopus* 4: 29–35.

———. 1980. Growth and plumage changes of the grey crowned crane (*Balearica regulorum gibbericeps*). *Bulletin of the British Ornithologists' Club* 100(4): 219–223.

Prange, H. 2008. The status of the common crane (*Grus grus*) in Europe—breeding, resting, migration, wintering and protection. In *Proceedings of the Tenth North American Crane Workshop*, edited by M. J. Folk and S. A. Nesbitt, 69–77. Gambier, OH: North American Crane Working Group.

Qian, F., H. Wu, L. Gao, H. Zhang, F. Li, X. Zhong, X. Yang, and G. Zheng. 2009. Migration routes and stopover sites of black-necked cranes determined by satellite tracking. *Journal of Field Ornithology* 80: 19–26.

Sauey, R. T. 1985. The range, status, and winter ecology of the Siberian crane (*Grus leucogeranus*). PhD dissertation. Cornell University, Ithaca, NY.

Scott, D. A. 1993. The black-necked cranes, *Grus nigricollis*, of Ruoergai Marshes, Sichuan, China. *Bird Conservation International* 3(3): 245–259.

Shaw, J. M., A. R. Jenkins, J. J. Smallie, and P. J. Ryan. 2010. Modeling power-line collision risk for blue cranes *Anthropoides paradiseus* in South Africa. *Ibis* 152: 590–599.

Steyn, P., and P. Ellman-Brown. 1974. Crowned crane nesting in a tree. *Ostrich* 45: 40–41.

Su, L. 1993. Comparative feeding ecology of the red-crowned and white-naped cranes. MS thesis. University of Missouri, Columbia.

Sundar, K. S. G., J. D. A. Grant, I. Veltheim, S. Kittur, K. Brandis, M. A. McCarthy, and E. C. Scambler. 2019. Sympatric cranes in northern Australia: Abundance, breeding success, habitat preference and diet. *Emu* 119: 79–89.

Tao, Y., and L. Peixun. 1991. Observations on mating behavior of white-naped cranes in the wild. In *The Cranes of China: Proceedings of the 1987 International Crane Workshop, 1–10 May 1987, Qiqihar, Heilongjiang Province, People's Republic of China*, edited by J. Harris, 63–66. Baraboo, WI: International Crane Foundation.

van Ee, C. A. 1966. Notes on the breeding behavior of the blue crane *Tetrapteryx paradisea*. *Ostrich* 37: 23–39.

Viniter, S. V. 1981. Nesting of the red-crowned crane in the Central Amur Region. In *Crane Research Around the World: Proceedings of the International Crane Symposium at Sapporo, Japan, in 1980 and Papers from the World Working Group on Cranes, International Council for Bird Preservation*, edited by J. C. Lewis and H. Masatomi, [74–80]. Baraboo, WI: International Crane Foundation.

Walkinshaw, L. H. 1963. Some life history studies of the Stanley crane. In *Proceedings XIII International Ornithological Congress, Ithaca, 17–24 June 1962*, 2 vols., edited by C. G. Sibley, J. J. Hickey, and M. B. Hickey, 344–353. Baton Rouge, LA: American Ornithologists' Union.

Yang, R., H. Q. Wu, X. J. Yang, W. G. Jiang, L. Zuo, and Z. R. Xiang. 2005. A preliminary observation on breeding behavior of black-necked cranes at Ruoergai, Sichuan Province. In *Status and Conservation of Black-necked Cranes on the Yunnan and Guizhou Plateau*, edited by F. S. Li, X. J. Yang, and F. Yang, 163–169. Kunming, People's Republic of China: Yunnan Nationalities Publishing House. (In Chinese)

Multispecies Studies and Symposia

Archibald, G. W., and R. F. Pasquier, eds. 1987. *Proceedings of the 1983 International Crane Workshop*. Baraboo, WI: International Crane Foundation. 595 pp.

Aynalem, S., G. Nowald, and W. Schröder. 2013. Biology and ecology of cranes: Wattled cranes (*Grus carunculatus*), black-crowned cranes (*Balearica pavonina*), and Eurasian cranes (*Grus grus*) at Lake Tana, Ethiopia. In *Proceedings of the 7th European Crane Conference*, edited by G. Nowald, A. Weber, J. Fanke, E. Weinhardt, and N. Donner, 126–133. Groß Mohrdorf, Germany: Crane Conservation Germany.

Bankovics, A., ed. 1987. *Proceedings of the International Crane Foundation Working Group on European Cranes, 1985*. Budapest, Hungary: Aquila. 326 pp.

Beilfuss, R. D., T. Dodman, and E. K. Urban. 2007. The status of cranes in Africa in 2005. *Ostrich* 78(2): 175–184.

Carwardine, M. 2013. *Natural History Museum Book of Animal Records*. Richmond Hill, ON: Firefly Books. 256 pp.

Chong J., H. Higuchi, and P. U-il. 1994. The migration routes and important rest-sites of cranes on the Korean Peninsula. In *The Future of Cranes and Wetlands*, edited by H. Higuchi and J. Minton, 41–50. Tokyo, Japan: Wild Bird Society of Japan.

Fengshan, Li. 2020. Developing a land management system for Cao Hai and its watershed to safeguard resources for black-necked crane and people. PhD dissertation. University of Wisconsin, Madison.

Goroshko, O. A. 2012. Global climate change and conservation of cranes in the Amur River Basin. In *Cranes, Agriculture and Climate Change: Proceedings of the Workshop Organized by the International Crane Foundation and Muraviovka Park for Sustainable Land Use*, edited by J. Harris, 143. Baraboo, WI: International Crane Foundation.

Halvorson, C. H., J. T. Harris, and S. M. Smirenski, eds. 1995. *Cranes and Storks of the Amur River: The Proceedings of the International Workshop*. 3–12 July 1992, Khaborovsk and Poyarkovo, Russia. The Amur Program of the Socio-Ecological Union, International Crane Foundation, and Moscow State University. Moscow, Russia: Arts Literature Publishers. 200 pp.

Harris, J. ed. 1991. *Proceedings 1987 International Crane Workshop, 1–10 May 1987, Qiqihar, Heilongjiang Province, People's Republic of China*. Baraboo, WI: International Crane Foundation. 456 pp.

———. 2012. [Abstracts] *Cranes, Agriculture, and Climate Change: Proceedings of a Workshop Organized by the International Crane Foundation and Muraviovka Park for Sustainable Land Use*. Baraboo, WI: International Crane Foundation.

Harris, J. T. 2008. Cranes respond to climate change. *The Bugle* (ICF Newsletter) 34(4): 1–3, 13–15.

Harris, J. T., and C. Mirande. 2013. A global overview of cranes: Status, threats and conservation priorities. *Chinese Birds* 4(3): 189–209.

Heilongjiang Forest Bureau. 1987. Summaries. *Proceedings 1987 International Crane Workshop, Qiqihar, Heilongjiang Province, People's Republic of China*. Beijing: China Forestry Press. 143 pp. (In Chinese. See also Heilongjiang Forest Bureau, 1990 and Harris, 1991.)

———. 1990. *International Crane Protection and Research: Proceedings of the 1987 International Crane Workshop, 1987*. Beijing: China Forestry Press. 285 pp. (In Chinese. See also Harris, 1991.)

Higuchi, H., and J. Minton, eds. 1994. *The Future of Cranes and Wetlands: Proceedings of the International Symposium, June 1993*. Tokyo and Sapporo, Japan: Wild Bird Society of Japan. 181 pp.

Howell, S. N. G., I. Lewington, and W. Russell. 2014. *Rare Birds of North America*. Princeton, NJ: Princeton University Press. 448 pp.

Ilyashenko, E. I., A. F. Kovshar, and S. V. Winter, eds. 2008. *Cranes of Eurasia (Biology, Distribution, Migrations)*. Vol. 3. Moscow, Russia: Moscow Zoo.

IUCN [International Union for Conservation of Nature]. 2013. *IUCN Red List of Threatened Species*. Version 2013.2. www.iucnredlist.org

———. 2019. *IUCN Red List of Threatened Species*. Version 2018.2. www.iucnredlist.org

Johnson, R. L., Zou Hongfei, and R. C. Stendell, eds. 2001. *Cranes in East Asia: Proceedings of the Symposium held in Harbin, People's Republic of China*. Fort Collins, CO: Geological Survey, Midcontinent Ecological Science Center.

Lewis, J. C., and H. Masatomi, eds. 1981. *Crane Research around the World: Proceedings of the International Crane Symposium*. Baraboo, WI: International Crane Foundation.

Li, F., J. Wu, J. Harris, and J. Burnham. 2012. Number and distribution of cranes wintering at Poyang Lake, China, during 2011–2012. *Chinese Birds* 3(3): 180–190.

Litvinenko, N. M., and I. A. Neufeldt, eds. 1982. *Cranes of East Asia*. Vladivostok, USSR: Far East Branch, Academy of Sciences of the USSR. 120 pp. (In Russian with English abstracts)

———. 1988. *The Palearctic Cranes: Biology, Morphology, and Distribution: Papers from the Fifth Meeting of the Soviet Working Group on Cranes, 1986*. Vladivostok, USSR: Far East Branch, Academy of Sciences of the USSR, and Amur-Ussuri Branch of the USSR Ornithological Society. 236 pp. (In Russian with English abstracts)

Lundin, G., ed. 2005. *Cranes—Where, When and Why? A Guidebook for Visitors in European Crane Areas and Ideas How to Manage Cranes in an Agricultural Environment*. Stockholm: Sveriges Ornitologiska Förening. 228 pp. (Guidebook for finding cranes in Europe and elsewhere)

Ma, J., and Y. Ma. 2001. The status and conservation of cranes in China. In *Cranes in East Asia: Proceedings of the Symposium Held in Harbin, People's Republic of China*, edited by R. L. Johnson, H. Zou, and R. C. Stendell, 3–9. Fort Collins, CO: Geological Survey, Midcontinent Ecological Science Center.

Ma Yiqing, ed. 1986. *Crane Research and Conservation in China: Proceedings of the First Symposium on Crane Research in China, 1984*. Harbin, China: Heilongjiang Education Press. 253 pp. (In Chinese with English abstracts)

Matsuda, Y. 1999. Cranes that cross the Himalaya. *The Himalayan Journal* 55: unpaginated.

Matthiessen, P. 1996. Accidental sanctuary. *Audubon Magazine*, July–August 1996. (Wintering Asian cranes and the Korean demilitarized zone)

Moll, K. H. 1963. Kranichbeobachtungen aus dem Mürirutzgebiet. *Beitrage zur Vogelkunde* 8: 221–253, 368–388, 412–439.

Neufeldt, I. A., ed. 1982. *Cranes of the USSR: Papers Presented at the Second Meeting of the Soviet Working Group on Cranes*. Leningrad, USSR: Zoological Institute of the Academy of Sciences of the USSR. 163 pp. (In Russian with English titles)

Neufeldt, I. A., and J. Kespaik, eds. 1987. *Crane Studies in the USSR: Papers Presented at the Fourth Meeting of the Soviet Working Group on Cranes, 1984*. Tartu, USSR (Estonia): Communications of the Baltic Commission for the Study of Bird Migration No. 19. 224 pp. (In Russian with English titles)

Porter, D. J., H. S. Craven, D. N. Johnson, and M. J. Porter, eds. 1992. *Proceedings of the First Southern African Crane Conference, 1989*. Durban, South Africa: Southern African Crane Foundation. 156 pp.

Prange, H., ed. 1995. *Crane Research and Protection in Europe*. Halle-Wittenberg, Germany: European Crane Working Group and Martin Luther-Universität. 580 pp.

Winkler, D. W., S. M. Billerman, and I. J. Lovette. 2020. *Family Gruidae: Cranes*. Version 1.0. In *Birds of the World*, edited by S. M. Billerman, B. K. Keeney, P. G. Rodewald, and T. S. Schulenberg. Ithaca, NY: Cornell Lab of Ornithology. https://doi.org/10.2173/bow.gruida1.01

Zimmerman, D. R. 1981. A fragile victory for beauty on an old Asian battleground. *Smithsonian* 12(7): 57–60. (Crane conservation in Korea)

Crane Lore, Legend, and Myth

Armstrong, E. A. 1943. Crane dance in East and West. *Antiquity* 17: 71–76.

Coern, E. 1977. *Sadako and the Thousand Cranes*. New York: Puffin Books.

Hattori, U. 1928. *Mythology of All Races*. Vol. 8. Cambridge, UK: Cambridge University Press.

Jensen, J. 2000. *Legends of the Crane*. Inverness, Scotland: Sandstone Press. 261 pp.

Johnsgard, P. A. 2008. *Wind Through the Buffalo Grass: A Lakota Story Cycle*. Lincoln, NE: Plains Chronicles Press. 214 pp. https://digitalcommons.unl.edu/johnsgard/51/

———. 2010. A place called Pahaku. *Prairie Fire*, June 2010, pp. 1, 19, 20, 23.

Lake-Thom, B. 1997. *Spirits of the Earth: A Guide to Native American Nature Symbols, Stories, and Ceremonies*. New York: Plume Press. 221 pp.

Leach, M., ed. 1972. *Funk and Wagnalls Standard Dictionary of Folklore, Mythology and Legends*. New York: Funk and Wagnalls.

Mewes, W., G. Nowald, and H. Prange. 2003. *Kraniche: Mythen, Forschung, Fakten* [Cranes: Myths, research, facts]. Karlsruhe, Germany: G. Braun Buchverlag.

Nelson, E. W. 1899. The Eskimo about Bering Strait. *18th Annual Report of the Bureau of American Ethnology for the Years 1896–1897*. Part 1. Washington, DC: US Government Printing Office. 518 pp.

Price, A. L. 2001. *Cranes: The Noblest Fliers*. Albuquerque: Alameda Press.

Rowland, B. 1979. *Birds with Human Souls: A Guide to Bird Symbolism*. Knoxville: Tennessee University Press.

Russell, N., and J. McGowan. 2003. Dance of the cranes: Crane symbolism at Çatalhöyük and beyond. *Antiquity* 77(297): 445–455.

Salisbury, J. E. 1993. *The Beast Within: Animals in the Middle Ages*. New York: Routledge.

Tate, P. 2008. *Flights of Fancy: Birds in Myth, Legend, and Superstition*. New York: Delacorte Press. 180 pp.

Topsell, E. 1972. *The Fowles of Heauen* [Heaven], *or History of Birdes*. Edited by T. P. Harrison and F. D. Hoeniger. Austin: University of Texas Press.

Toynbee, J. M. C. 1973. *Animals in Roman Life and Art*. London: Thames and Hudson.

Other Printed, Electronic, and Visual Resources

Regional Birding and Wildlife-Viewing Guides

Note: Some of these references may not contain specific crane-finding information.

National and Interregional Guides

Finlay, J. C., and J. Cams. 1984. *The Bird Finding Guide to Canada*. Edmonton, AB: Hurtig Publishers. 387 pp.

Jones, J. O. 1990. *Where the Birds Are: A Guide to All 50 States and Canada*. New York: William Morrow. 400 pp. (Incudes 319 national wildlife refuges, 51 national parks, and 307 Audubon and Nature Conservancy sanctuaries plus more than 200 Canadian locations)

Pettingill, O. S. 1977. *A Guide to Bird Finding East of the Mississippi*. New York: Oxford University Press. 689 pp.

———. 1981. *A Guide to Bird Finding West of the Mississippi*. New York: Oxford University Press. 783 pp.

Riley, L., and W. Riley. 1979. *Guide to the National Wildlife Refuges*. Garden City, NY: Anchor Press/Doubleday. 653 pp. (Includes 175 refuges)

White, M. 1999a. *Guide to Birdwatching Sites: Western US*. Washington, DC: National Geographic Society. 224 pp. (Includes states east to ND, SD, KS, OK, and western TX)

———. 1999b. *Guide to Birdwatching Sites: Eastern US*. Washington, DC: National Geographic Society. 320 pp. (Includes states west to MN, IA, MO, and eastern TX)

Midwest and Great Plains

Brown, M. B., and P. A. Johnsgard. 2013. *Birds of the Central Platte River Valley and Adjacent Counties*. Lincoln: University of Nebraska–Lincoln Digital Commons and Zea Books. 182 pp. http://digitalcommons.unl.edu/zeabook/15/

Cooksey, M., and R. Weeks. 2006. *A Birder's Guide to the Texas Coast*. ABA/Lane Birdfinding Guide. Delaware City, DE: American Birding Association. 344 pp. (More than 200 sites described, including Aransas National Wildlife Refuge)

Dinsmore, S. J., L. S. Jackson, B. L. Ehresman, and J. J. Dinsmore. 1995. *Iowa Wildlife Viewing Guide*. Wildlife Viewing Guides Series. Helena, MT: Falcon Press. 96 pp. (77 sites described)

Farrar, J. 2004, Birding Nebraska. *Nebraskaland Magazine* 82(1): 1–178.

Gress, B., and G. Potts. 1993. *Watching Kansas Wildlife: A Guide to 101 Sites*. Lawrence: University Press of Kansas. 118 pp.

Gress, B., and P. Janzen. 2008. *The Guide to Kansas Birds and Birding Hot Spots*. Lawrence: University Press of Kansas. 368 pp.

Henderson, C. L., and A. L. Lambrecht. 1997. *Traveler's Guide to Wildlife in Minnesota*. Minneapolis: Minnesota's Bookstore. 326 pp. (120 sites described)

Holt, H. R. 1992. *A Birder's Guide to the Rio Grande Valley of Texas*. 2nd ed. ABA/Lane Birdfinding Guide. Delaware City, DE: American Birding Association. 189 pp.

Johnsgard, P. A. 2007. *A Guide to the Natural History of the Central Platte Valley of Nebraska*. Lincoln: University of Nebraska–Lincoln Digital Commons and Zea Books. 156 pp. https://digitalcommons.unl.edu/biosciornithology/40/

———. 2011. *A Nebraska Bird-Finding Guide*. Lincoln: University of Nebraska–Lincoln Digital Commons and Zea Books. 166 pp. https://digitalcommons.unl.edu/zeabook/5/

———. 2015. *Birding Nebraska's Central Platte Valley and Rainwater Basin*. Lincoln: University of Nebraska–Lincoln Digital Commons and Zea Books. 54 pp. https://digitalcommons.unl.edu/zeabook/36/

———. 2018. *A Naturalist's Guide to the Great Plains*. Lincoln: University of Nebraska–Lincoln Digital Commons and Zea Books. 161 pp. http://digitalcommons.unl.edu/zeabook/63/ (More than 400 Great Plains sites in the United States and Canada, from Texas to southern Canada, described)

Knue, J. 1992a. *North Dakota Wildlife Viewing Guide*. Helena, MT: Falcon Press. 96 pp. (81 sites described)

———. 1992b. *Nebraska Wildlife Viewing Guide*. Helena, MT: Falcon Press. 96 pp. (61 sites described)

Lane, J. A., and J. L. Tveten. 1984. *A Birder's Guide to the Texas Coast*. Denver, CO: L&P Press. 234 pp. (Includes Aransas National Wildlife Refuge)

Lingle, G. R. 1994. *Birding Crane River: Nebraska's Platte*. Grand Island, NE: Harrier Publishing.

Lockwood, M. W., W. B. McKinney, J. N. Paton, and B. R. Zimmer. 2008. *A Birder's Guide to the Rio Grande Valley*. 4th ed. Delaware City, DE: American Birding Association. 336 pp. (230 sites described)

McCarter, J. 1994. *New Mexico Wildlife Viewing Guide*. Helena, MT: Falcon Press. (74 sites described)

Parmeter, J. E., B. Neville, and D. Emkains. 2002. *New Mexico Bird Finding Guide*. 3rd ed. Albuquerque: New Mexico Ornithological Society.

Ritter, J. 2007. *Birding Corpus Christi and the Coastal Bend: More Than 75 Prime Birding Sites*. Helena, MT: Falcon Press. 284 pp. (Includes Aransas National Wildlife Refuge)

Shepard, L. 1996. *The Smithsonian Guides to Natural America: The Northern Plains: Minnesota, North Dakota, South Dakota*. New York: Random House. 286 pp.

Wauer, R. H., and M. A. Elwonger. 1998. *Birding Texas*. Helena, MT: Falcon Guides. 544 pp. (200 sites described)

White, M. 1996. *The Smithsonian Guides to Natural America: The South-Central States: Texas, Oklahoma, Arkansas, Louisiana, Mississippi*. New York: Random House. 284 pp.

Winkler, S. 1997. *The Smithsonian Guides to Natural America: The Heartland: Illinois, Iowa, Nebraska*. New York: Random House. 304 pp.

Zimmer, K. 1979. *A Birder's Guide to North Dakota*. Denver, CO: L&P Press.

Zimmerman, D., et al. 1997. *New Mexico Bird Finding Guide*. Albuquerque: New Mexico Ornithological Society.

Zimmerman, J. L., and S. T. Patti. 1988. *A Guide to Bird Finding in Kansas and Western Missouri*. Lawrence: University Press of Kansas. 244 pp.

Rocky Mountains

Canterbury, J. L., P. A. Johnsgard, and H. Downing. 2013. *Birds and Birding in Wyoming's Bighorn Mountains Region*. Lincoln: University of Nebraska–Lincoln Digital Commons and Zea Books. 260 pp. http://digitalcommons.unl.edu/zeabook/18

Fisher, C., and H. Fisher. 1995. *Montana Wildlife Viewing Guide*. Helena, MT: Falcon Publishing. 111 pp. (109 sites described)

Gray, M. T. 1992. *Colorado Wildlife Viewing Guide*. Helena, MT: Falcon Publishing. 128 pp. (110 sites described)

Johnsgard, P. A. 2011b. *Rocky Mountain Birds: Birds and Birding in the Central and Northern Rockies.* Lincoln: University of Nebraska–Lincoln Digital Commons and Zea Books. 274 pp. http://digitalcommons.unl.edu/zeabook/7/

———. 2013. *Yellowstone Wildlife: Ecology and Natural History of the Greater Yellowstone Ecosystem.* Boulder: University Press of Colorado. 228 pp.

———. 2019. *Wyoming Wildlife: A Natural History.* Lincoln: University of Nebraska–Lincoln Digital Commons and Zea Books. 242 pp. https://digitalcommons.unl.edu/zeabook/73/

Kingery, H. 2007. *Birding Colorado: Over 180 Premier Birding Sites at 93 Locations.* Guilford, CT: Falcon Guides. 336 pp.

Lamb, S. 1996. *The Smithsonian Guides to Natural America: The Southern Rockies: Colorado and Utah.* New York: Random House. 304 pp.

McEneaney, T. 1993. *The Birder's Guide to Montana.* Helena, MT: Falcon Press. 327 pp.

Raynes, B., and D. Wile. 1994. *Finding the Birds of Jackson Hole.* Jackson, WY: Darwin Wile. 159 pp.

Scott, O. 1992. *A Birder's Guide to Wyoming.* Delaware City, DE: American Birding Association. 246 pp.

Schmidt, T. 1995. *The Smithsonian Guides to Natural America: The Northern Rockies: Idaho, Montana, Wyoming.* New York: Random House. 304 pp.

Svingen, D., and K. Dumroese, eds. 1997. *A Birder's Guide to Idaho.* ABA/Lane Birdfinding Guide. Delaware City, DE: American Birding Association. 339 pp.

Wauer, R. 1993. *Visitor's Guide to the Birds of the Rocky Mountain Parks, US and Canada.* Santa Fe, NM: John Muir.

Wilkinson, T. 2004. *Watching Yellowstone and Grand Teton Wildlife.* Helena, MT: Riverbend Publishing.

Wyoming Game and Fish Department. 1996. *Wyoming Wildlife Viewing Guide.* Lander: Wyoming Game and Fish Department.

Pacific Coast

Cannings, R., and R. Cannings. 2013. *Birding in British Columbia.* Vancouver: Greystone Books. 400 pp.

Hadley, J., ed. 2015. *A Birder's Guide to Washington.* 2nd ed. Seattle: Washington Ornithological Society.

Rakestraw, J. 2014. *Birding Oregon: A Guide to the Best Birding Sites across the State.* 2nd ed. Create Space Publishing. 224 pp.

Newsletters, Bulletins, and Online Sources

Kentucky Coalition for Sandhill Cranes. This organization's quarterly electronic newsletter, the *Eastern Crane Bulletin,* provides detailed information on the Eastern Populations of sandhill and whooping cranes, and more general information on other crane populations. It can be accessed at http://kyc4sandhillcranes.com/eastern-crane-bulletin/

International Crane Foundation (ICF). Address: E-11376 Shady Lane Road, Baraboo, WI 55913. The foundation's quarterly newsletter *Bugle* (8 pp.) is sent to members. The ICF's Ron Sauey Memorial Library has a very large collection of crane-related materials that are available on loan to members. For more information, contact the ICF librarian Betsy Didrickson at Bugle@savingcranes.org

The North American Crane Working Group (NACWG). The NACWG is an informal group of ornithologists that specializes in cranes. Its newsletter, *Unison Call,* is published twice a year for its members; previous issues are free online at http://www.nacwg.org/news.html. The NACWG also provides free online access to the first 14 volumes (through 2017) of the *Proceedings of the North American Crane Workshop*: https://digitalcommons.unl.edu/nacwg/. The collection includes the following volumes:

> *Proceedings 1978 Crane Workshop,* Rockport, TX, December 6–8, 1978 (1979)
>
> *Proceedings 1981 Crane Workshop,* Grand Tetons, WY, August 25–27, 1981 (1982)
>
> *Proceedings 1983 International Crane Workshop,* Bharatpur, India, February 1983 (1987)
>
> *Proceedings 1985 Crane Workshop,* Grand Island, NE, March 26–28, 1985 (1987)
>
> *Proceedings 1987 International Crane Workshop,* Heilongjiang Province, China, May 1–10, 1987 (1991)
>
> *Proceedings 1988 Crane Workshop,* Lake Wales, FL, February 22–24, 1988 (1992)
>
> *Proceedings of the Sixth North American Crane Workshop,* Regina, SK, October 3–5, 1991 (1997)
>
> *Proceedings of the Seventh North American Crane Workshop,* Biloxi, MS, January 10–13, 1996 (1997)
>
> *Proceedings of the Eighth North American Crane Workshop,* Albuquerque, NM, January 11–14, 2000 (2001)

Proceedings of the Ninth North American Crane Workshop, Sacramento, CA, January 17–20, 2003 (2005)

Proceedings of the Tenth North American Crane Workshop, Zacatecas City, Mexico, February 7–10, 2006 (2008)

Proceedings of the Eleventh North American Crane Workshop, Wisconsin Dells, WI, September 23–27, 2008 (2010)

Proceedings of the Twelfth North American Crane Workshop, Grand Island, NE, March 13–16, 2011 (2014)

Proceedings of the Thirteenth North American Crane Workshop, Lafayette, Louisiana, 14–17 April 2014 (2016)

Proceedings of the Fourteenth North American Crane Workshop, Chattanooga, Tennessee, 11–15 January 2017 (2018)

Whooping Crane Conservation Association. This association is an informal group open to all people who are interested in whooping cranes and their conservation. No permanent address; phone 251-626-7804. Its newsletter is *Grus Americana* and older issues are available online, http://www.whoopingcrane.com/. A Facebook website also provides recent news about whooping cranes: https://www.facebook.com/pg/WhoopingCraneConservationAssociation/posts/

Websites

Aransas National Wildlife Refuge (Austwell, TX): https://www.fws.gov/refuge/Aransas/

Bosque Del Apache National Wildlife Refuge (Socorro, NM): https://www.fws.gov/refuge/Bosque_del_Apache/

The Crane Trust (Wood River, NE): https://cranetrust.org/

Friends of the Wild Whoopers: https://friendsofthewildwhoopers.org/

Government of Canada. 2010. Whooping crane (*Grus americana*): COSEWIC [Committee on the Status of Endangered Wildlife in Canada] assessment and status report 2010. https://www.canada.ca/en/environment-climate-change/services/species-risk-public-registry/cosewic-assessments-status-reports/whooping-crane-2010.html

International Crane Foundation (Baraboo, WI): https://www.savingcranes.org/

International Union for Conservation of Nature (IUCN) (Whooping crane conservation status): https://www.iucnredlist.org/species/22692156/155547970

IUCN Red List of Threatened Species: https://www.iucn.org/resources/conservation-tools/iucn-red-list-threatened-species

Lillian Annette Rowe Sanctuary (Iain Nicolson Audubon Center) (Gibbon, NE): https://rowe.audubon.org/

Mississippi Sandhill Crane National Wildlife Refuge (Gautier, MS): https://www.fws.gov/refuge/mississippi_sandhill_crane/

Necedah National Wildlife Refuge (Necedah, WI): https://www.fws.gov/refuge/necedah/

North American Crane Working Group: http://www.nacwg.org/

Patuxent Wildlife Research Center (Laurel, MD): https://www.usgs.gov/centers/pwrc

Platte River Recovery Implementation Program (Kearney, NE, and Denver, CO): https://platteriverprogram.org/

Whooping Crane Conservation Association: https://whoopingcrane.com/

Whooping Crane Eastern Partnership (WCEP): http://www.bringbackthecranes.org/

Wikipedia entry "Crane (bird)": https://en.wikipedia.org/wiki/Crane_(bird)

Wood Buffalo National Park (Alberta and Northwest Territories, Canada): https://www.pc.gc.ca/en/pn-np/nt/woodbuffalo/index

Documentary Films

Cranes of the Gray Wind. 1980. 50 minutes. T. D. Mangelsen, filmmaker. PBS/Nature, BBC film.

Crane Song. 2007. One-hour (50-minute) documentary on the sandhill crane migration in the Platte River valley and related information about the whooping crane. Produced by Nebraska Educational Television, Lincoln, NE. http://netnebraska.org/basic-page/television/crane-song

Flight of the Whooping Crane. 1984. 50 minutes. T. D. Mangelsen et al., filmmakers. Documentary on whooping crane migration from wintering grounds to nesting area. National Geographic TV special.

Journey of the Whooping Crane. 2018. One-hour documentary on the natural history of the whooping crane, produced by Red Sky Productions and Georgia Public Broadcasting. Available from Amazon, Google Play, and iTunes. http://whooping-crane.org/

Photo by Scott Johnsgard

Paul Johnsgard is Foundation Regents Professor Emeritus in the School of Biological Sciences at the University of Nebraska. He is the author of about 100 books on ornithology, avian behavior, ecology, and natural history. He is a Fellow of the American Ornithologists' Union and the recipient of lifetime awards from the National Wildlife Federation and the National Audubon Society. His publications have appeared in eight different decades.

Tom Mangelsen is a photographer, cinematographer, and filmmaker. He is recognized as one of the world's premier nature photographers, with works appearing in *National Geographic, Audubon, Smithsonian, Natural History, Newsweek, Wildlife Art, American Photo,* and *National Wildlife.* His photos have been exhibited around the world and received international awards. He is an advisor and collaborator with Jane Goodall on her African conservation projects.

Also by Paul Johnsgard and Tom Mangelsen—*Wyoming Wildlife: A Natural History* (Lincoln: Zea Books, 2019).
ISBN: 978-1-60962-150-6   https://digitalcommons.unl.edu/zeabook/73/